CREEPY CUTE DOODLES

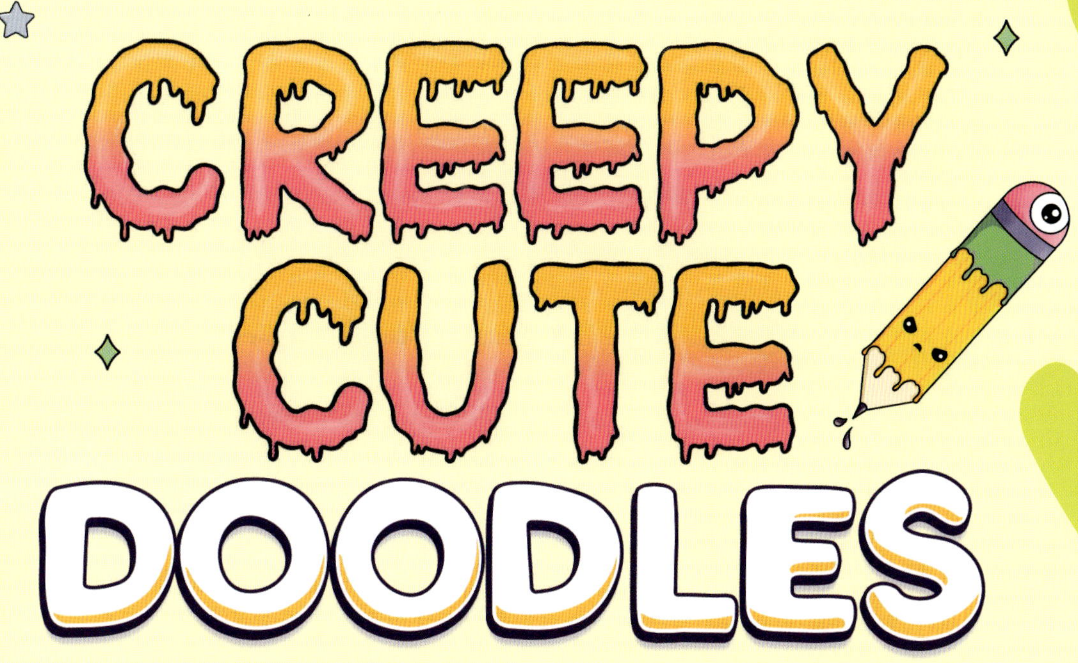

HOW TO DRAW 100 SWEET & SPOOKY DESIGNS

Illustrated by Gaynor Carradice

ADAMS MEDIA

NEW YORK   AMSTERDAM/ANTWERP   LONDON   TORONTO
SYDNEY/MELBOURNE   NEW DELHI

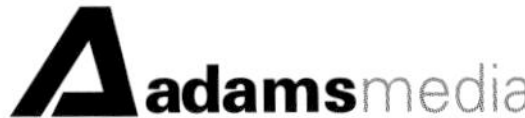

Adams Media
An Imprint of Simon & Schuster, LLC
100 Technology Center Drive
Stoughton, MA 02072

First Adams Media trade paperback edition October 2025

Interior design by Kellie Emery
Illustrations by Gaynor Carradice

Manufactured in China

10 9 8 7 6 5 4 3 2 1

ISBN 978-1-5072-2385-7

TABLE OF CONTENTS

HOW TO DRAW

INTRODUCTION

Super sweet cupcakes topped with creepy skulls...

Spooky ghosts that love to garden...

*Eye-catchingly cute sushi rolls that
stare into your soul...*

Creepy Cute Doodles combines the eerily macabre and the utterly sweet for something even more endearing, with how-tos for drawing haunted gingerbread houses, monstrous plants, devious treats, and more—the perfect fit for doodle enthusiasts who enjoy a splash of adorable with a ghoulish twist.

Here you'll find easy steps for recreating one hundred sinisterly lovely images, including noodles with skulls, an evil snowman, a batwing boom box, and vengeful bumblebees. You'll also sink your teeth (or fangs) into a quick guide to following the steps in this book, as well as tips and tools for making doodles so lively they could crawl right off the page.

So grab your pencils, pens, and drawing paper, and get ready to spend hours buried in creepy cute fun!

GETTING STARTED

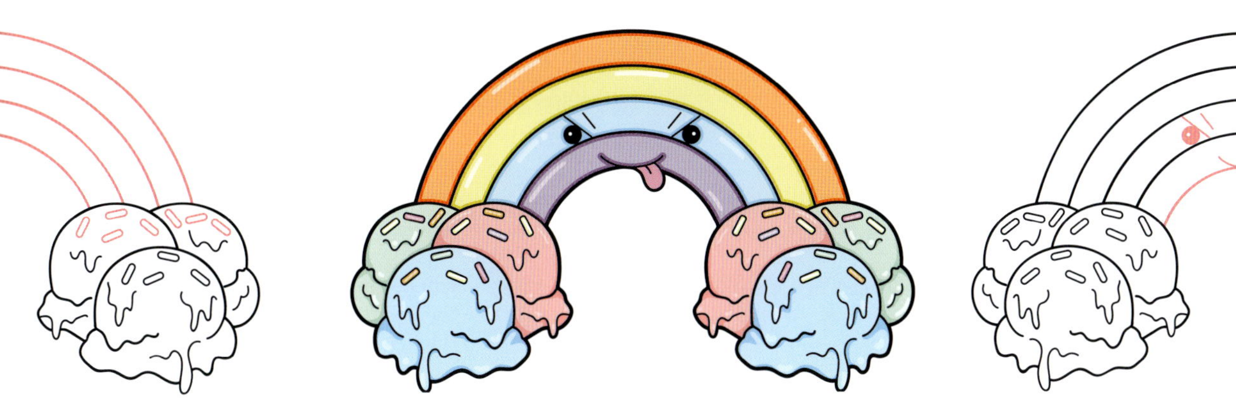

Drawing your own creepy cute doodles is easy with a few (delightful) tricks and materials! Keep reading to find everything you'll need to make the charming, spooky doodles in this book come alive (laboratory not included).

HOW TO USE THIS BOOK

Each of the one hundred ghastly doodles in this book is broken up into six easy steps: Each step shows you in pink ink exactly what to draw and where, and the instructions tell you how:

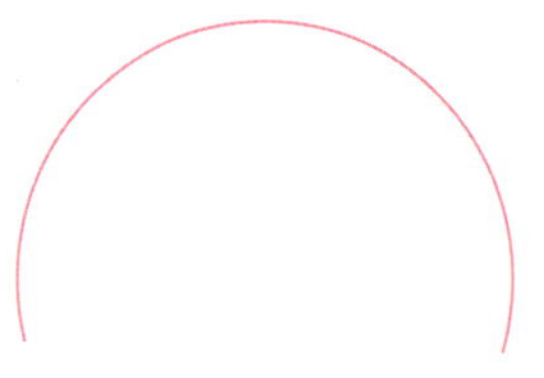

1. Start by drawing a little more than half of a circle. Leave the bottom open.

Cobwebs, sprinkles, eyeballs, frosting, and any other cute or creepy lines and shapes from previous steps are shown in black ink so you can easily spot what was already drawn and what you'll be adding next:

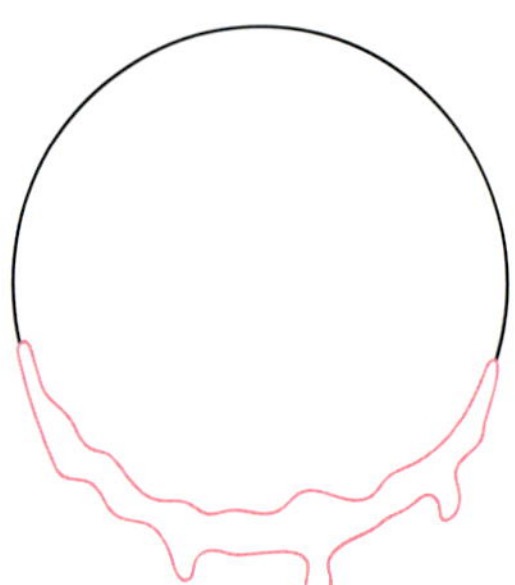

2. Add a wiggly line and drips at the bottom.

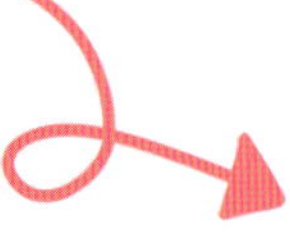

Draw along to each step, and in no time you'll be bringing these ghoulish doodles to life (or death)!

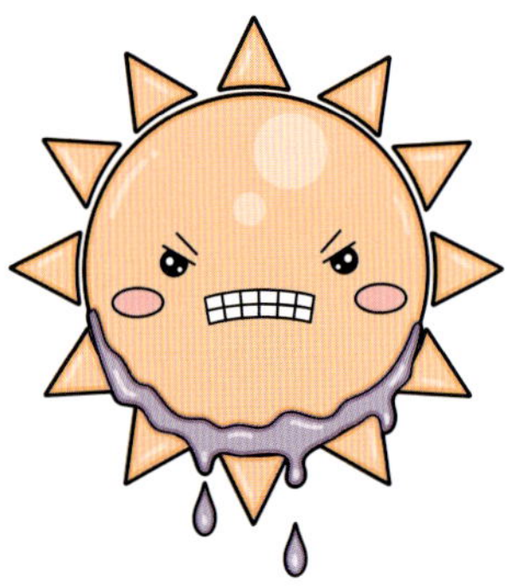

DRAWING TOOLS AND OTHER MATERIALS

Want to summon devilish boba tea? Or call on the frightfully delightful spirits of vampire chocolates? Or turn that sweet drawing app on your tablet a little sour with "rotten" milk? There are a few tools you'll want to have on hand—or claw—as you follow the steps for each doodle:

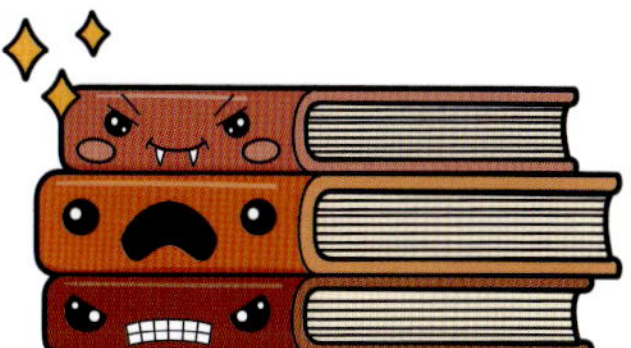

- **Paper or a designated drawing notebook or sketchbook:** You can doodle on any paper you have lying around or use a designated notebook or your go-to sketchbook.

- **Pens and/or pencils:** Use fine-tipped pens or a well-sharpened pencil to draw your outline.

- **Colored pencils, markers, crayons, etc.:** Use your favorite colors to make each doodle really haunt the page. Colored pencils, markers, crayons, gel pens, pastels, or even paint can help you put a unique spin on the images in this book.

- **Optional alternative:** Instead of paper, if your morbid heart desires, you can make your doodles in an art app with a tablet and stylus!

From pen and paper to paint and canvas to stylus and tablet, what you choose to awaken your disturbingly adorable doodles is up to you.

DRAWING TIPS

Whatever materials you choose, a few tips can help you draw your creepiest, cutest creations:

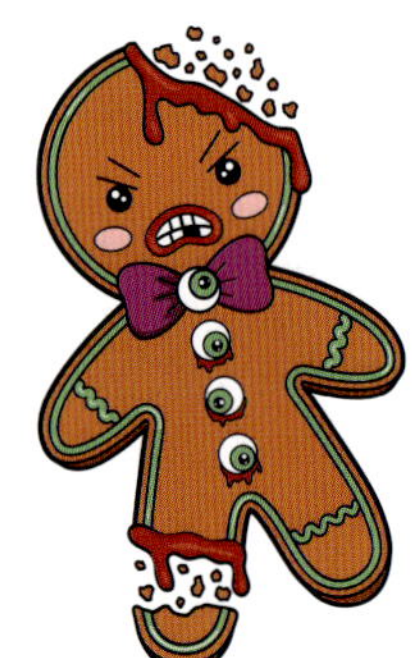

- **Give yourself room to change or redo things.** It's best to start a doodle with a pencil. Draw lightly at first so it's easier to erase your lines if you make a mistake or want to change or redo part of your doodle.

- **Trace what you love so you can redo what you don't.** Love how one part of a doodle turned out but want to touch up another? You can use a second piece of paper to trace the elements you want to keep, then draw the rest better than before.

- **Use shading and detail lines to make a doodle pop.** To add liveliness and depth, shade eyeballs with blank spots for pupils and/or a shiny effect—or add wavy or jagged lines for texture, or draw background outlines for different shapes.

- **Practice makes creepy cute!** Nothing is perfect, but a bit of practice can help you sharpen your creepy cute doodling skills. Return to your favorite images in this book again and again to see how your skills grow!

- **Add your own gruesome details.** After you have the basics of an image down, you can put your own unique twist on it. Give that haunted gingerbread house window boxes filled with glaring roses, or zombify that frog wizard. This book is meant as a helpful guide, not some firm manual, so let that wicked creativity possess your pencil!

- **Solidify the final doodle.** Once you have a pencil outline you're happy with, go over it in pen or a fine-tipped marker so it really stands out and is ready to use however you please!

Once you have a finished doodle, it's up to you whether you want to keep it in your notebook, cut it out and paste it somewhere you'll see it every day, turn it into a spooky greeting card—whatever your sinisterly sweet heart desires. So now that you've got the essential tools and tips at the ready, let's conjure up some creepy cute fun!

HAUNTED GINGERBREAD HOUSE

1.

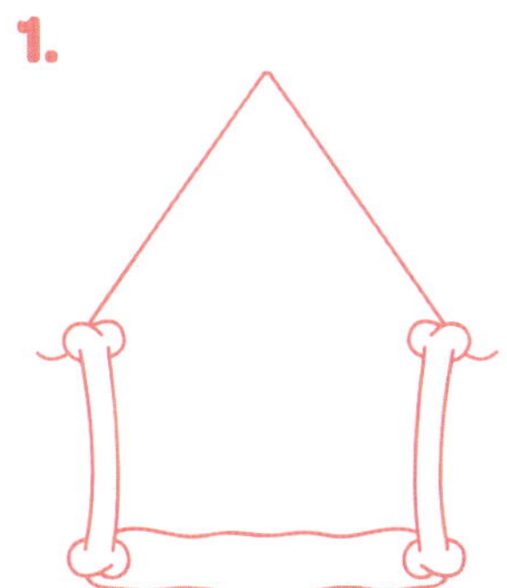

Start by drawing an upside-down V. Add a vertical bone shape under each line of the V. Add a small curve on the outside of the top of each bone and two wiggly lines connecting the bones at the bottom.

2.

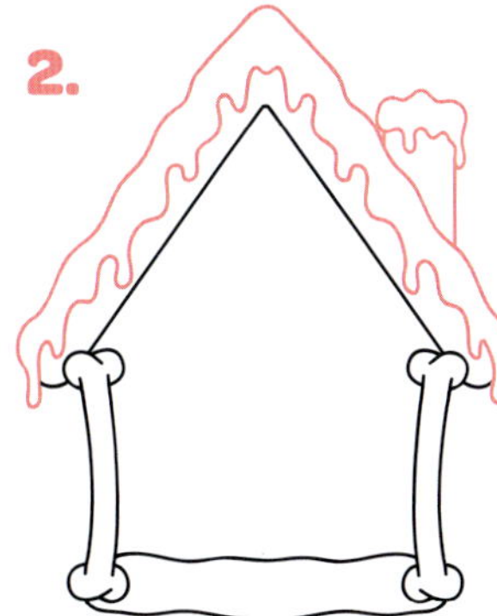

Draw a dripping wiggly triangle for the top of the roof. Add two lines to the top right for the chimney and a dripping wiggly rectangle for the chimney top.

3.

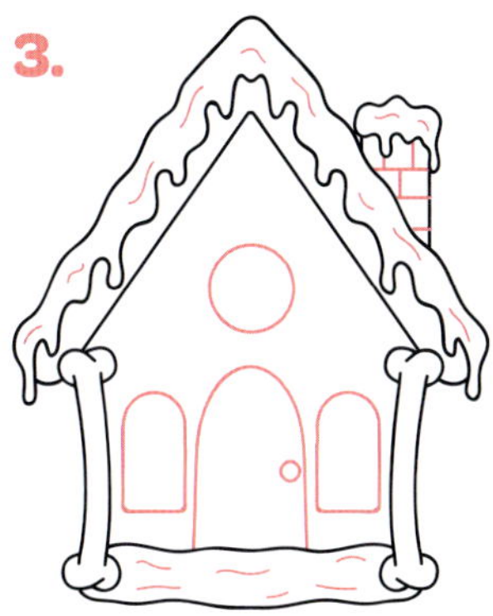

Draw a circle in the top middle of the house and an arched door with a round handle. Draw a smaller arched rectangle on either side of door. Add brick pattern on chimney and squiggly lines for snow texture.

4.

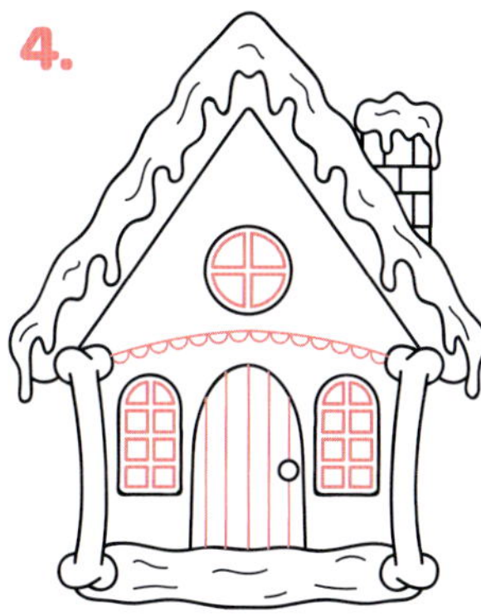

Add little square panes to the arched windows and quarter-circle panes to the circular window. Add vertical lines to the door. Across the middle of the house, add a curved line with a scalloped bottom.

5.

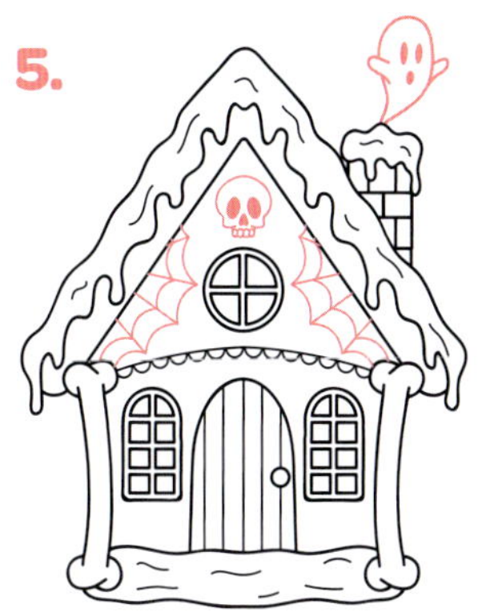

Give the gingerbread house some creepy details, like cobwebs, a skull, and a ghost flying out of the chimney.

6.

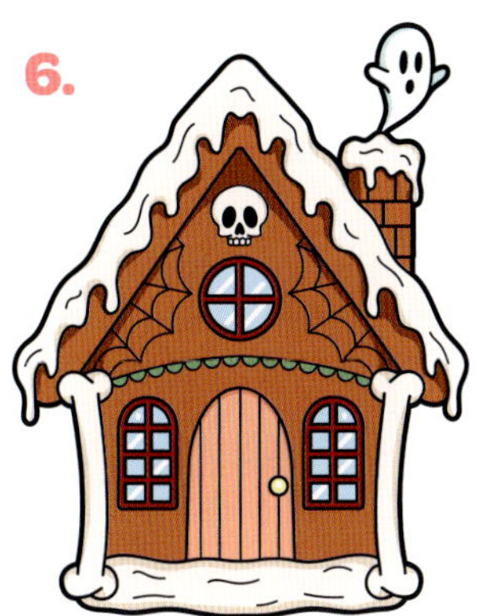

Color in your Haunted Gingerbread House!

HAUNTED COCOA

1.

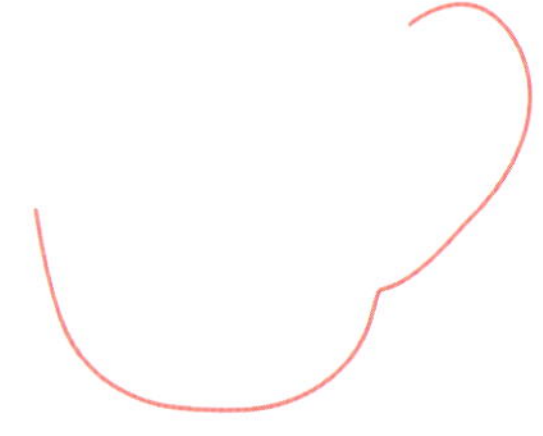

Start by drawing the base of the mug and the outside of the handle.

2.

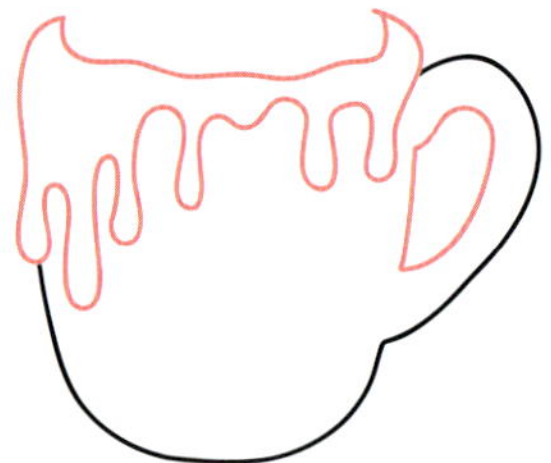

Draw the inside of the handle and a dripping shape along the top.

3.

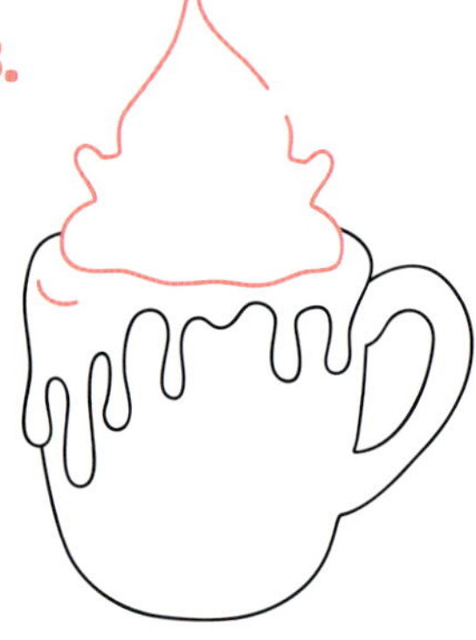

On top of the mug, draw a squished teardrop shape with little arms. Leave a small gap on the right side. Add a small, curved line to make the rim of the mug stand out.

4.

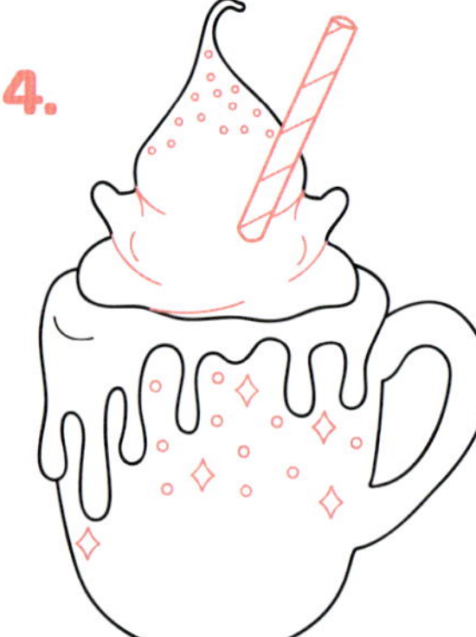

For the straw, draw a long rectangle with curved ends, then add diagonal stripes. Draw curved lines and circular sprinkles on cream topping. Decorate top half of mug with diamonds and tiny circles.

5.

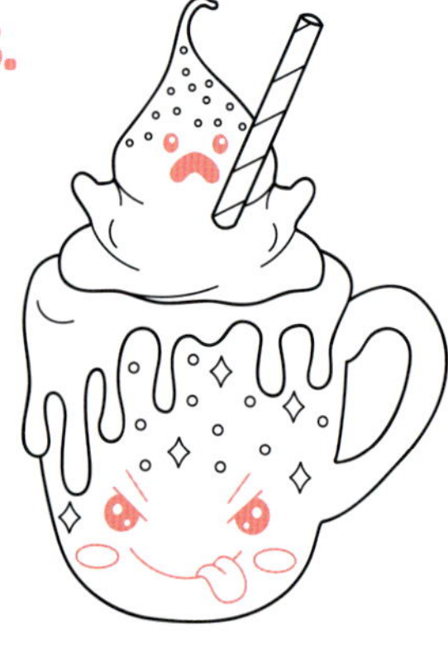

Add creepy cute faces to the mug and the cream topping.

6.

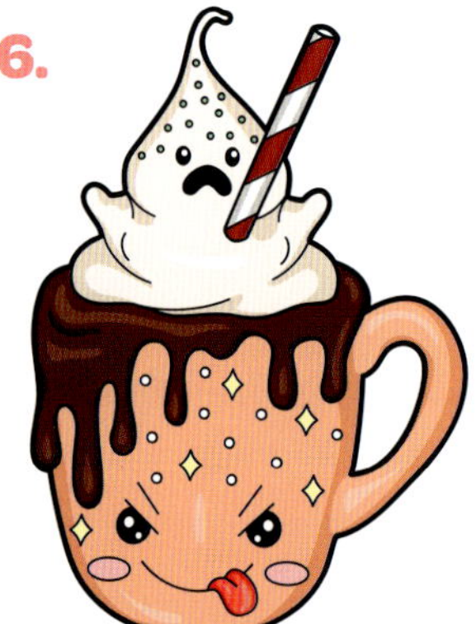

Color in your Haunted Cocoa!

CREEPY GINGERBREAD COOKIE

1.

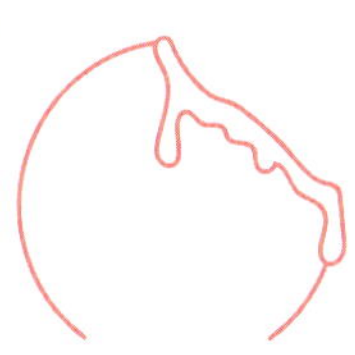

Start by drawing the head of the cookie as a circle with a dripping section at the top right. Leave the bottom open.

2.

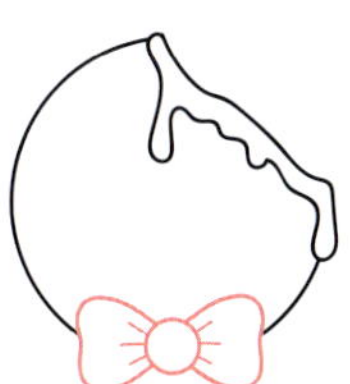

For the bow, draw a circle (which will become an eyeball) with a triangular shape on each side. Add three lines inside each triangle for folds in the bow.

3.

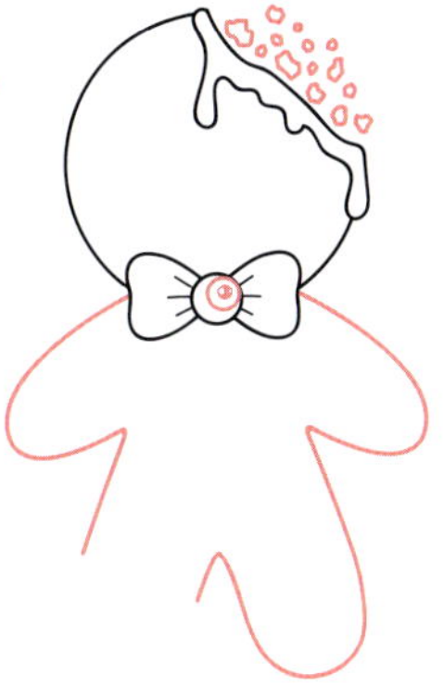

Draw an iris and shaded pupil inside the eyeball bow. Then draw the cookie's body, leaving the leg on the left side open. Add some crumbs to the top of the head.

4.

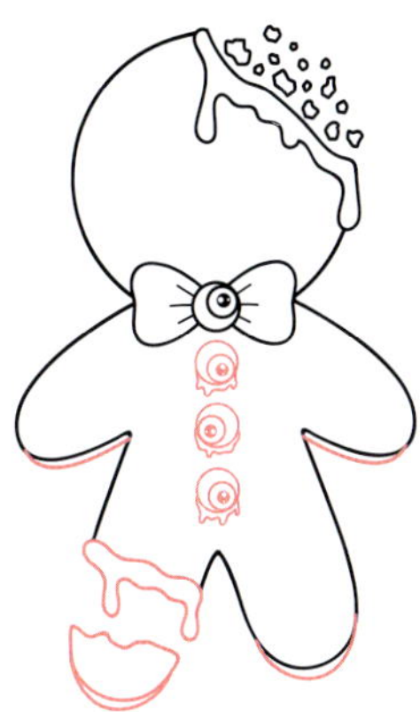

Add three dripping eyeballs as buttons. Add dripping icing to the open section of the leg. Draw in the broken-off leg as a semicircle with a wiggly line at the top. Draw some extra lines under arms and legs for dimension.

5.

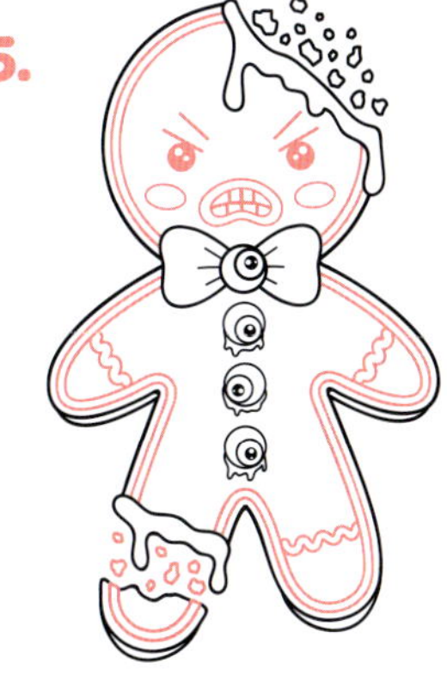

Make two close-together lines close to the edge of the cookie all the way around. Draw some wiggly lines of icing across each arm and the intact leg. Add crumbs above the broken-off leg, and draw a creepy cute face.

6.

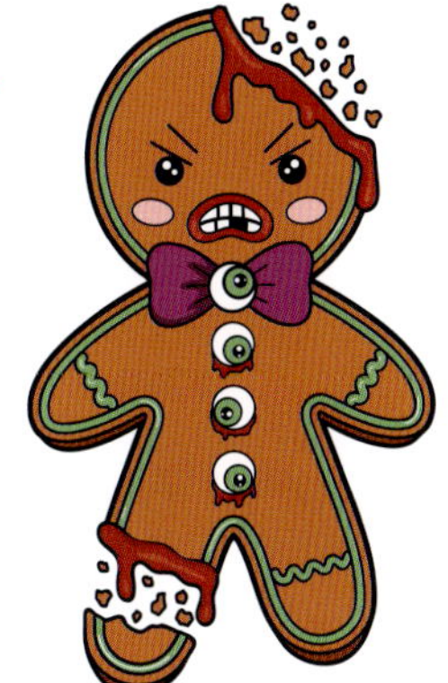

Color in your Creepy Gingerbread Cookie!

EVIL SNOWMAN

1.

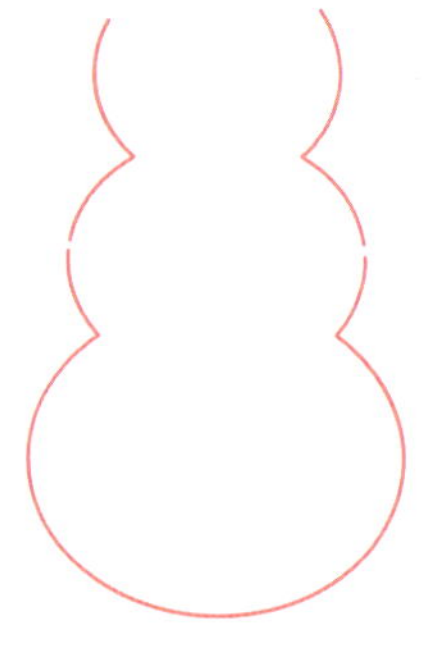

Start by drawing a stack of three overlapping circles, each slightly smaller than the one below it. Leave the smallest circle open on top. Leave a small gap on each side of the middle circle. Erase the inner lines to leave the outline of the snowman's body.

2.

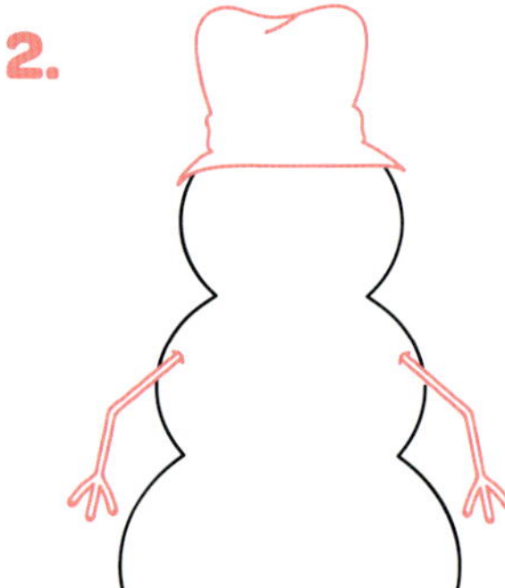

Draw the outline of the top hat and two bent, stick-like arms.

3.

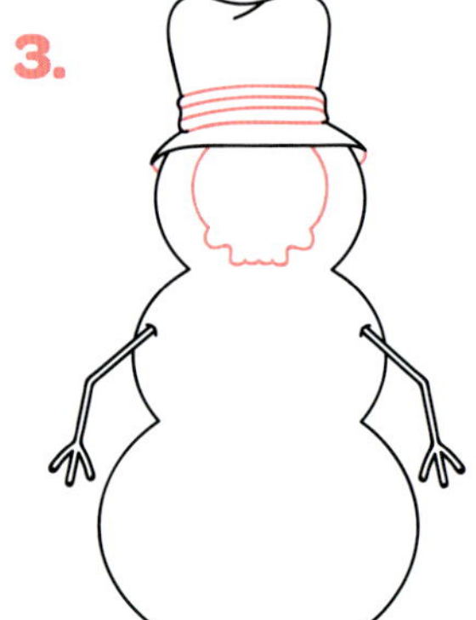

Draw stripes at the bottom of the top hat, and add two small lines connecting the base of the hat to the snowman's head. Inside the head, draw a simple skull shape.

4.

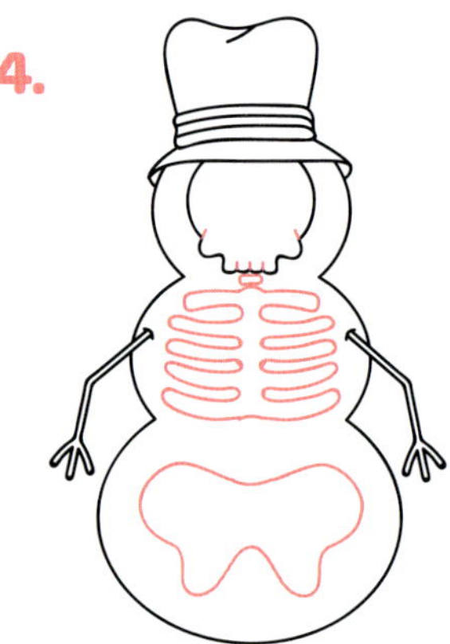

Add three short lines to the skull for teeth. Draw two more short lines for the cheekbones. Draw a small, rounded rectangle below the skull and a simple rib cage. In the bottom circle, draw a bow shape for the hip bone.

5.

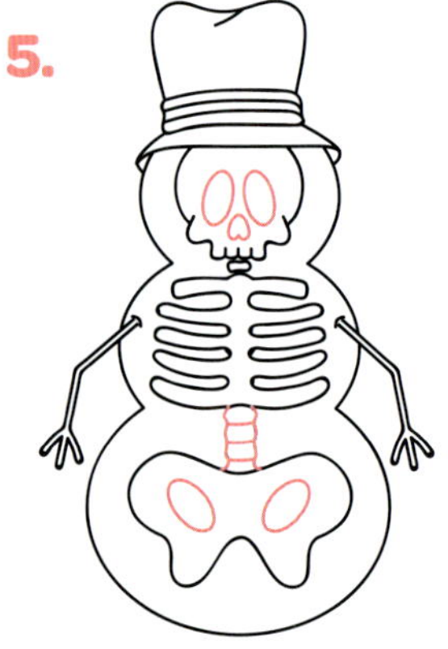

Draw two big eye sockets and a triangle nose on the skull, and add the spine connecting the rib cage to the hips. Draw an oval inside each half of the hip bone.

6.

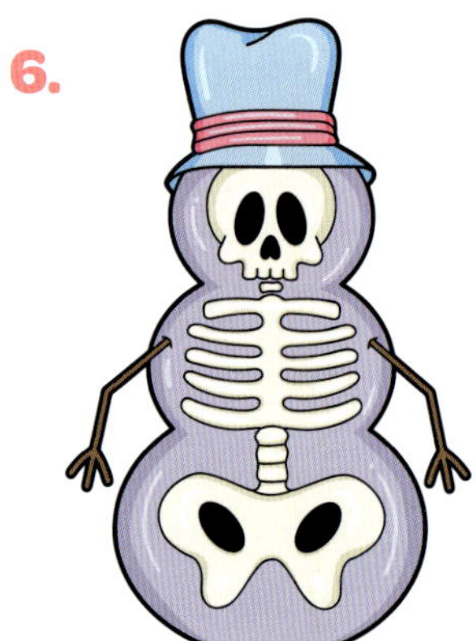

Color in your Evil Snowman!

POSSESSED MITTEN

1.

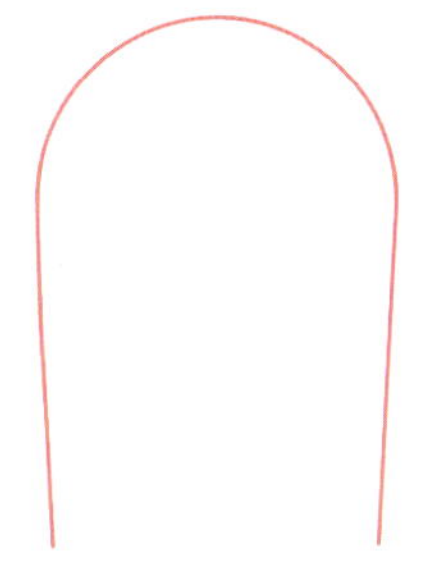

Start by drawing a simple coffin shape, leaving the bottom open.

2.

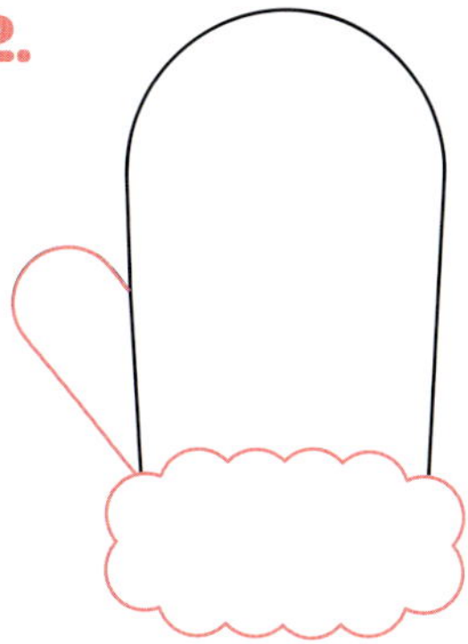

Add a cloud shape to the bottom and a smaller, angled coffin shape on the left side for a thumb.

3.

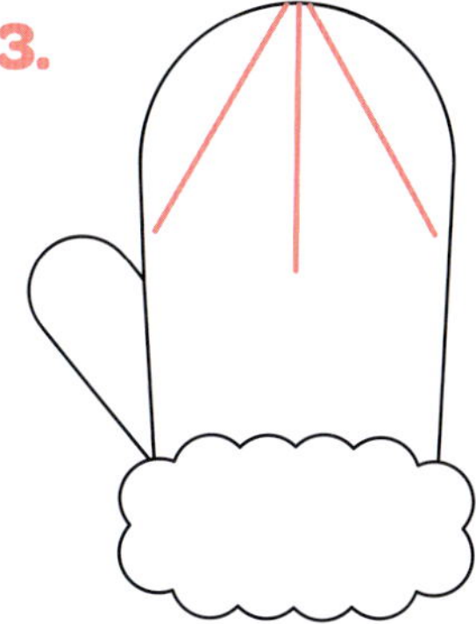

Starting at the top center of the mitten, draw one line straight to the middle of the mitten and two lines, about the same length, angled toward the sides.

4.

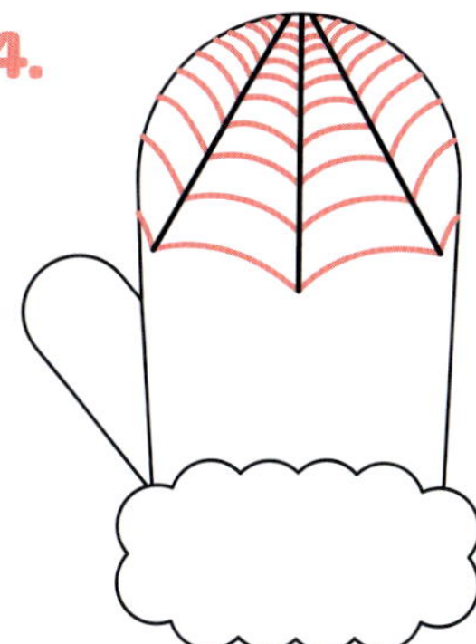

To make the cobweb, draw curved lines connecting the three straight lines and the edges of the mitten.

5.

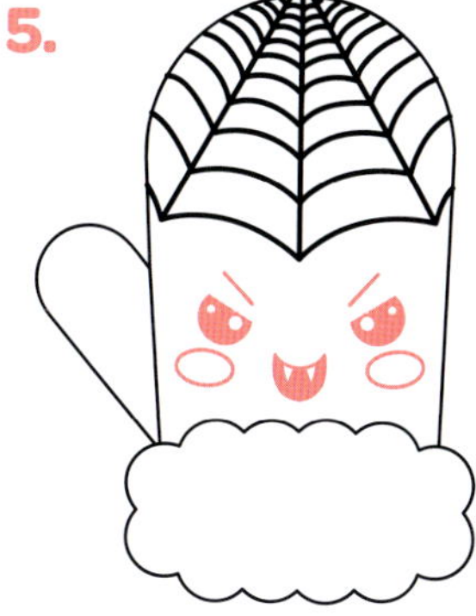

Draw a creepy cute face under the cobweb.

6.

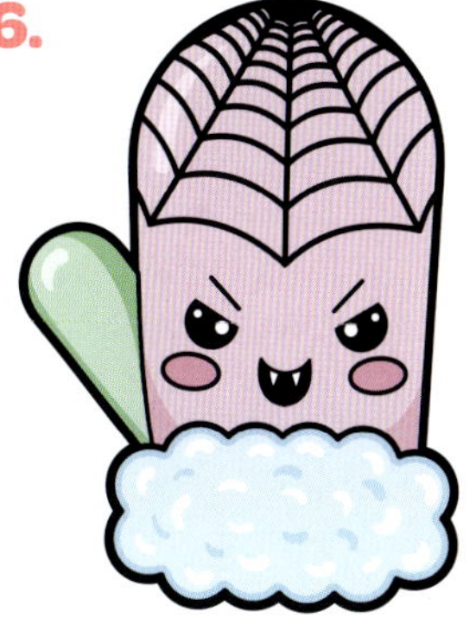

Color in your Possessed Mitten!

YETI SNOW GLOBE

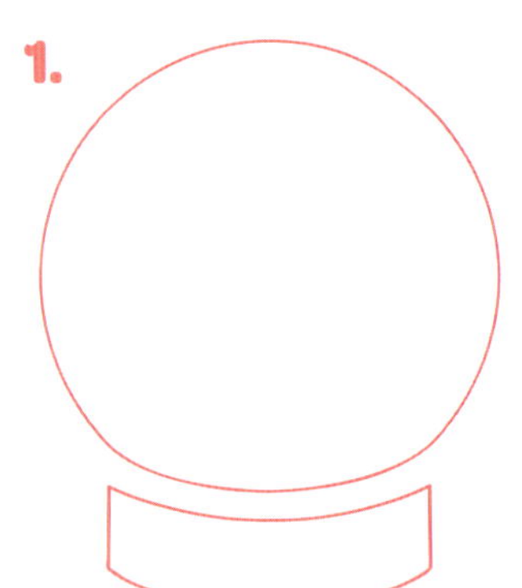

1. Start by drawing a curved rectangle for the base and a circle for the globe.

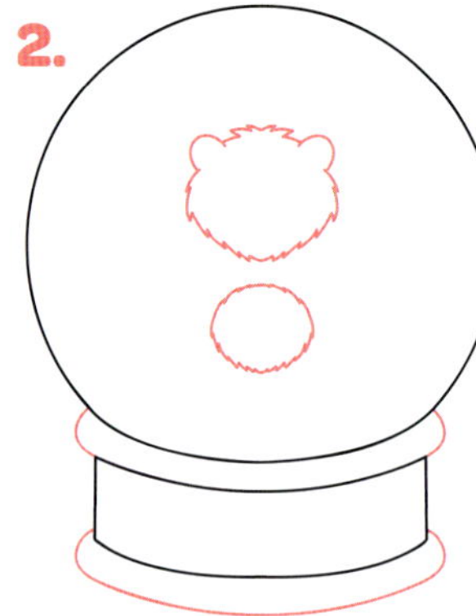

2. Add a curved line below the base, and join the base and the globe with a curved line on either side. Inside the globe, draw a teddy bear head shape and a furry circle underneath.

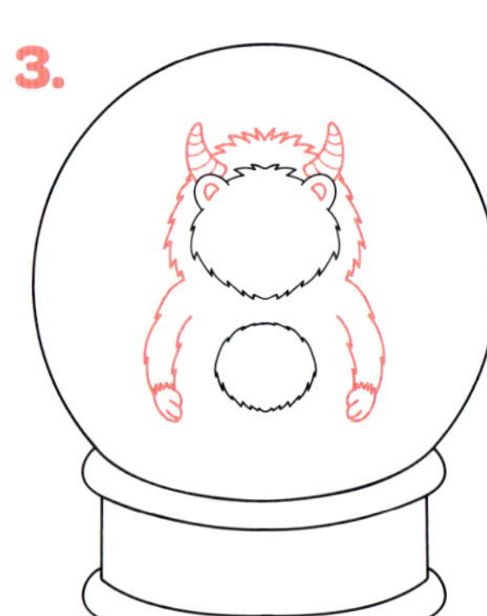

3. Draw the outline of the top of the yeti, arms and hands at either side, and horns above the ears. Draw a half circle inside each ear. Add curved horizontal lines inside both horns.

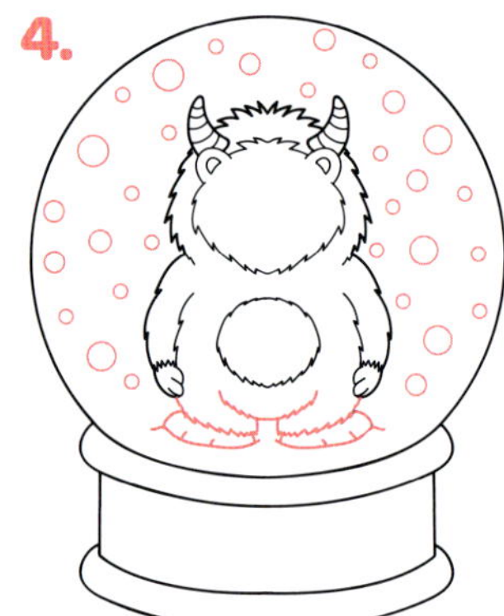

4. Add a curved furry line under the belly and short legs with big feet. Add lines for the toes and a short line at either side for the snow. Add circles all around for snowflakes.

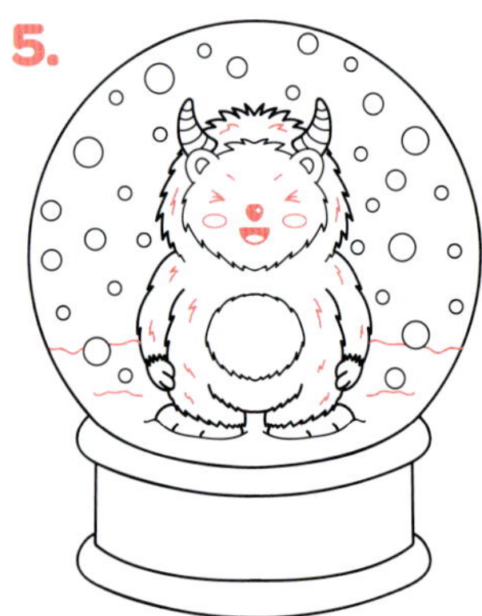

5. Add two wavy lines on either side of the yeti for the snow-covered ground. Draw a cute face, and use squiggly lines to add fur.

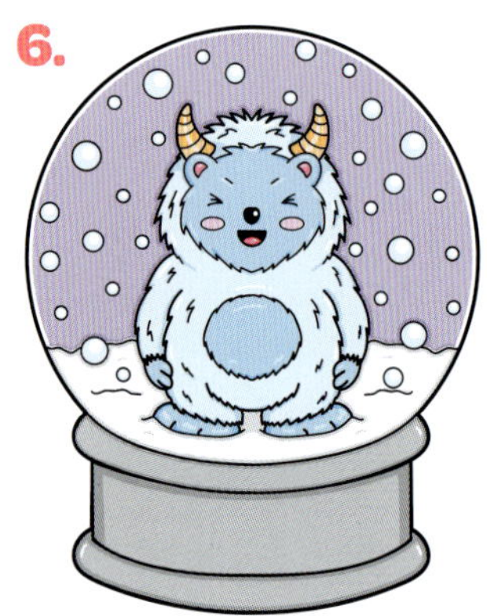

6. Color in your Yeti Snow Globe!

SKULL BOW TIE

1. 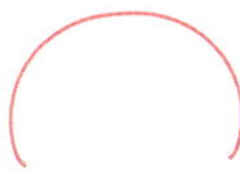

Start by drawing an oval with an open bottom. This is the top of the skull.

2. 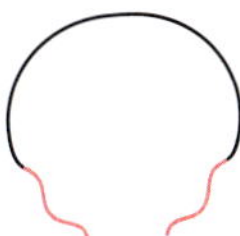

From each end of the first line, draw a wavy line stepping down toward the center of the drawing.

3. 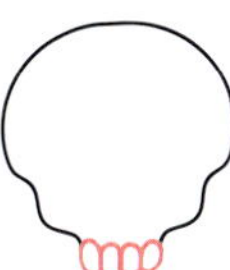

Draw four little rounded rectangles for teeth.

4. 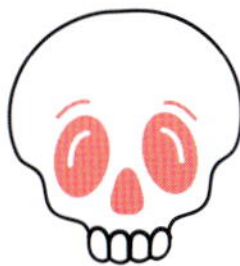

Draw two shaded ovals for eye sockets. For the nose, draw a filled-in triangle with rounded edges. Add curved lines above the eyes.

5. 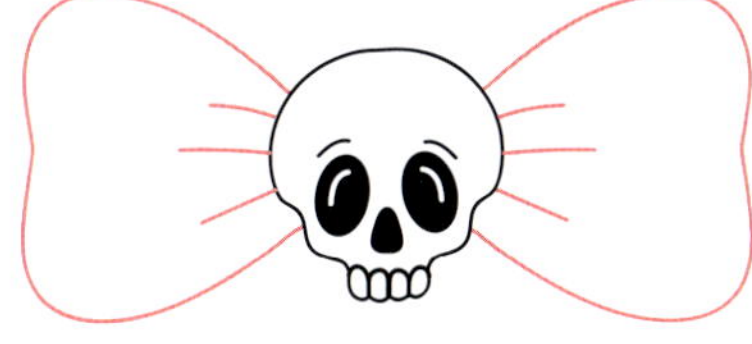

On either side of the skull, draw a rounded triangle, and add lines inside for the creases of the bow.

6. 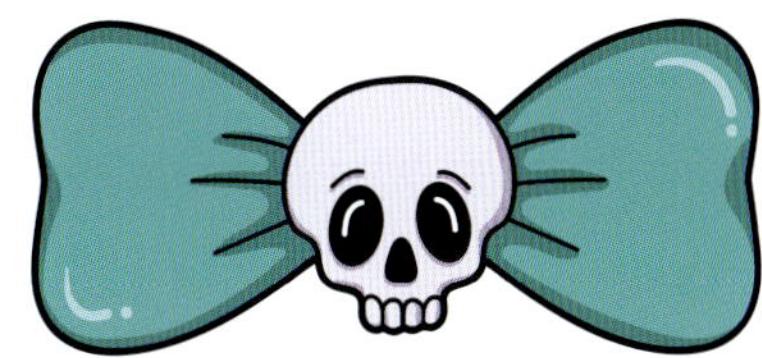

Color in your Skull Bow Tie!

BATWING EYEBALL

1. 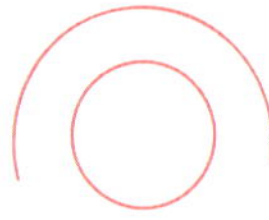

Start by drawing a circle with a half circle above it.

2. 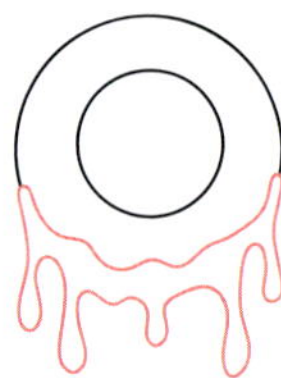

Draw a wavy line to complete the outer circle, and draw drips at the bottom.

3. 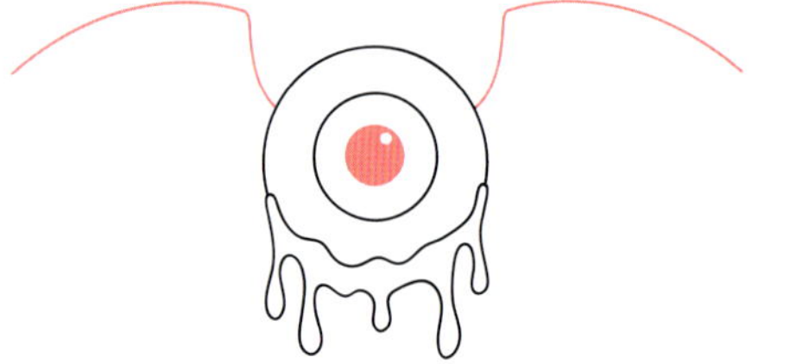

Inside the inner circle, draw a shaded circle for the pupil. Draw the tops of the wings.

4. 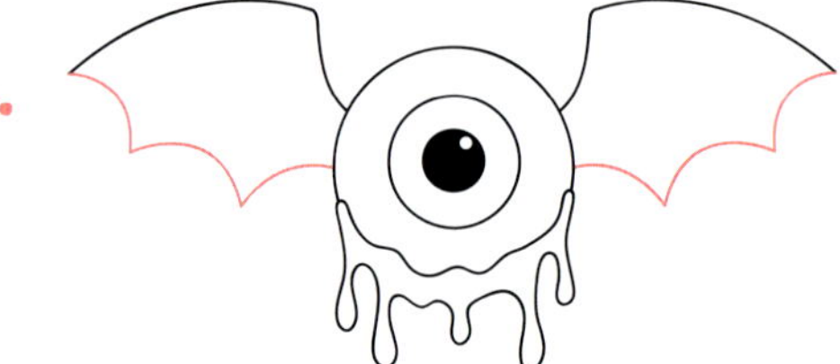

Draw the bottoms of the wings using three curved lines on each side.

5. 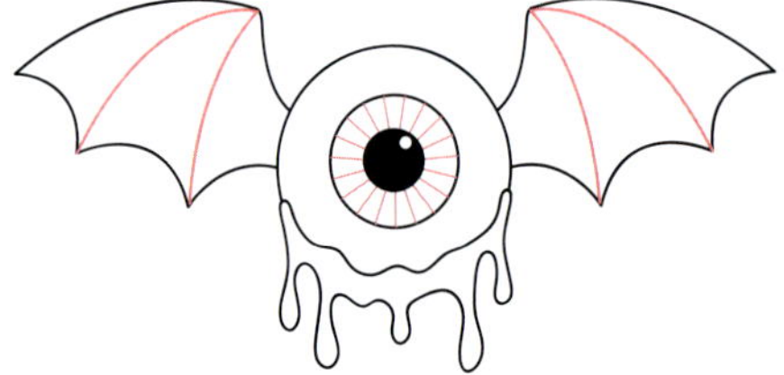

Add little lines inside the iris. Inside each wing, draw lines connecting the top point with each bottom point.

6. 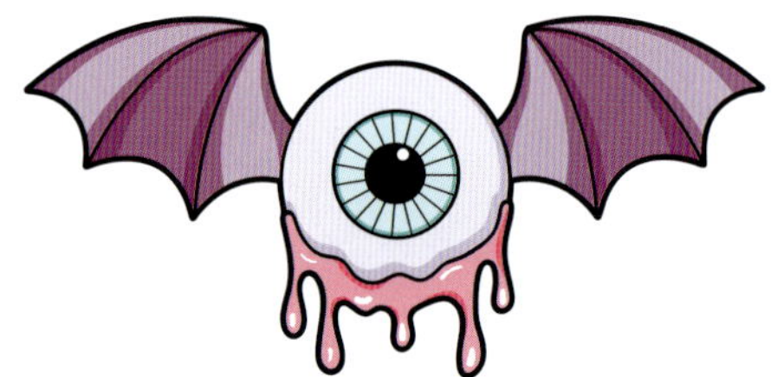

Color in your Batwing Eyeball!

SNOWBOARDING BEAR

1.

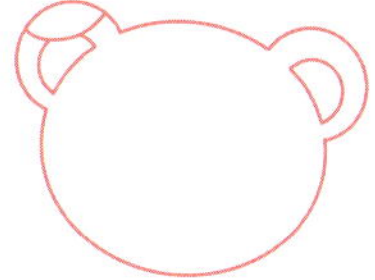

Start by drawing a circle for the head and semicircles for ears. Add a half circle inside each ear. On the left side, draw a semicircular patch at the top of the ear.

2.

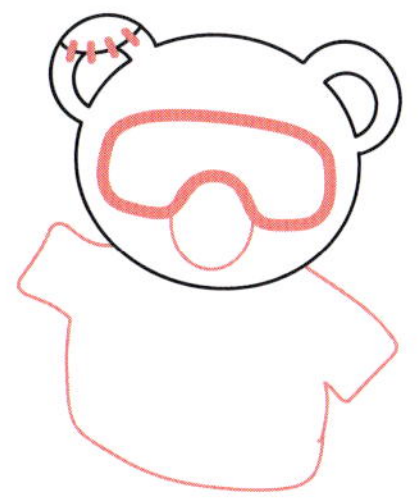

Use a thick line to draw the shape of the goggles. At the bottom of the goggles, make an oval for the bear's muzzle. Draw little stitches on the ear patch. Outline the bear's sweater.

3.

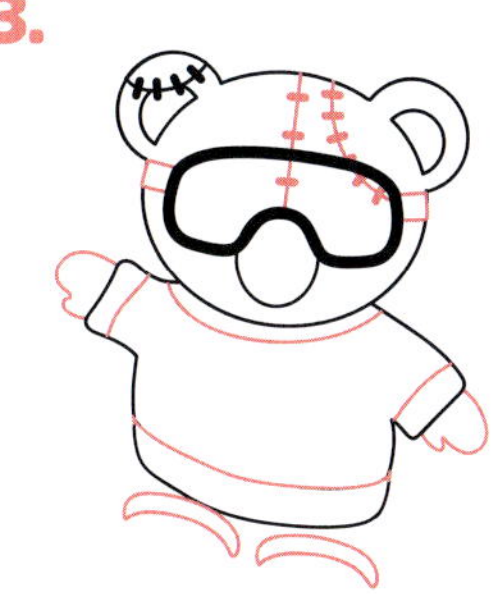

Draw two stitched lines from the top middle of the head—one straight to the bottom of the goggles and one curved to the right. Add a strap for the goggles. Draw hands. Add trim at the cuffs, neckline, and hem of the sweater. Below the sweater, draw two curved rectangles.

4.

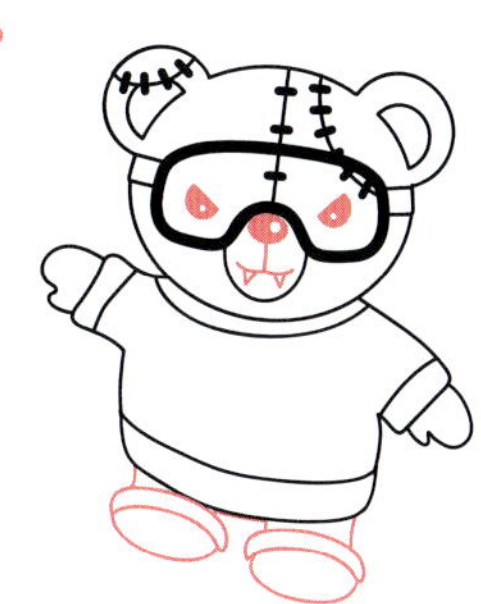

Below the curved rectangles, draw rounded feet. For legs, draw four short horizontal lines connecting the hem of the sweater to the curved rectangles. For the face, draw and shade two slanted eyes and an oval-shaped nose. Add a creepy cute smile.

5.

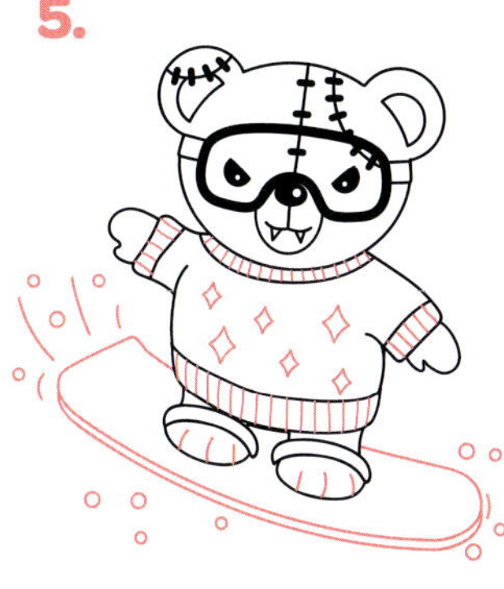

Draw in the snowboard, then add little details: lines on sweater trim, diamonds to decorate sweater, curved lines for toes, movement lines behind the snowboard, and circles for flying snow.

6.

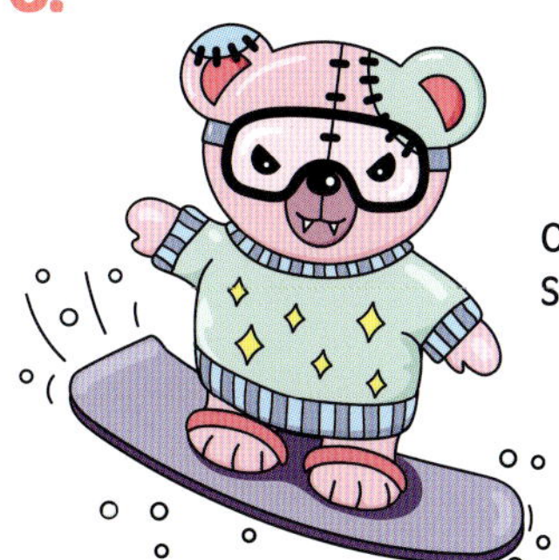

Color in your Snowboarding Bear!

SKIING PENGUIN

1.

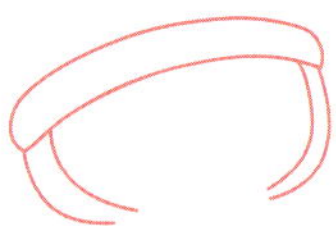

Start by drawing the bottom of the hat as a curved rectangle with rounded edges. Add two curved vertical lines below the hat—the sides of the head.

2.

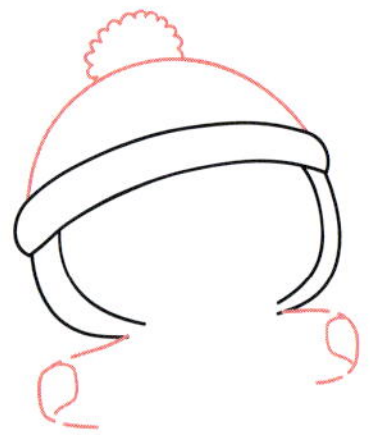

Draw the wings, leaving a tiny gap at the top and bottom of each wing. Draw the top of the hat as a half circle, and add a fluffy pom-pom to the top.

3.

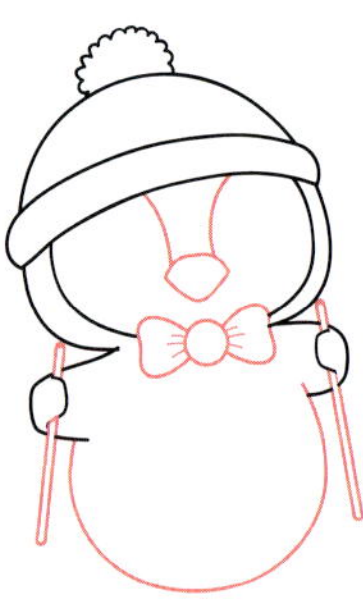

Add a straight pole to each wing. Draw a rounded body. For the nose, draw a triangle, then a curved line from each side of the triangle to the hat. To make the bow tie, draw a small circle, a triangle on either side, and little lines for the folds in the bow.

4.

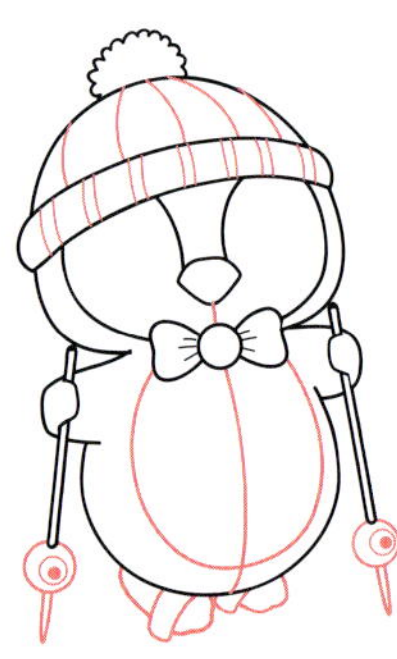

Draw an oval down from the bottom corners of the bow tie. Add a curved line to the middle of the body. Add feet and ski straps. At the end of each pole, draw an eyeball and then a pointy end. Draw in curved lines on middle and bottom of hat.

5.

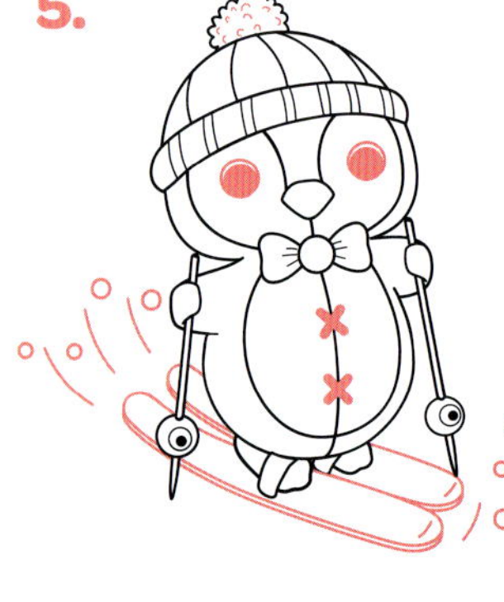

Add two shaded circles for eyes. Draw in the skis, then add details: X's along the belly line to look like stitches, movement lines, and circles for snow.

6.

Color in your Skiing Penguin!

SKULL NOODLES

1.

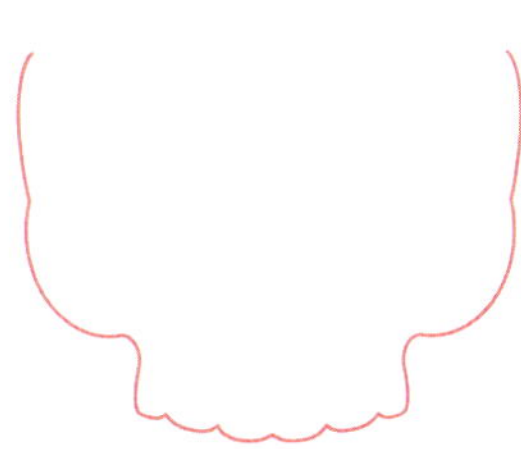

Start by drawing the outline of the skull bowl. Use curved lines for the sides and a squared-off, scalloped bottom.

2.

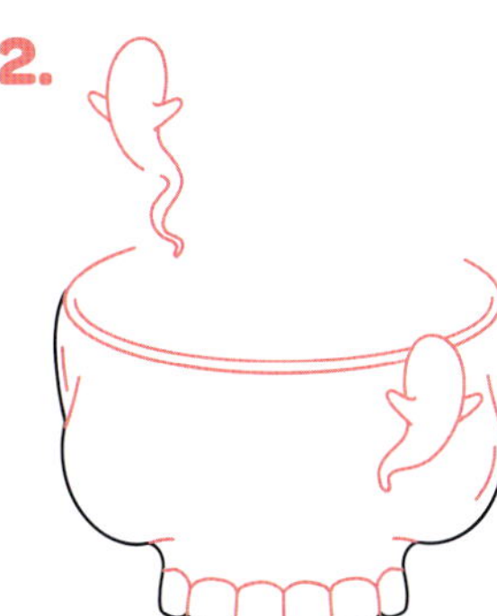

At the top, draw a flattened oval for the rim of the bowl. Use a double line for the front part, and leave the top open. Add upside-down teardrop shapes (outlines of ghosts) at the right and top. Draw teeth, and make curved lines for the cheekbones.

3.

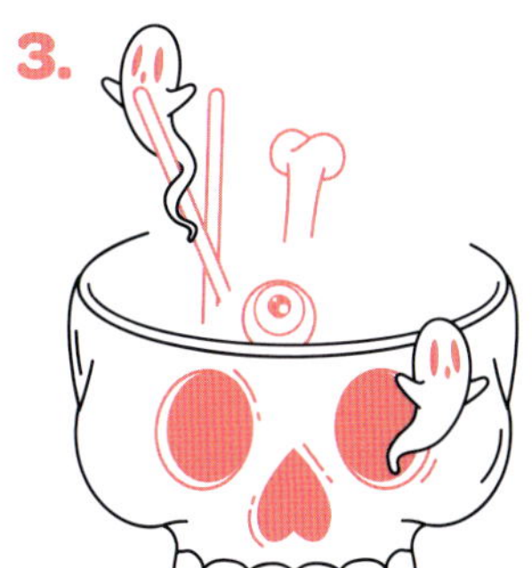

Inside the bowl, add chopsticks, a bone shape, and an eyeball. Draw and fill in two big oval eye sockets and an upside-down heart nose. Add spooky faces to the ghosts and some little detail lines around the eyes and nose of skull.

4.

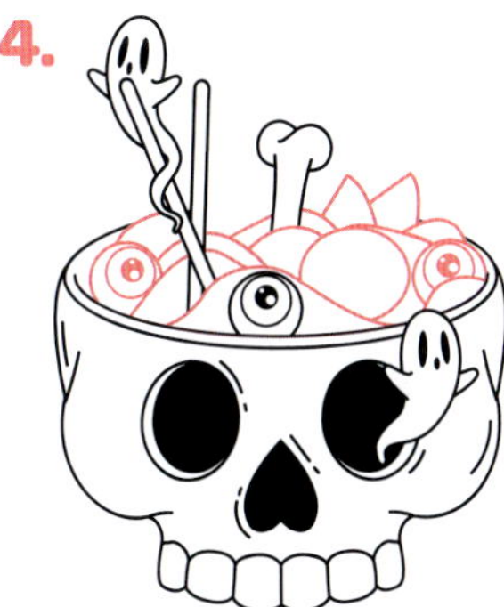

Draw a circle (cucumber slice) to the right of the eyeball with two triangles (radish slices) above it. Add more eyeballs and wavy outlines of noodles.

5.

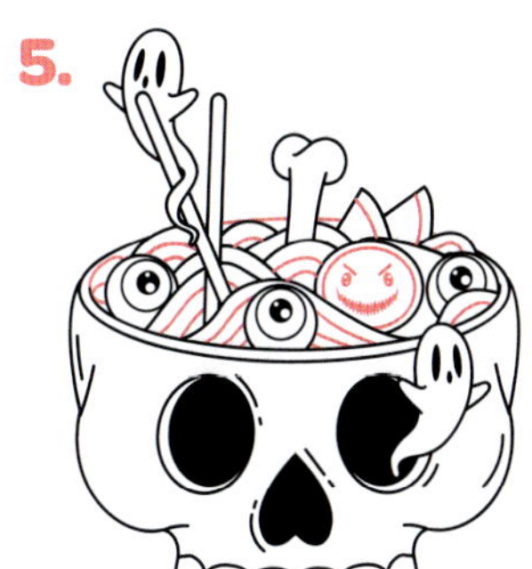

Add more wavy lines to detail the noodles. Add peels for the vegetables, and make a creepy cute face inside the cucumber.

6.

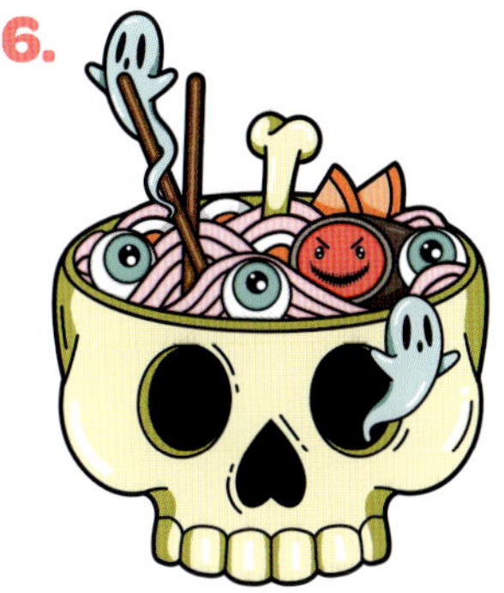

Color in your Skull Noodles!

TENTACLE SUSHI

1.

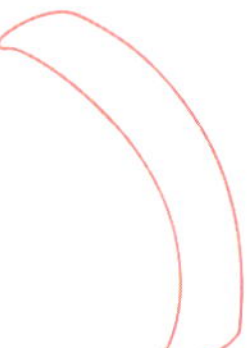

Start by drawing a thin, curved rectangle.

2.

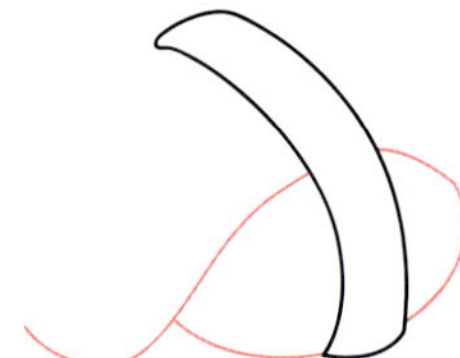

Add a sideways teardrop (rice) behind the bottom half of the rectangle. Extend the top line (the bottom of the tentacle) to the left with a curve.

3.

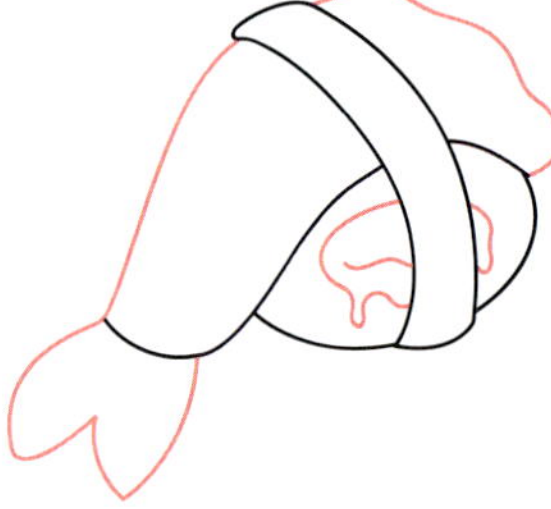

Add a lumpy line for the top of the tentacle, and then continue past the curve to add a mermaid-like tail. Inside the teardrop, add a dripping oval of yummy-looking filling.

4.

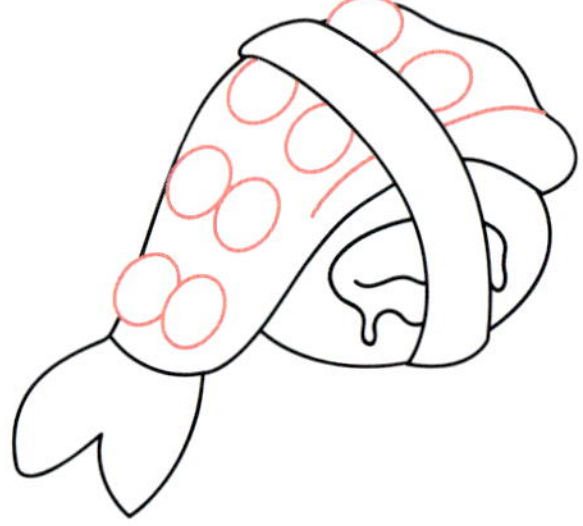

Inside the tentacle, draw two rows of ovals (suckers), and add a curved line to make the edge look folded.

5.

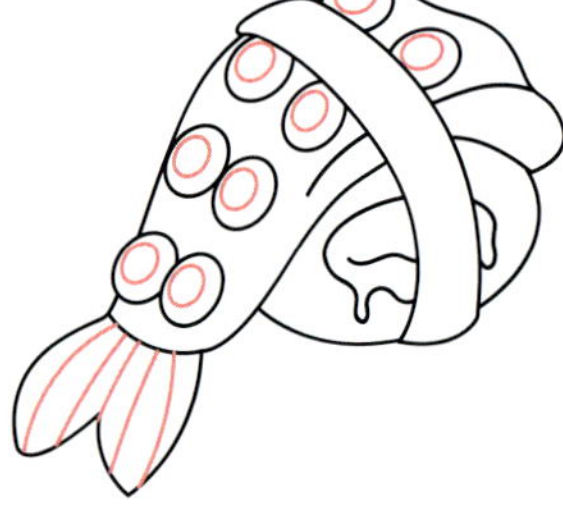

Add more ovals to finish the suckers, and add lines inside the tail for extra detail.

6.

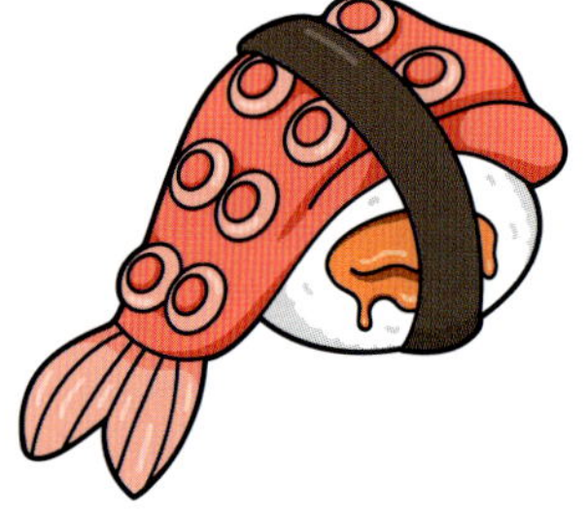

Color in your Tentacle Sushi!

CHOPSTICKS AND EYEBALL ROLL

1.

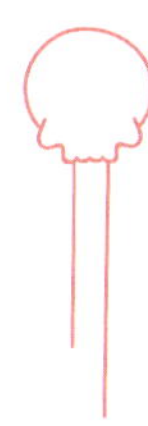

Start by drawing a skull shape: a circle with a square jaw at the bottom. Draw two straight lines down from the bottom, the right line slightly longer than the left.

2.

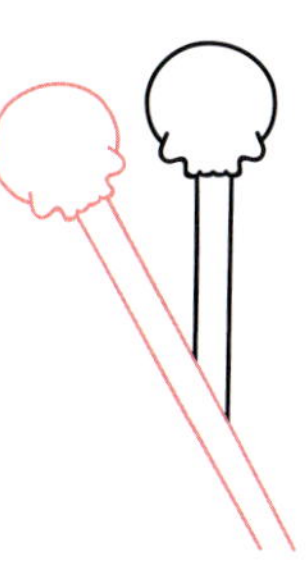

Add another skull shape, this one with two diagonal lines.

3.

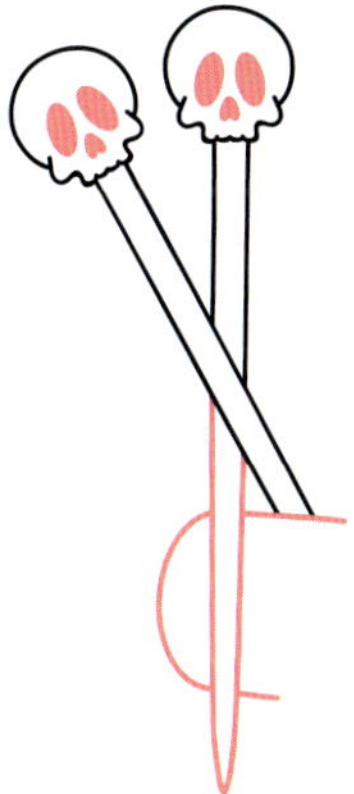

Continue the straight lines of the first chopstick and join them at the bottom. Draw in sushi roll as a curved line on the left and two straight top and bottom lines. Add faces to skulls.

4.

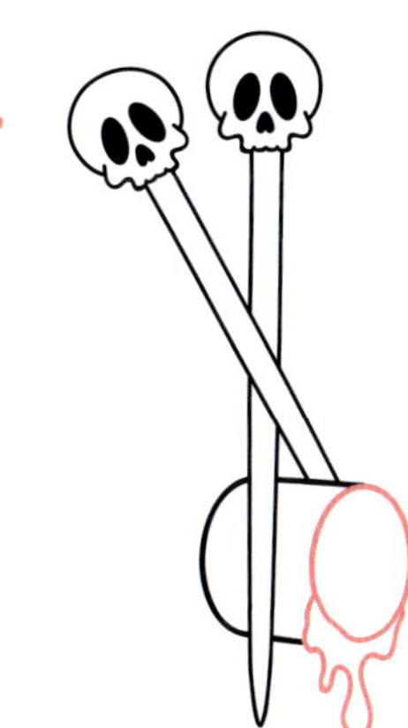

Draw a dripping oval for the end of the sushi roll.

5.

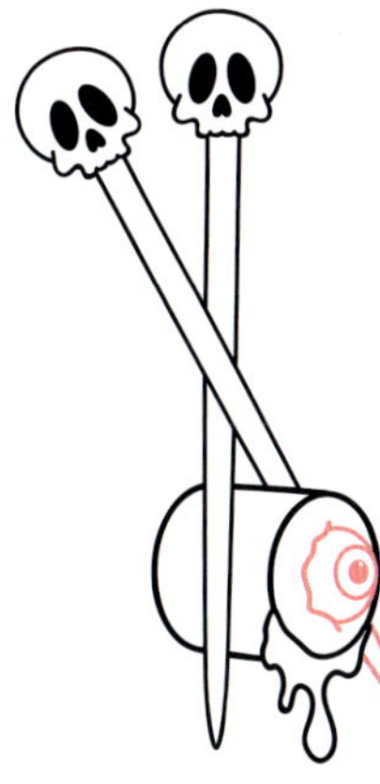

Add an eyeball in the middle of the roll, making the edge of the eyeball wavy. Then add the pointed end of the second chopstick.

6.

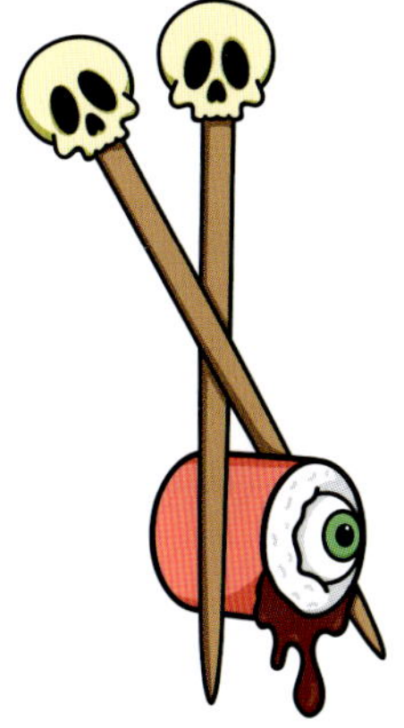

Color in your Chopsticks and Eyeball Roll!

CREEPY CUTE CUPCAKE

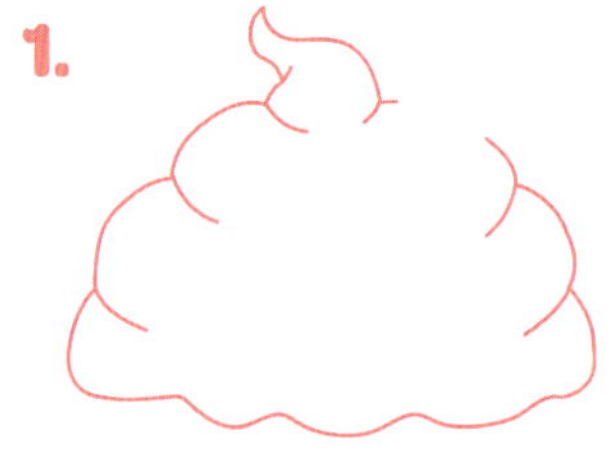

1. Start by drawing the top of the cupcake as a lumpy half circle with a wavy bottom and curved lines for the frosting. Leave a gap for the skull.

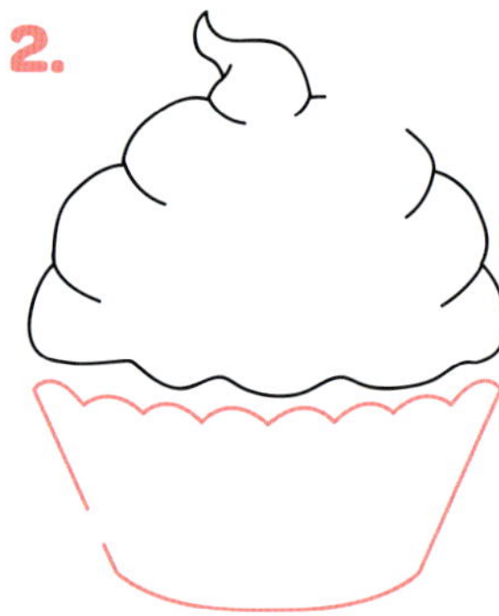

2. Leaving a gap below the frosting, add the cupcake bottom: a rectangle with a wider top, leaving a gap on the left side, and a scalloped top edge for the cupcake wrapper.

3. Draw a circle with a square bottom for the skull at the top, and add curved diamond sparkles at the bottom. Add lines to fill in the cupcake wrapper.

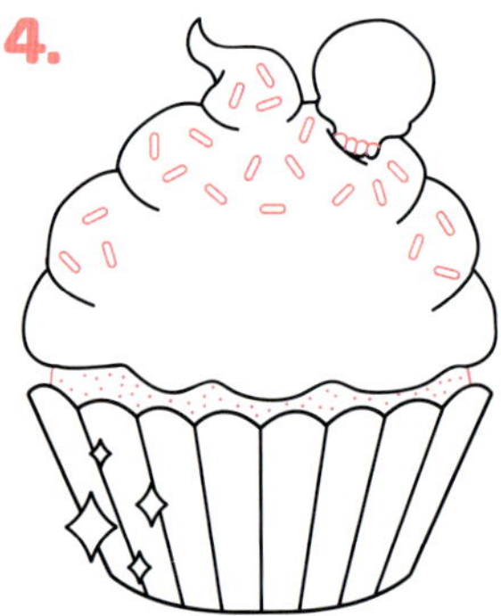

4. Draw two short lines to connect the frosting and the wrapper, and fill this area with tiny dots to make cake look extra moist. Draw tiny rectangles for sprinkles, and add teeth to skull.

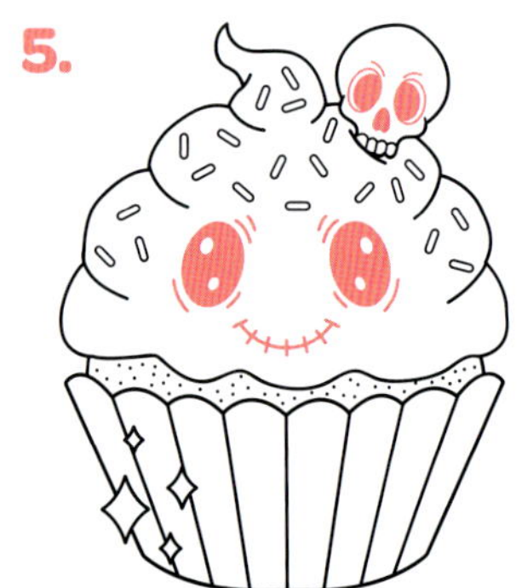

5. Give the cupcake a creepy cute smile and big eyes, and draw the skull's eye sockets and nose.

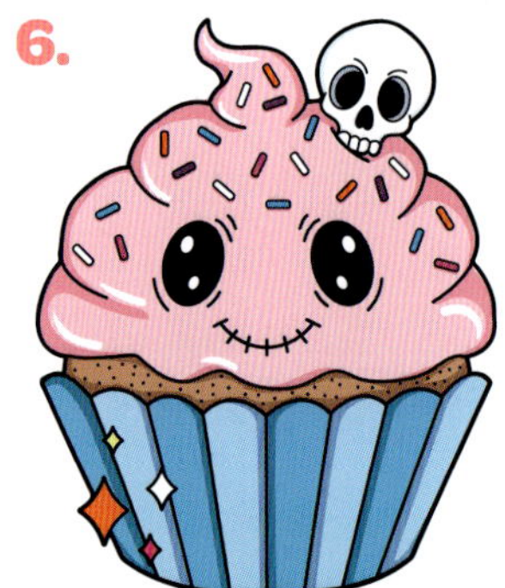

6. Color in your Creepy Cute Cupcake!

ROTTEN MILK

1.

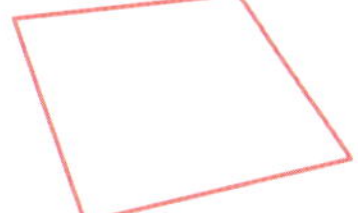

Start by drawing the top of the milk carton as a slanted rectangle.

2.

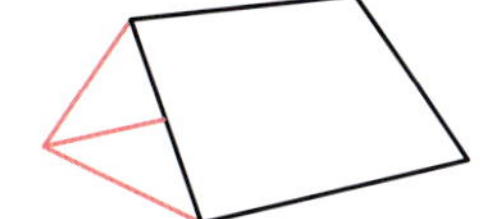

Draw a triangle to the left of the rectangle and add a line across the middle.

3.

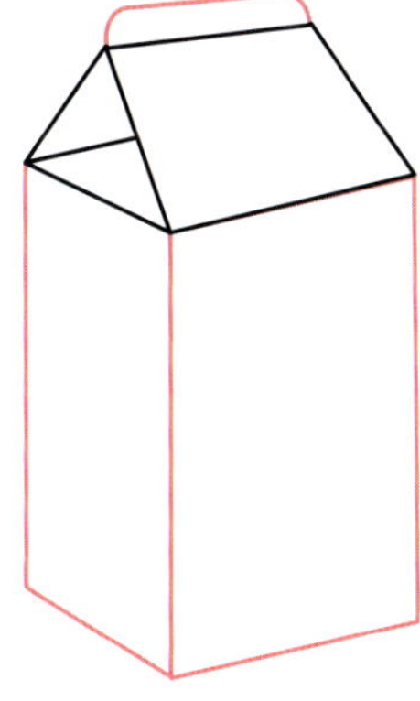

For the carton itself, draw a tall rectangle and, on the left side, a slanted rectangle. At the very top, add a narrow rectangle with curved corners.

4.

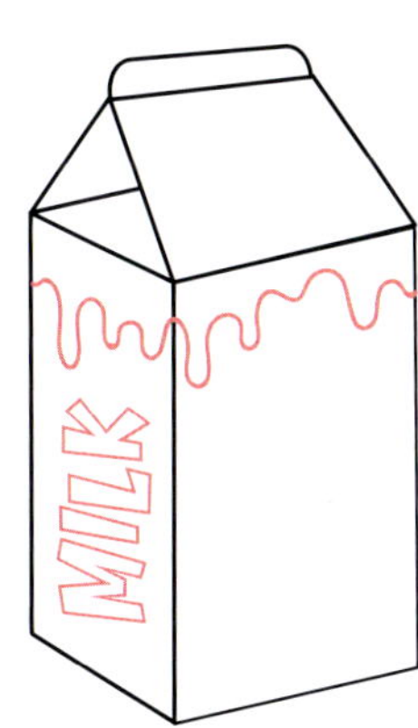

Add a wavy dripping line to the carton front and side, and write "MILK" on the side.

5.

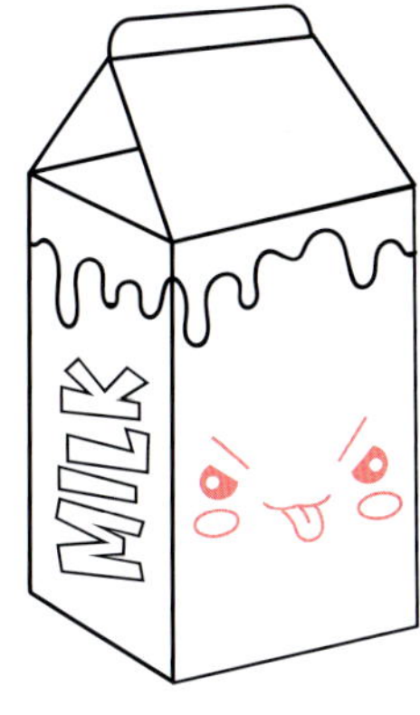

Draw a creepy cute face under dripping line, perhaps with its tongue sticking out.

6.

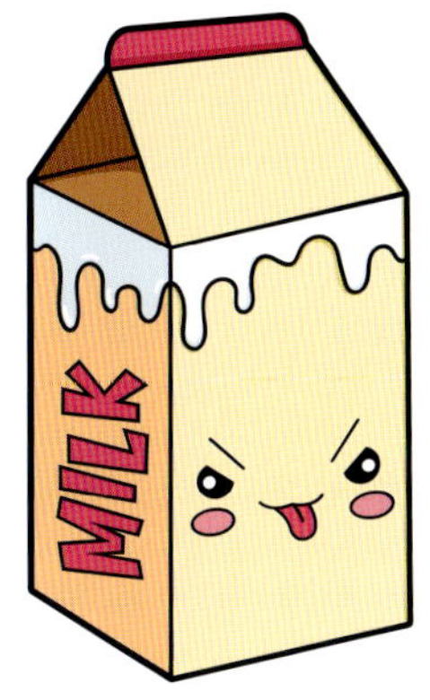

Color in your Rotten Milk!

SKULL ROLLING PIN

1.

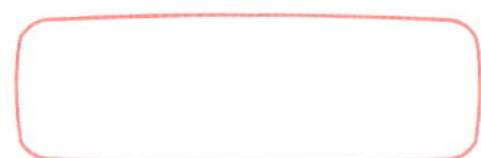

Start by drawing a rectangle with rounded corners.

2.

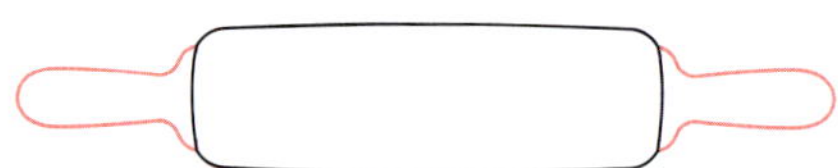

Add a handle to either side.

3.

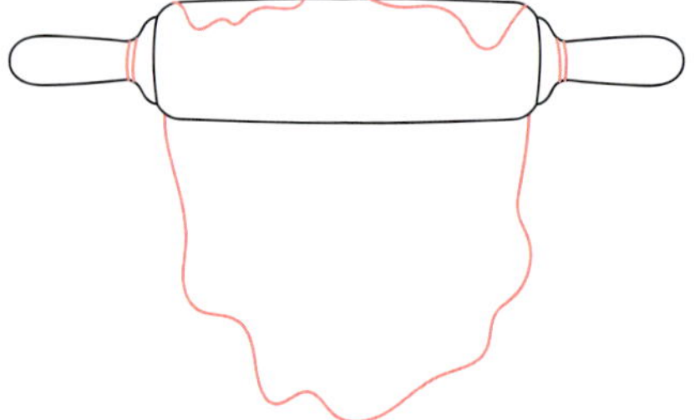

Draw two curved lines on each handle. Then draw a wavy line under the rolling pin for the dough. Add some more wavy dough lines to the top of the rolling pin.

4.

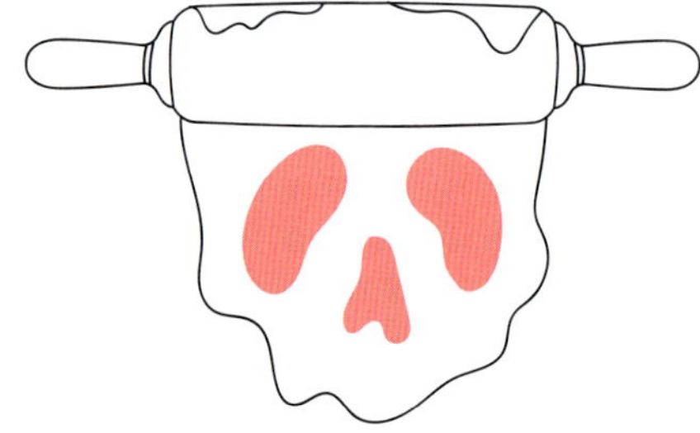

Draw a skull face on the dough: two curved, filled-in ovals for eye sockets and a filled-in upside-down heart for the nose.

5.

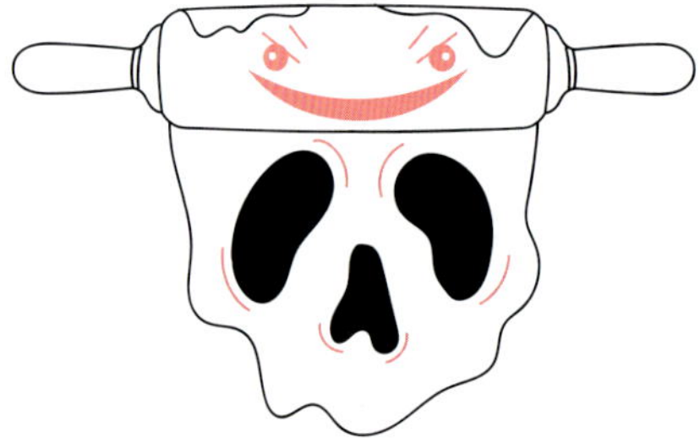

Give the rolling pin a creepy face with a wide smile. Add lines around the skull's eye sockets and nose to make it look extra gooey.

6.

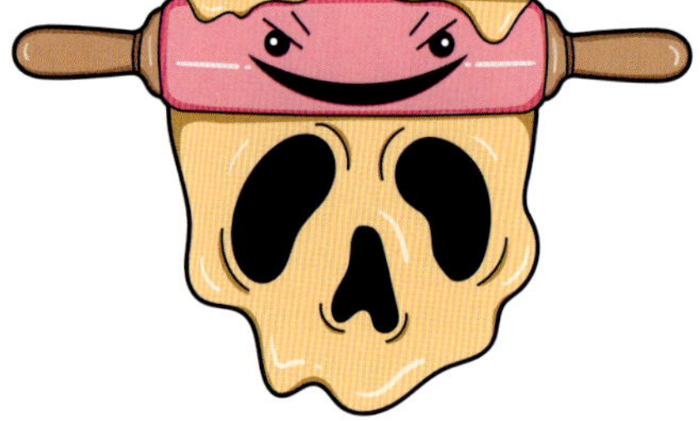

Color in your Skull Rolling Pin!

GOOPY GOGGLES

1.

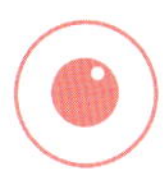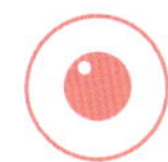

Start by drawing the insides of the eyeballs: two circles, each with a shaded circle inside it.

2.

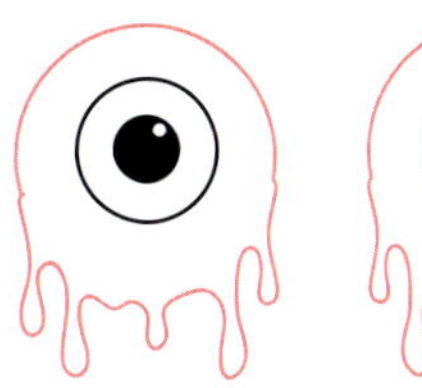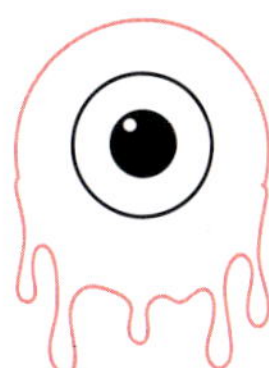

For the outside lines of the eyeballs, draw half circles on top and dripping lines at the bottom.

3.

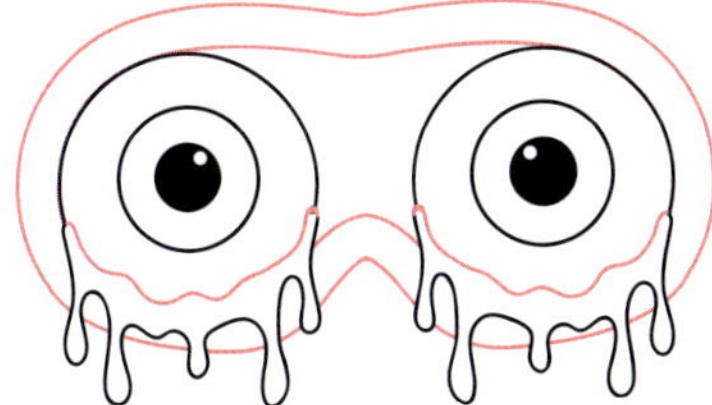

Draw a goggle shape around the eyeballs using two parallel lines. In the area below the eyeballs, make the inner line wiggly.

4.

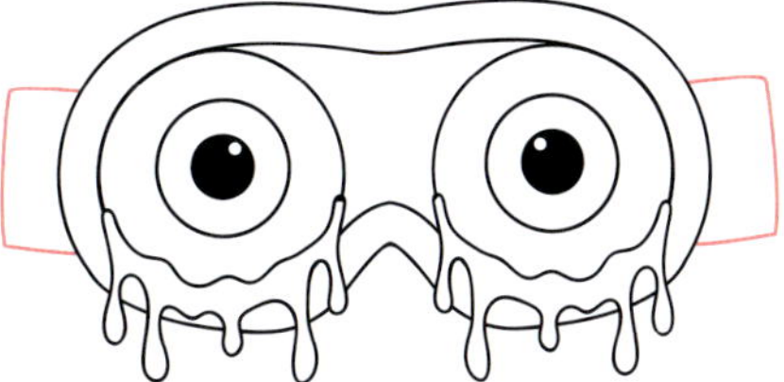

For the strap, draw a rectangle on each side of the goggles.

5.

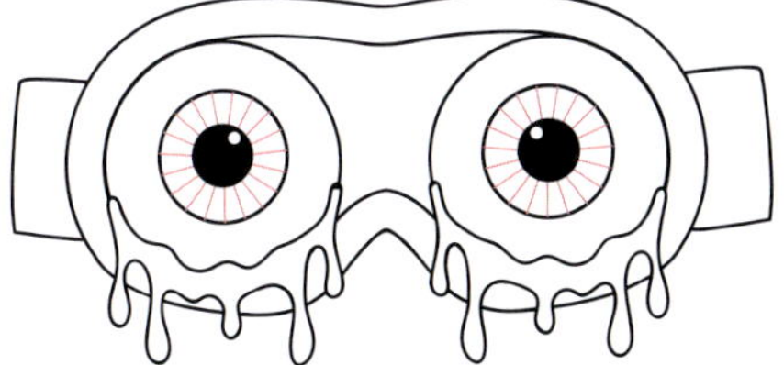

Draw some lines on the eyeballs for extra detail.

6.

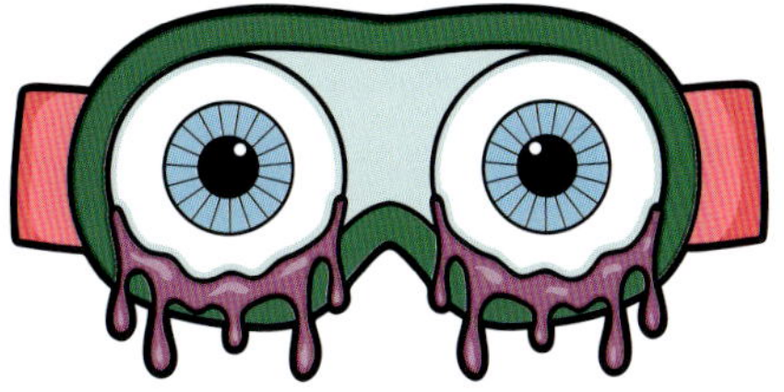

Color in your Goopy Goggles!

BROKEN TEDDY

1.

Start by drawing the snowball as a little scalloped circle.

2.

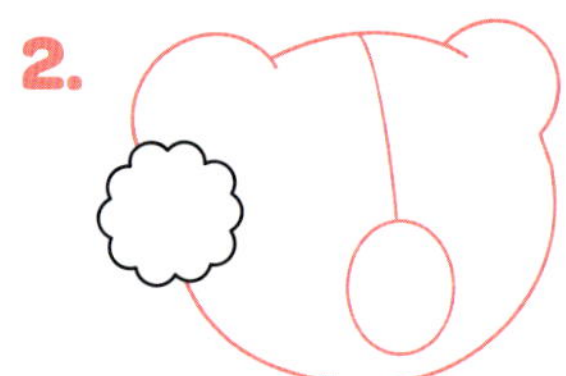

Draw the outline of the teddy bear's head as a circle with a small half circle (ear) on either side. Draw an oval inside the head and a curved line connecting it to the top of the head.

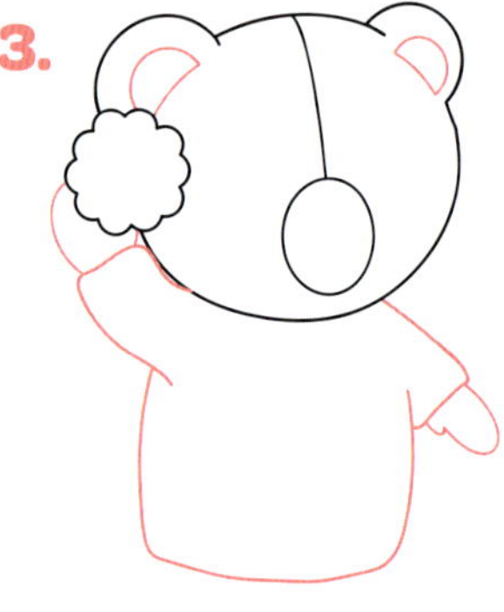

Add a round body with rectangular arms, one of them raised close to the snowball. Add paws, and draw a half circle inside each ear.

4.

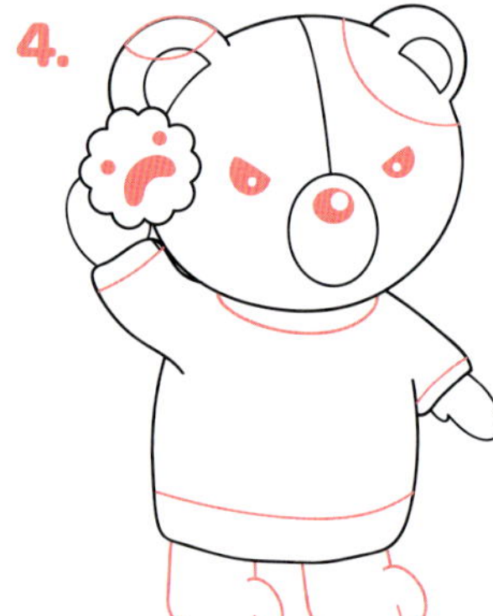

Draw short legs and feet with rounded toes. Add trim at the cuffs, neckline, and hem of the sweater. Draw a half circle at the top of one ear and another under the other ear. Draw the bear's eyes and nose, and add a face to the snowball.

5.

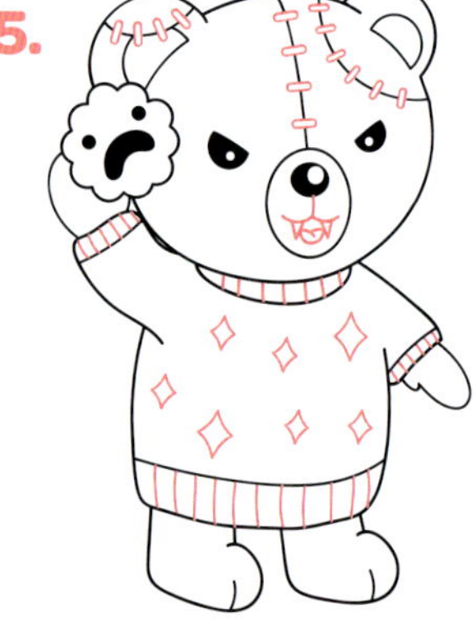

Give the bear a creepy cute smile and stitches. Then add lines to the sweater trim and little diamonds on the front of the sweater.

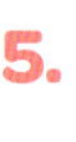

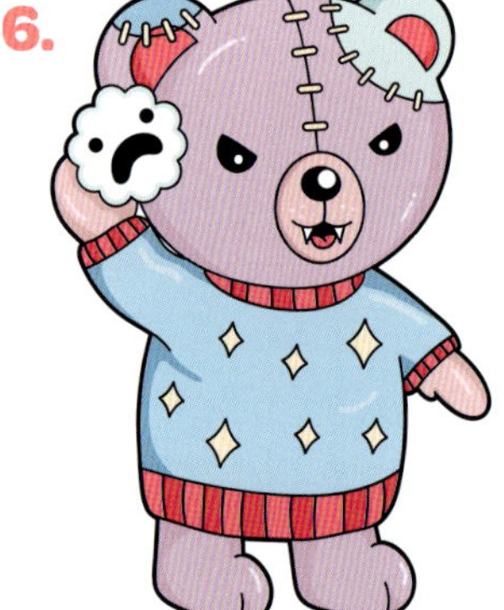

Color in your Broken Teddy!

EVIL SLED

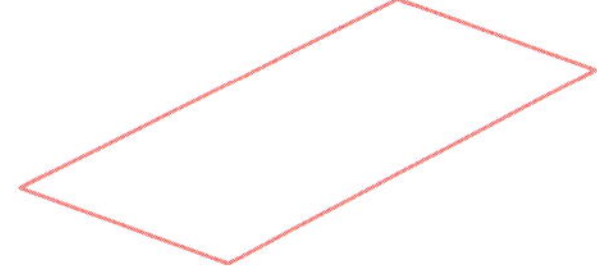

1. Start by drawing the top of the sled as a slanted rectangle.

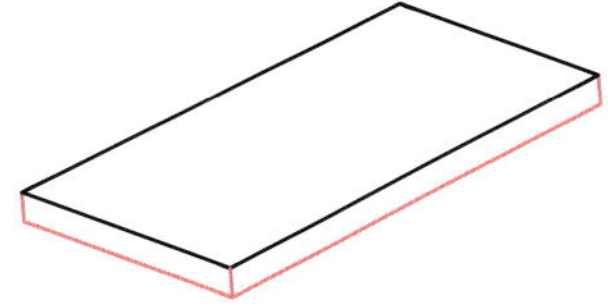

2. Add lines below the slanted rectangle, and join them to the rectangle at the corners with straight vertical lines.

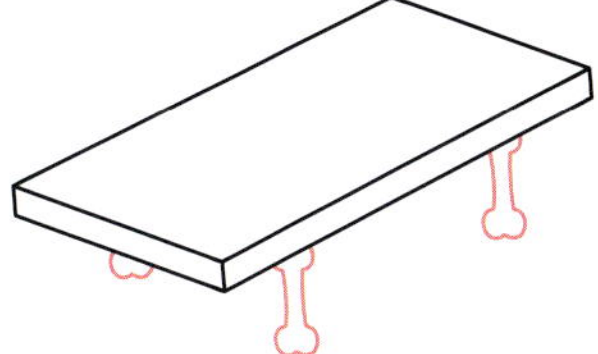

3. Add vertical bone shapes underneath the rectangle.

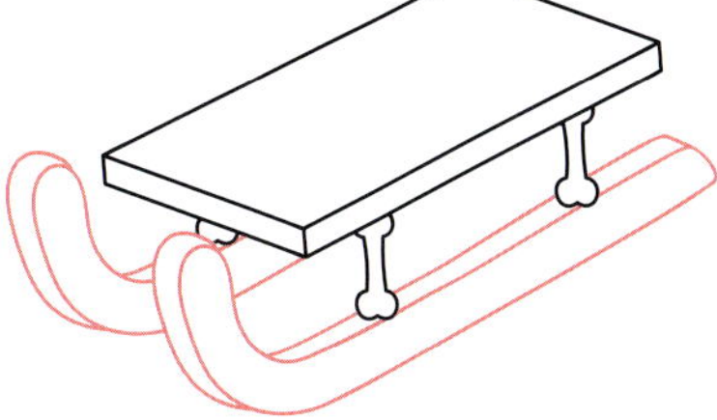

4. Draw in the blades as sideways J shapes.

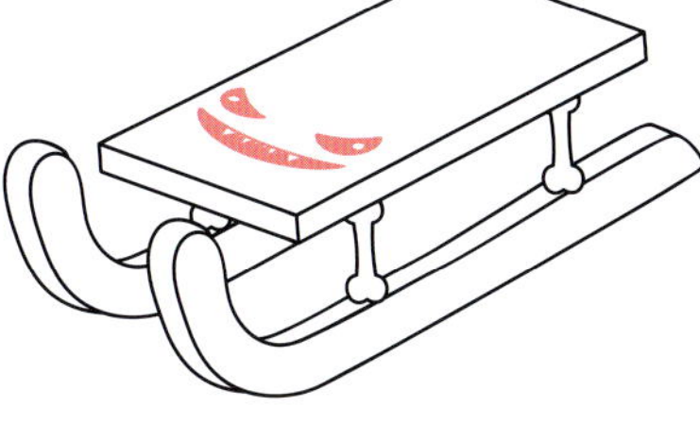

5. On the top of the sled, add a creepy face with a wide smile and slanted eyes.

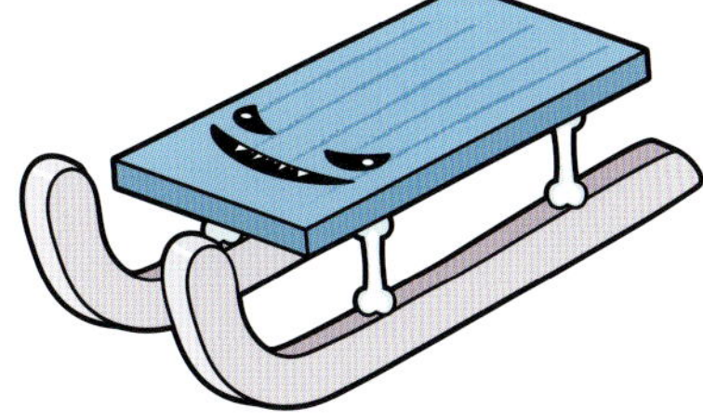

6. Color in your Evil Sled!

BONEY BOOT

1.

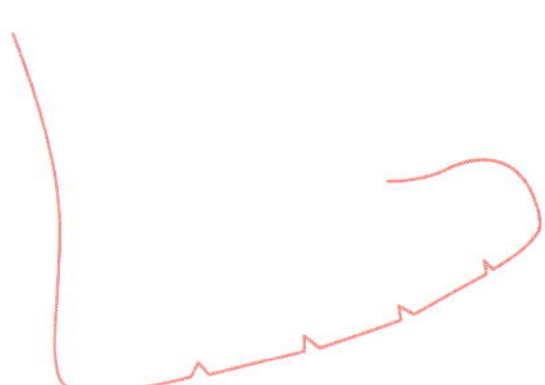

Start by drawing the outline of the boot: a curved vertical line on the left, continuing into most of a rounded rectangle on the bottom. Give the bottom of the boot treads.

2.

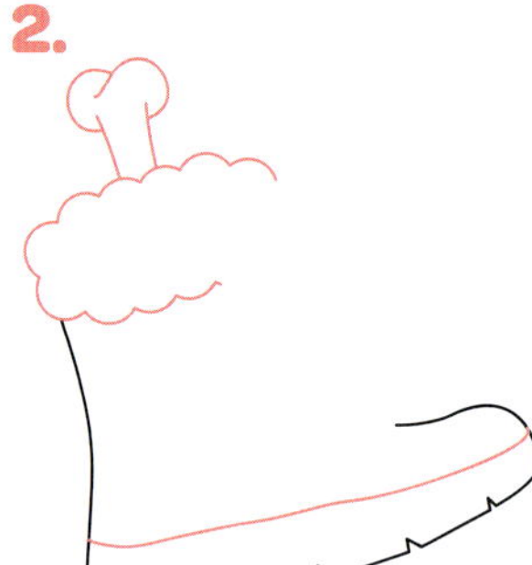

Draw a scalloped oval on top of the boot, leaving the lower right corner open. Add a bone shape to the top. Add a line at the bottom for the boot sole.

3.

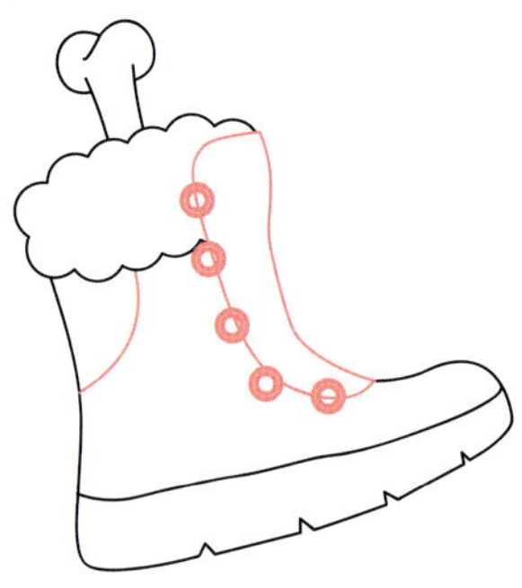

Close up the open front of the boot with a curved, triangular tongue. Add round eyelets along the edge. Add a quarter circle to the back of the boot.

4.

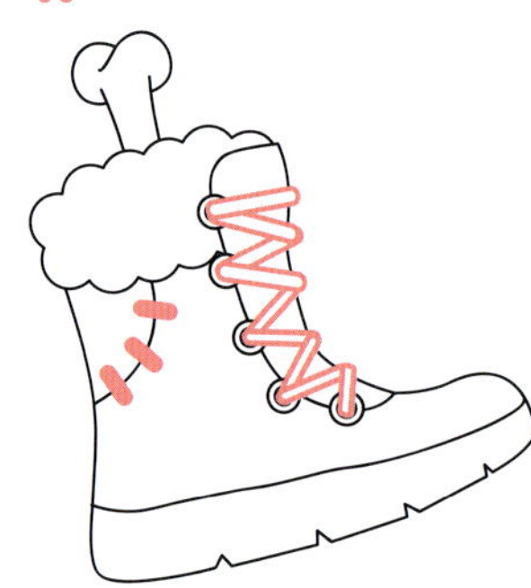

For the laces, add a zigzag line connecting to the eyelets. Then draw stitch lines along the quarter circle.

5.

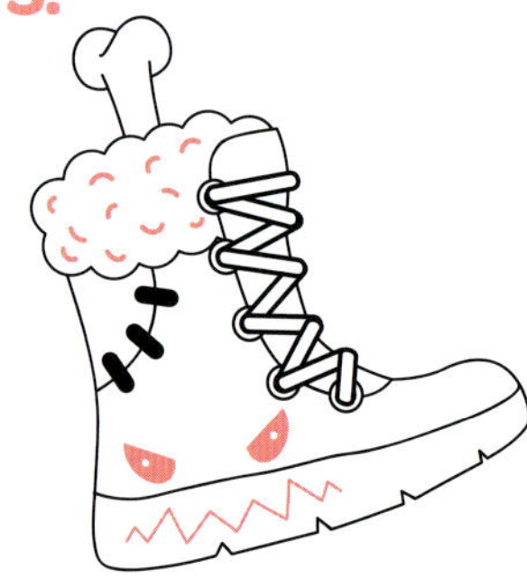

Give the boot a creepy cute zigzag smile and big eyes. Add small, curved lines to the top to make the boot lining look fluffy.

6.

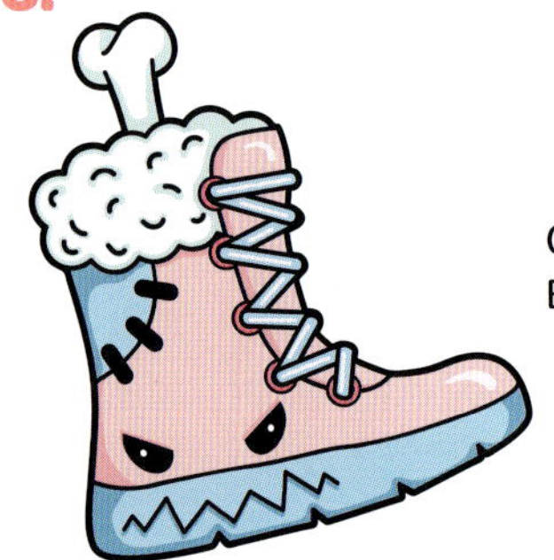

Color in your Boney Boot!

EYEBALL PLANT

1.

Start by drawing the base of the plant pot.

2.

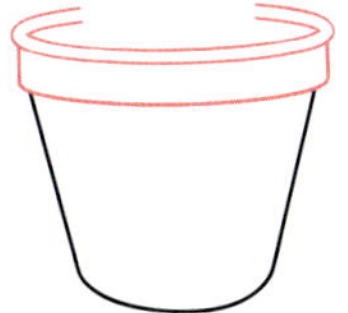

Draw the top of the pot as a curved rectangle. Add an oval above it, leaving the top of the oval open. Extend the top line of the rectangle to double the oval line.

3.

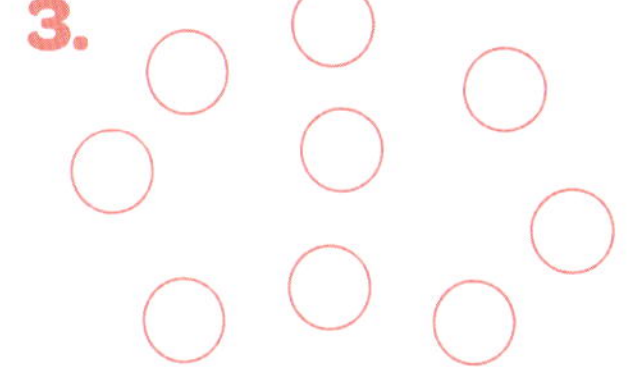

Add some circles to outline the eyeballs.

4.

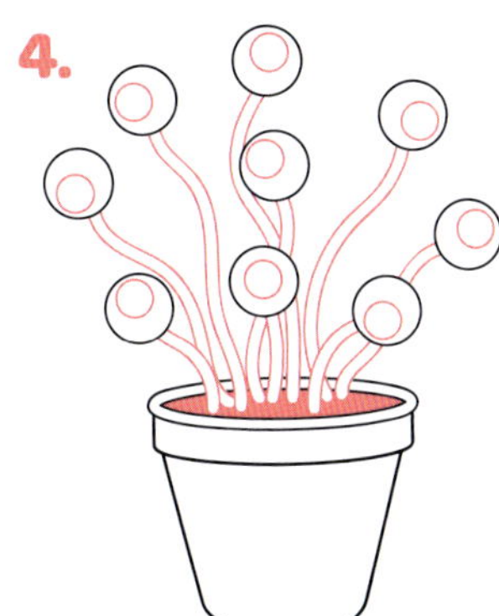

To form stalks, add double curved lines from the bottom of each eyeball to the pot. Add a circle inside each eyeball. Then fill in the soil inside the pot.

5.

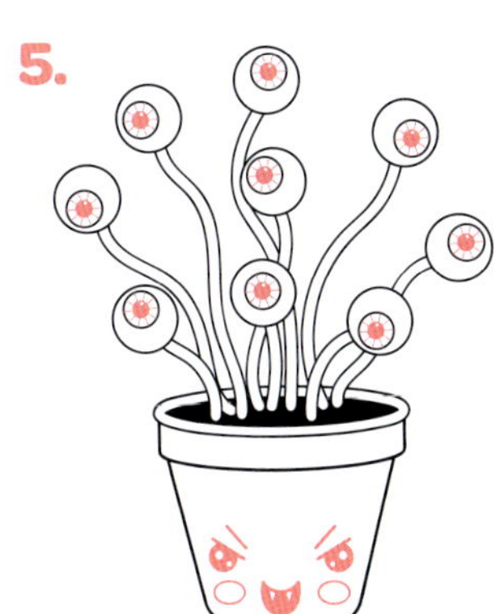

Add filled-in pupils with vein lines to the eyeballs, and draw an evil face on the pot.

6.

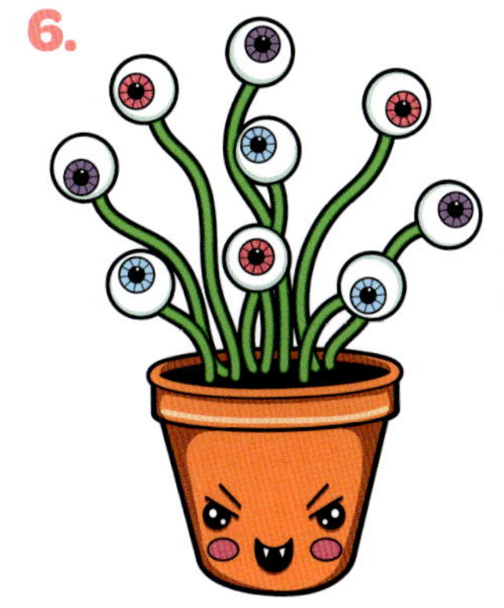

Color in your Eyeball Plant!

MONSTER PLANT

1.

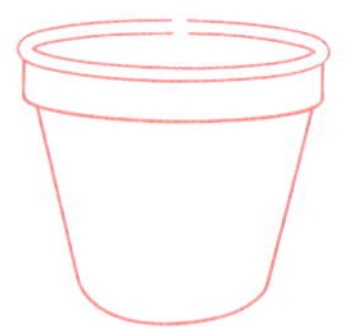

Start by drawing the base of the plant pot. Add a curved rectangle to the top and an oval above that with a small gap at the top. Extend the top line of the rectangle to double the oval line.

2.

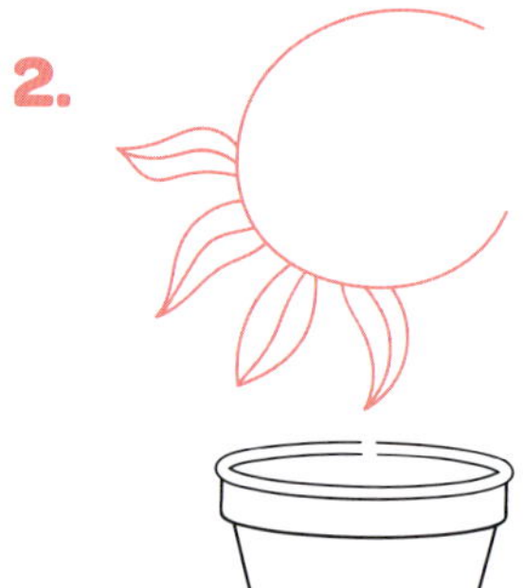

Draw a circle above the pot, leaving the right side open. Add leaf shapes to the left side of the circle.

3.

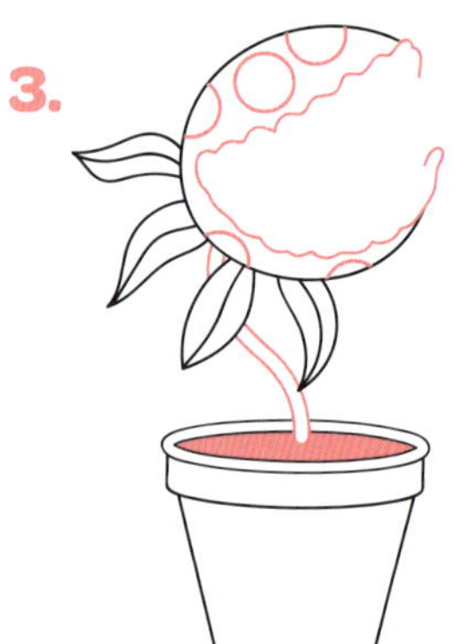

Add a wavy line inside the circle for an open mouth. Add circles inside head. Draw the plant stalk and fill in the soil in the plant pot.

4.

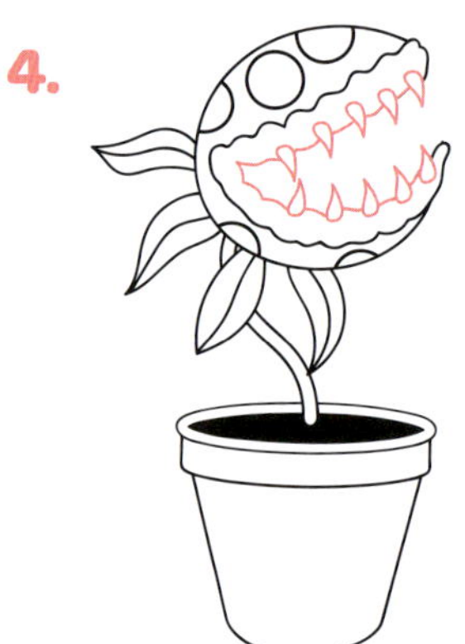

Add pointy teeth and a second wavy line to finish the mouth.

5.

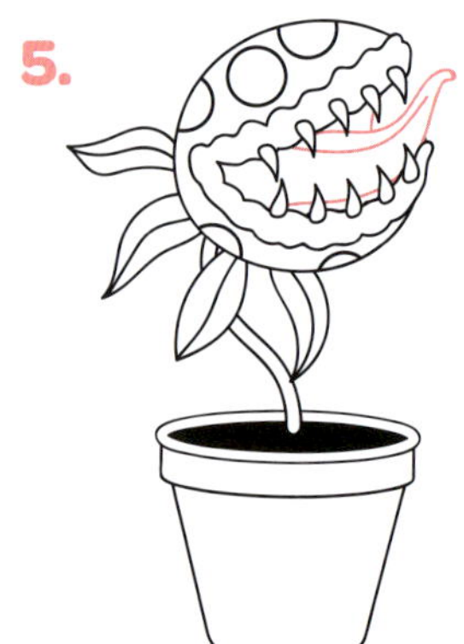

Add a creepy curly tongue in mouth. Add a small vertical line above the tongue.

6.

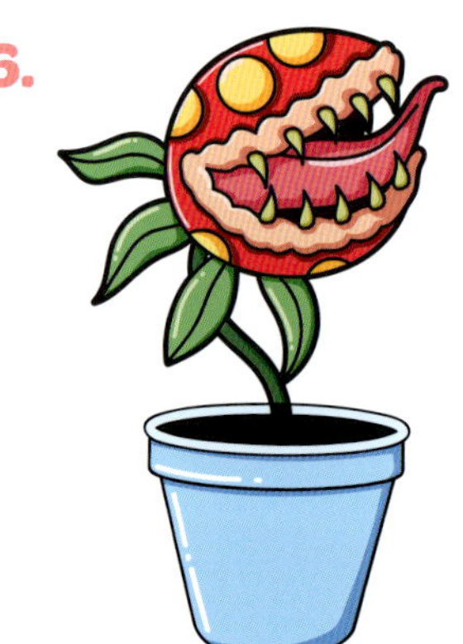

Color in your Monster Plant!

GARDENING GHOST

1.

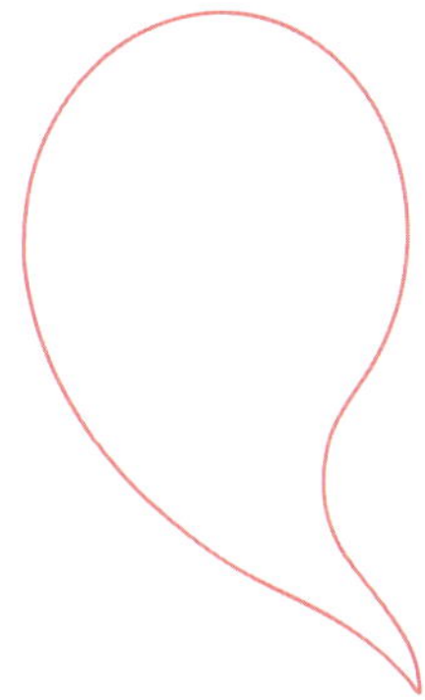

Start by drawing a bendy teardrop shape for the outline of the ghost.

2.

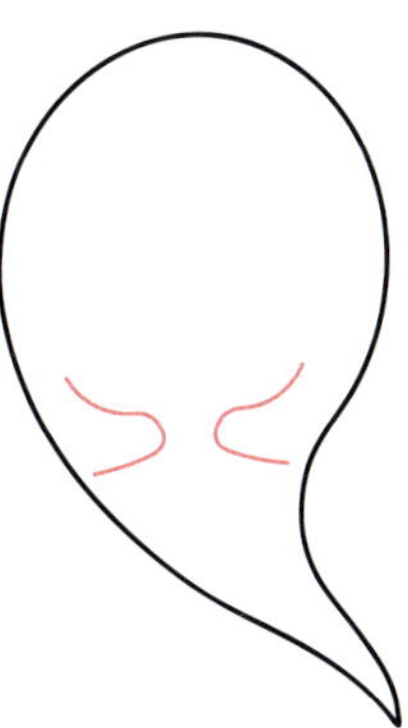

Add two arm shapes just below the middle of the ghost outline.

3.

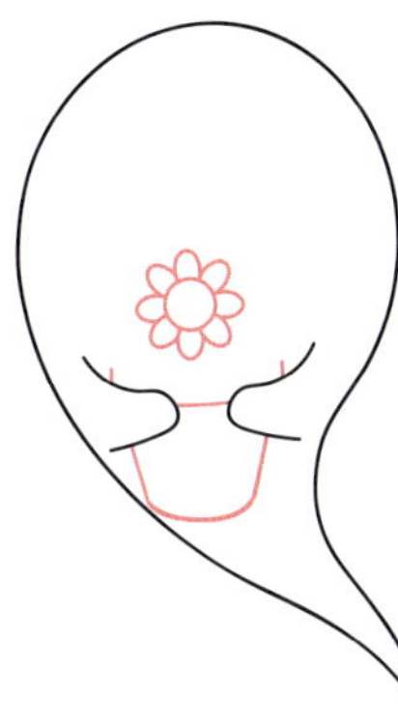

Add two symmetrical slanted lines below the arms and a line between the arms. For the bottom of the pot, add a curved horizontal line to connect the ends of the slanted lines below the arms. Add two little vertical straight lines above the arms. Draw a circle with little ovals around it for the flower.

4.

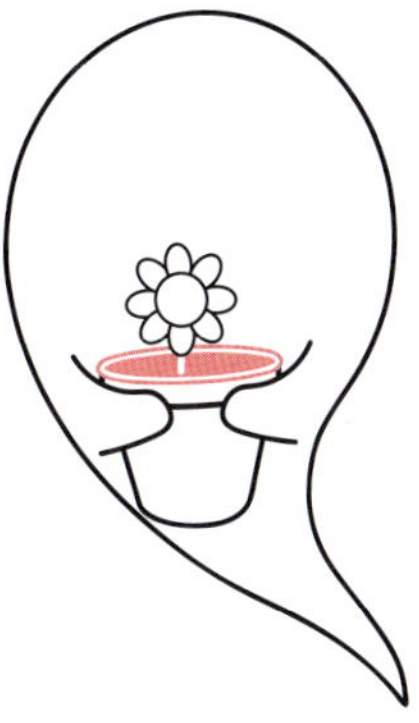

Add a small rectangle below the flower for the stalk, and add an oval joining the two sides of the flower pot. Fill in the middle of the oval, leaving the stalk blank. Add a line around the oval for the lip of the pot.

5.

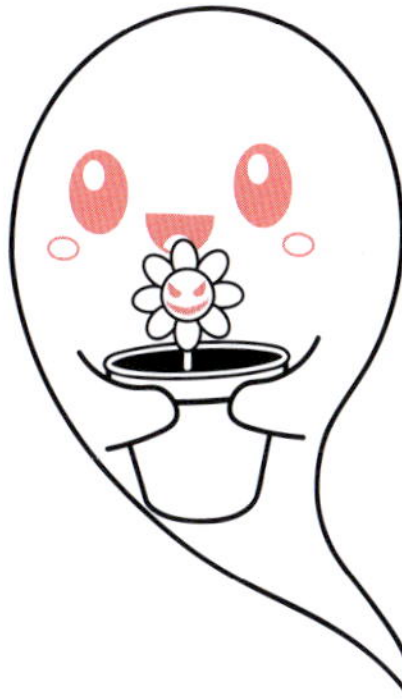

Add a spooky cute face to the inside of the flower, and add a cute face to the ghost.

6.

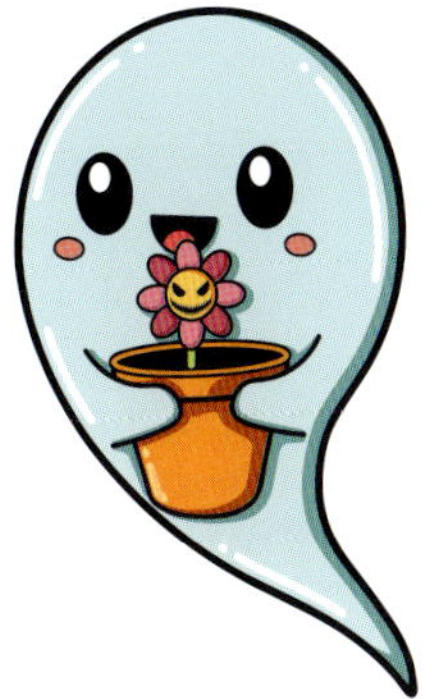

Color in your Gardening Ghost!

COBWEB MUSHROOM AND FRIEND

1.

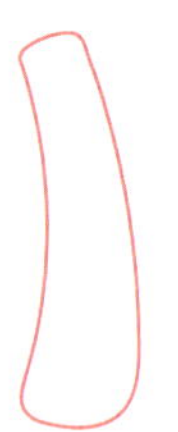

Start by drawing a curved rectangle with rounded edges, wider at the bottom, for the mushroom's stalk.

2.

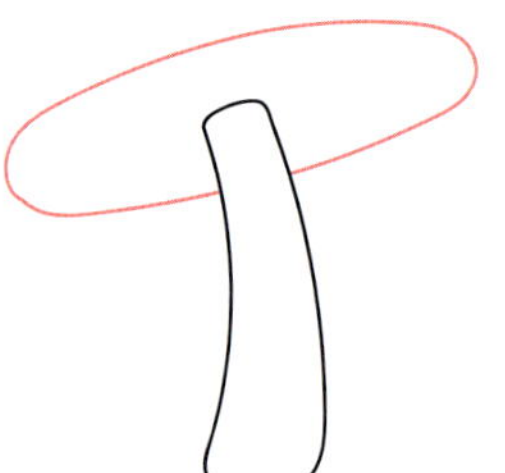

Add an oval at the top of the stalk.

3.

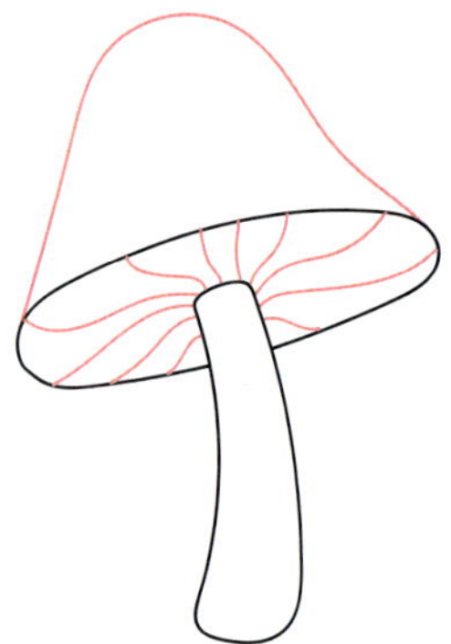

Draw a bell shape joining the sides of the oval. Then draw wavy lines from the stalk to the edges of the oval.

4.

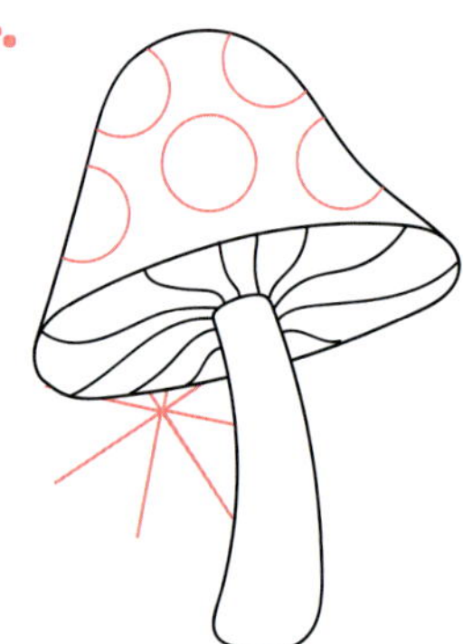

Start the cobweb with four straight lines crossing one another in a star shape. Add circles inside the mushroom cap.

5.

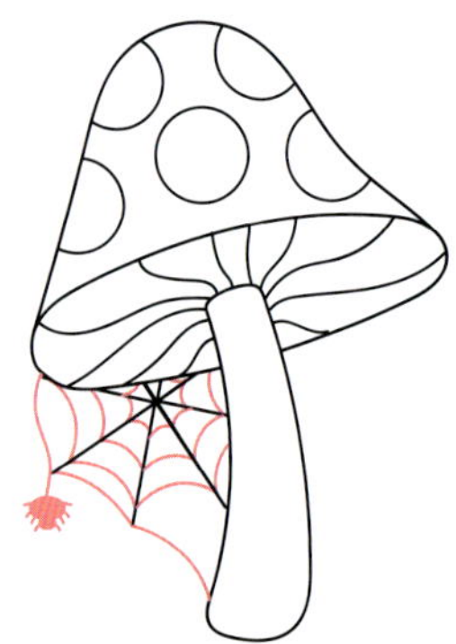

Add curved lines to the cobweb, and then draw a little spider hanging from the cobweb.

6.

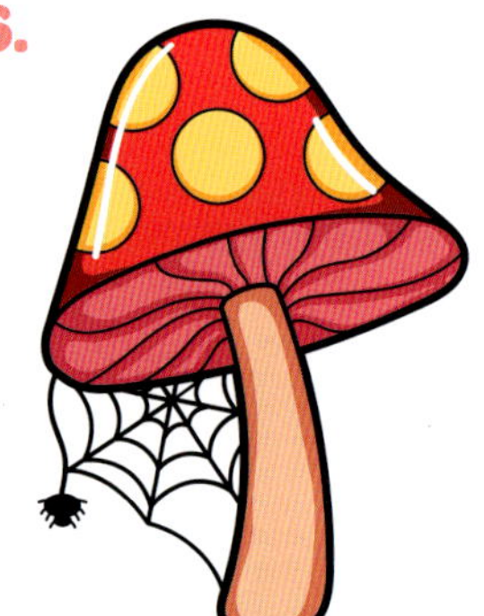

Color in your Cobweb Mushroom and Friend!

GARDENING GRIM REAPER

1. 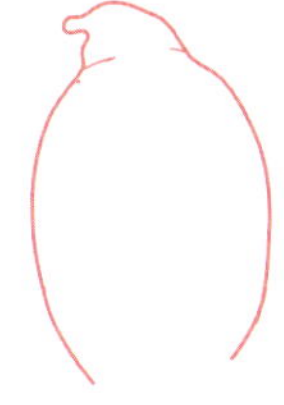

Start by drawing the outline of the hood as an oval with a bending point at the top. Leave the bottom open.

2. 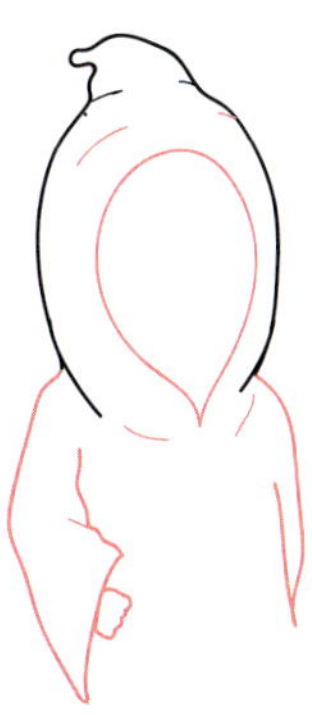

Draw a sleeve shape on the left and a thinner one on the right. Add torso lines. Draw a rectangle for the hand. Inside the hood, add an upside-down teardrop and some lines to make the edge look folded.

3. 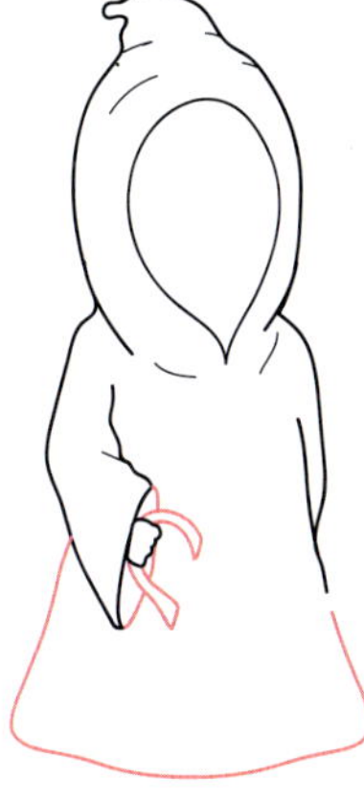

Draw the bottom of the cloak, leaving a small gap on the right side, and add a handle for the watering can. Add a curved line to finish the sleeve.

4. 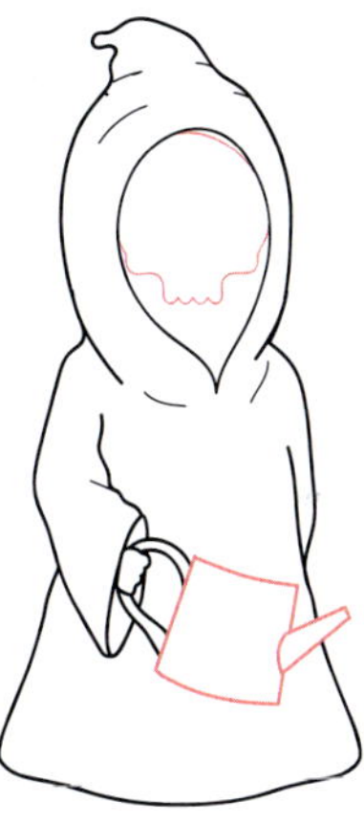

Add the cylinder shape of the watering can, then the spout. Inside the hood, draw a skull with a square jaw.

5. 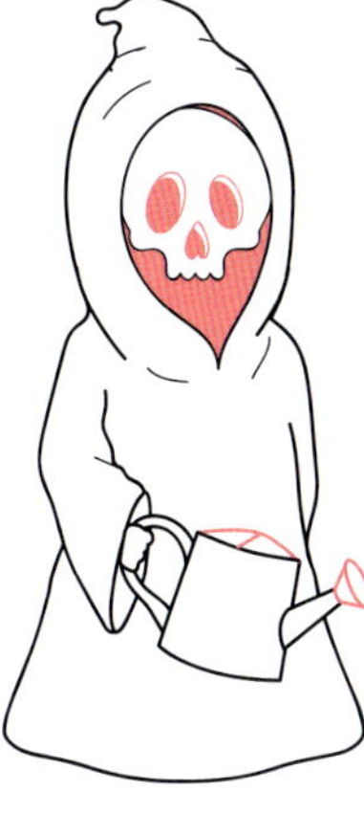

Add two big oval eye sockets to the skull and an upside-down heart nose. Shade them in, and fill in the area around the skull. Add the cap and nozzle to the watering can.

6. 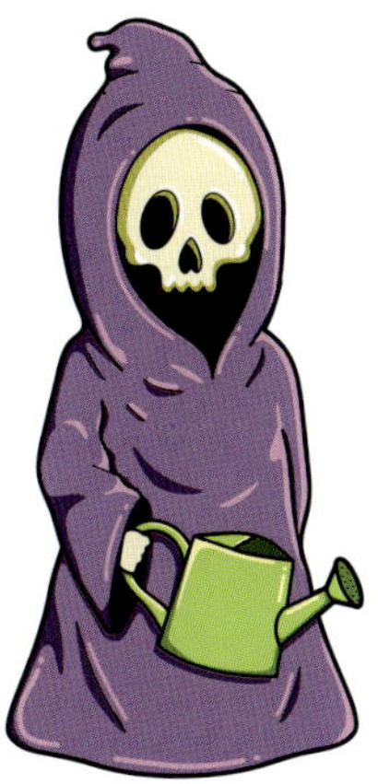

Color in your Gardening Grim Reaper!

EVIL BEE

1.

Start by drawing the head: a furry circle with two gaps at the top and a larger gap at the bottom right.

2.

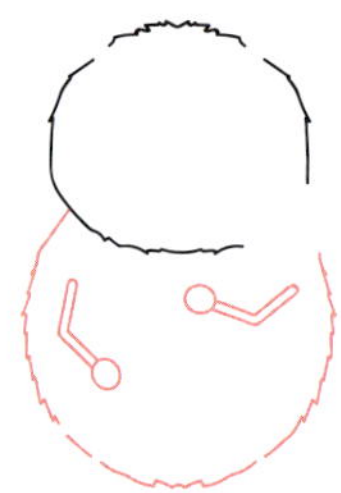

Draw a furry oval for the body with three small gaps along the bottom, then add thin rectangles for arms and circles for hands.

3.

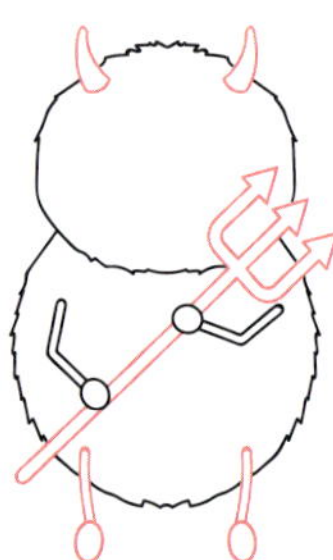

Make the pitchfork with an E shape with triangular tips at the top, then a straight stick passing through the hands. Then draw curved triangles for the horns. Add two legs with circles for feet.

4.

For the wings, draw two ovals on each side of body—one large and one smaller. Add an upside-down triangle for the stinger. Put curly antennae on the head, with furry circles at the ends.

5.

Add wiggly lines to the wings and stripes and fuzzy details to the body. Draw an evil face on the bee.

6.

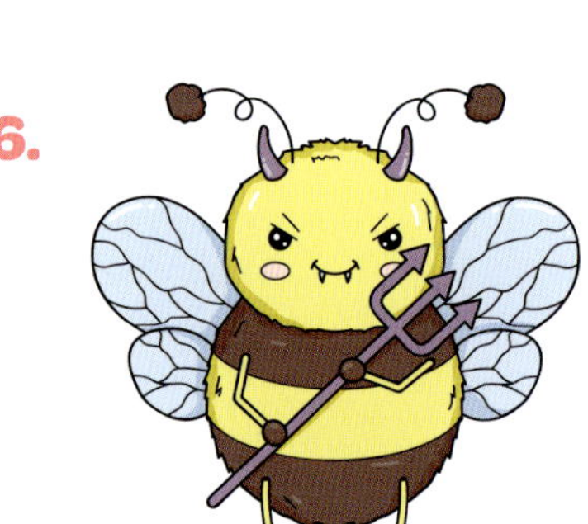

Color in your Evil Bee!

SKULL BUTTERFLY

1.

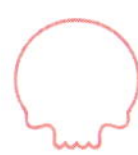

Start by drawing the skull shape: a circle with a square jaw.

2.

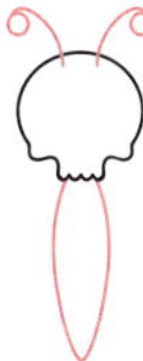

Draw a narrow, petal-shaped body, then draw two antennae coming out of the top of the skull.

3.

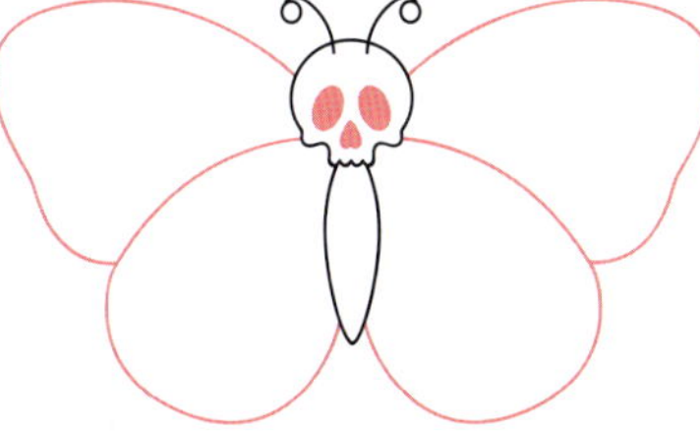

Inside the skull outline, add two oval eye sockets and an upside-down heart nose. Fill them in. Then add the wings on either side. Start with the bottom wings, then add the top ones.

4.

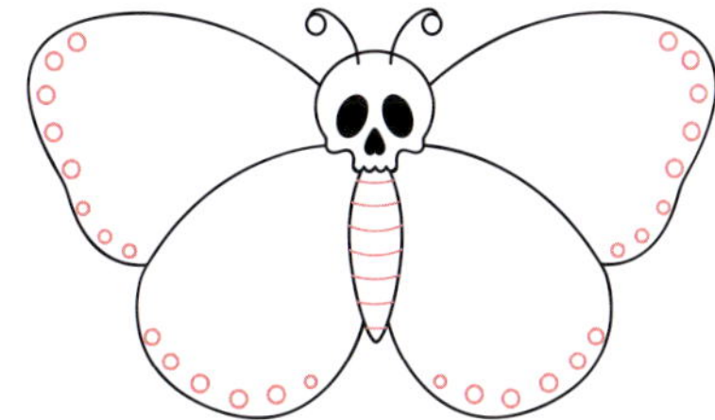

Draw little circles around the edges of the wings, and add stripes to the body.

5.

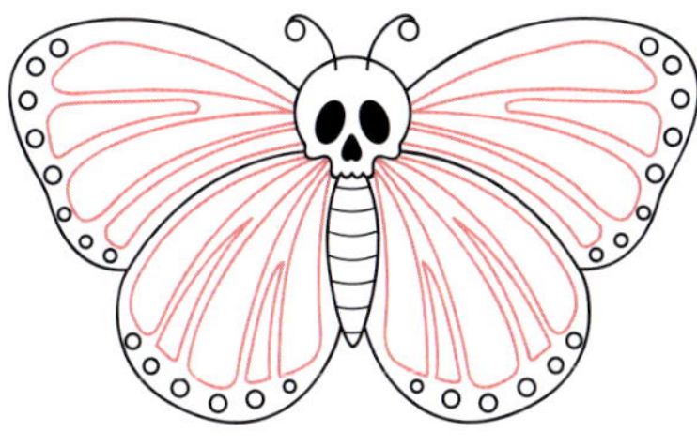

Add a triangular pattern inside the wings.

6.

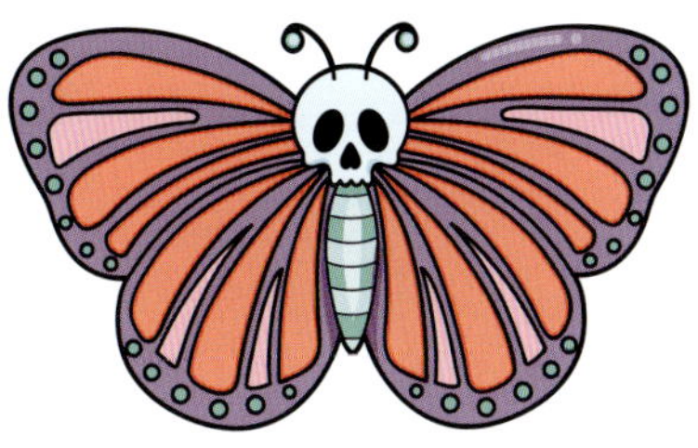

Color in your Skull Butterfly!

UNDEAD KITTY BALLOON

1. 

Start by drawing a circle.

2. 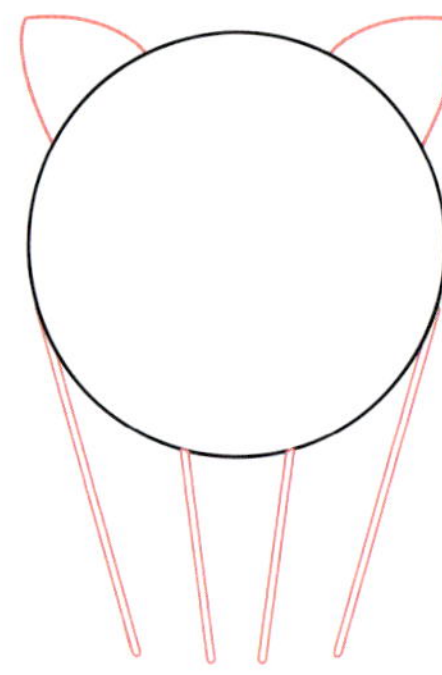

Add curved triangles for ears. Then draw four slanted double lines from the bottom of the circle downward.

3. 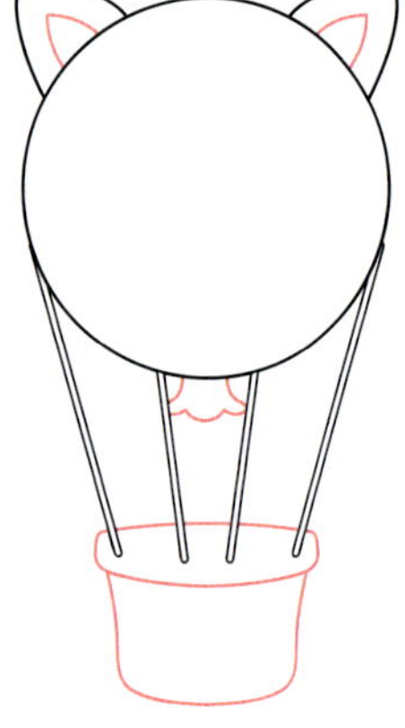

Add a smaller triangle inside each ear. Then draw the basket as a square with rounded corners and an oval on top. Under the circle, draw a triangle with a scalloped edge.

4. 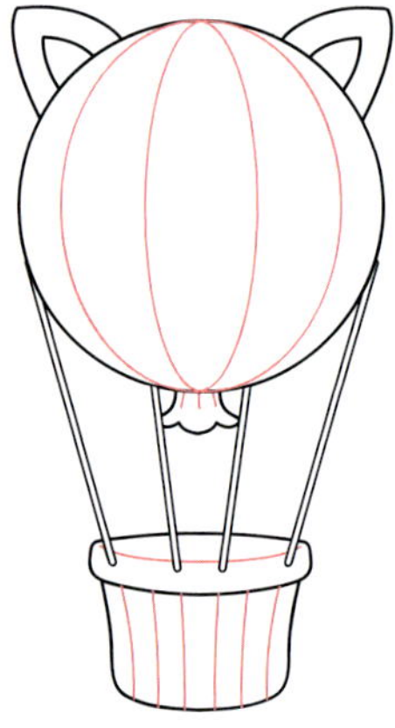

Draw a curved horizontal line connecting the bases of the rope lines. Draw vertical lines on the basket, and add some curved vertical lines to the balloon.

5. 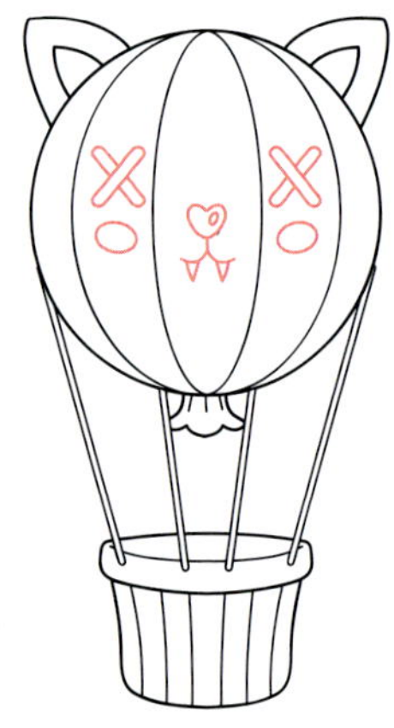

Draw X shapes for eyes, a heart-shaped nose, oval cheeks, and a creepy cat smile.

6. 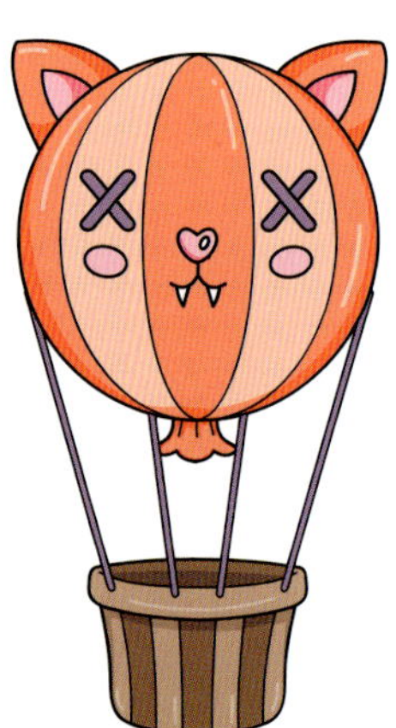

Color in your Undead Kitty Balloon!

GHOST WITH A FLOWER

1.

Start by drawing the flower shape: a circle surrounded by small oval petals.

2.

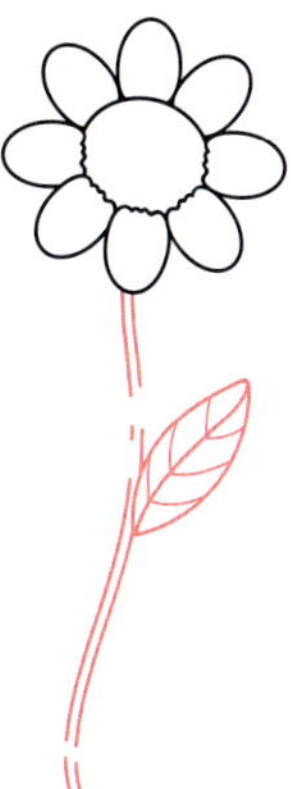

Add the stalk and a large leaf, leaving some gaps in the stalk for ghost hands and tail.

3.

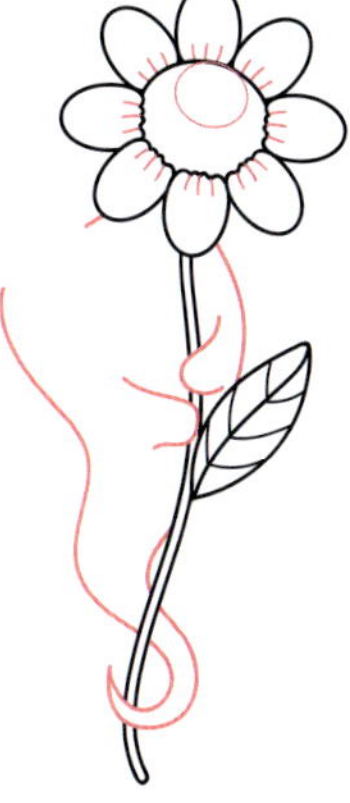

For the ghost, draw a curly teardrop, leaving the top open, and add arms wrapped around the stalk. Draw a circle inside the flower, and add some short lines to the petals.

4.

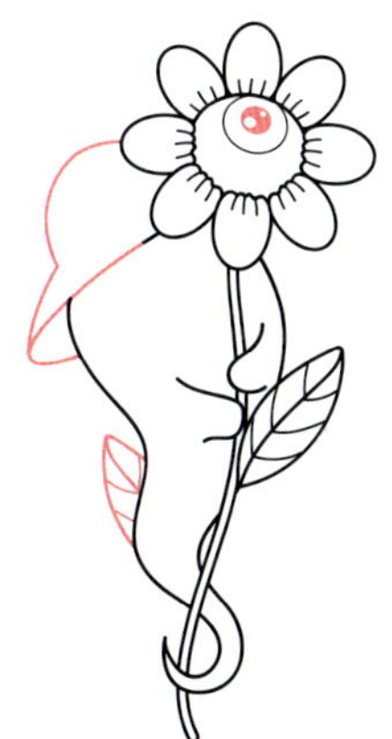

Draw the outline of the hat: a round top and a curved line. Draw and shade in a pupil to make the center of the flower an eyeball. Draw another leaf behind the ghost.

5.

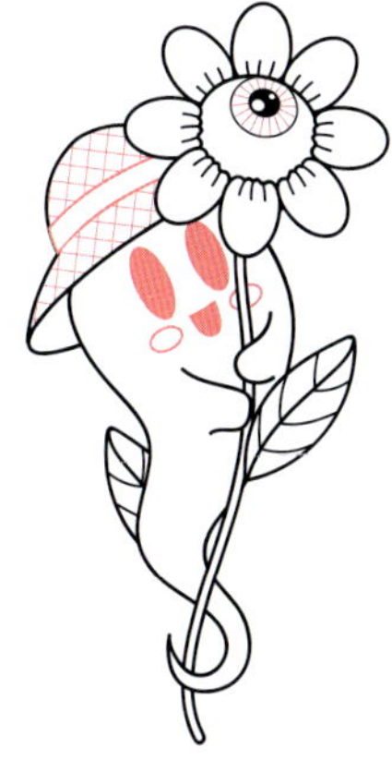

Give the ghost two big, filled-in oval eyes; oval cheeks; and a big, filled-in smile. Add a ribbon line to the hat, and shade the hat with a crosshatched pattern. Draw some lines on the eyeball of the flower for extra detail.

6.

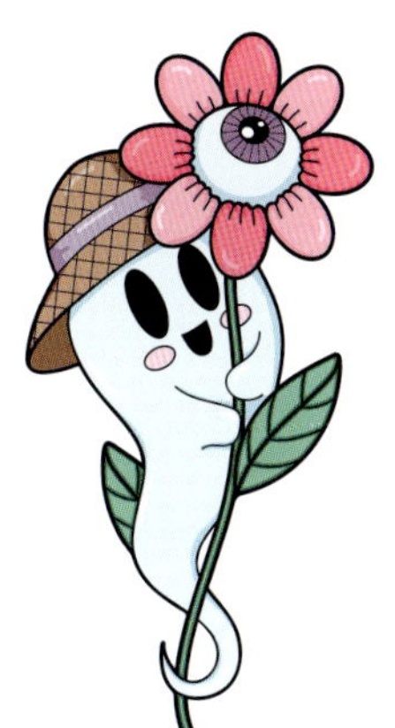

Color in your Ghost with a Flower!

ICE CREAM RAINBOW

1.

Start by drawing two half circles with a large gap between them.

2.

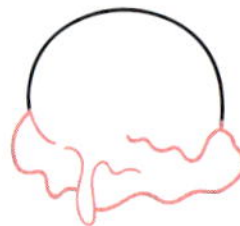

Add the bottoms of the ice cream scoops using wiggly lines. Add some drips.

3.

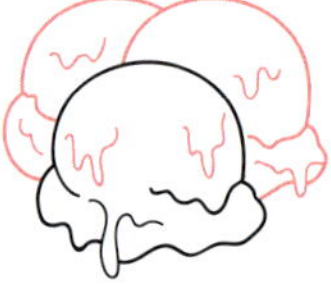
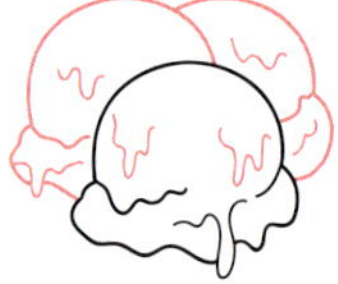

On each side, add two more scoops behind the first. Like before, use half circles on top and wavy lines at the bottom. Add dripping details to all of the ice cream.

4.

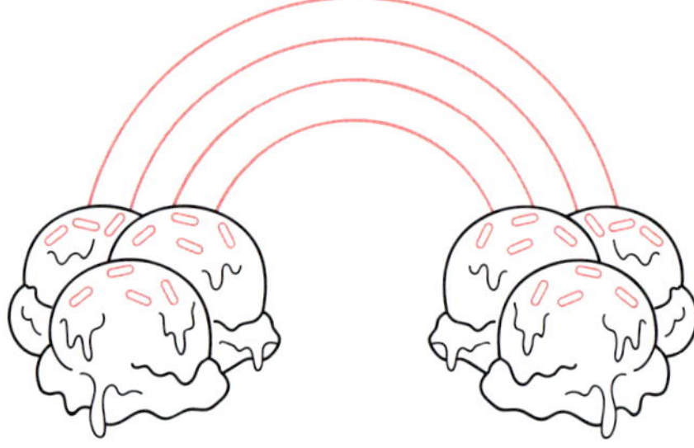

Add little rectangular sprinkles to each scoop. To make the rainbow, connect the two sets of scoops with four arched lines nested inside each other.

5.

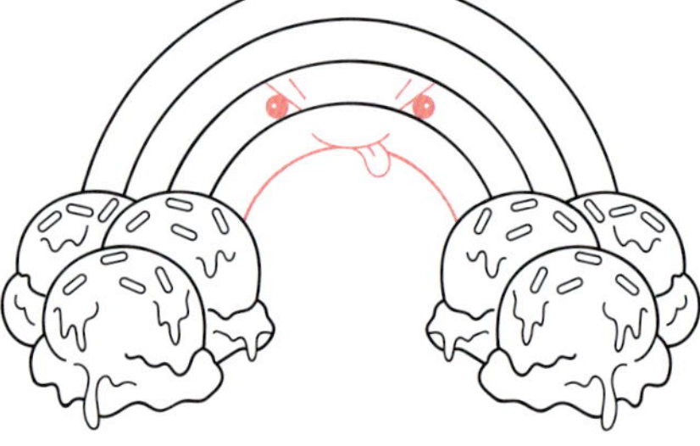

Draw a creepy cute face with its tongue sticking out. Then add a final bottom arch to the rainbow, touching the mouth.

6.

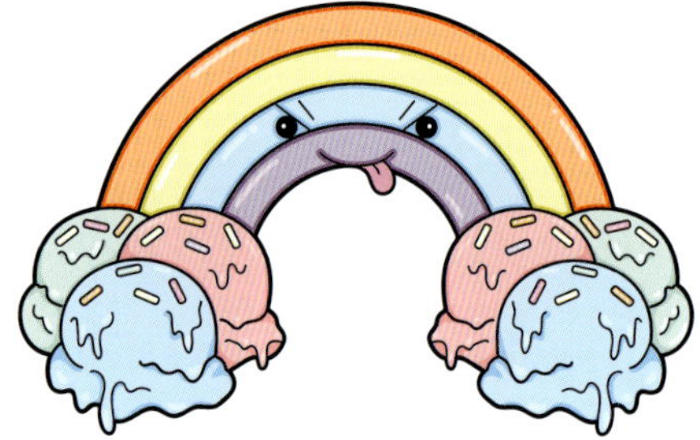

Color in your Ice Cream Rainbow!

ANGRY CLOUD

1.

Start by drawing the top of the cloud as a peaked shape with large scallops. Leave the bottom open.

2.

Add a short bone shape—made of a sideways heart and a rectangle—on either side.

3.

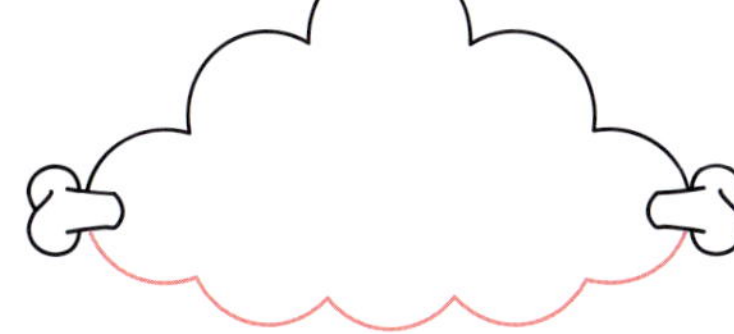

Draw the bottom of the cloud with large scallops.

4.

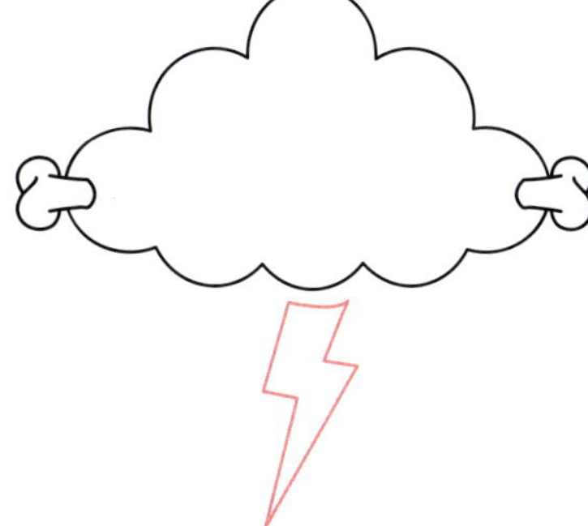

Draw a zigzag lightning bolt under the cloud.

5.

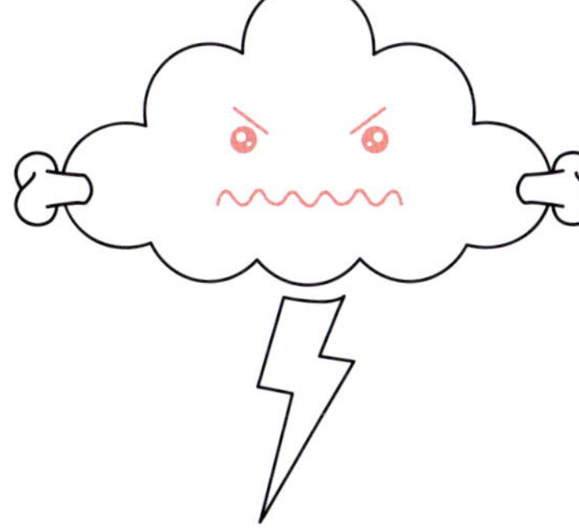

Give the cloud an angry face with a wiggly mouth and slanted eyebrows.

6.

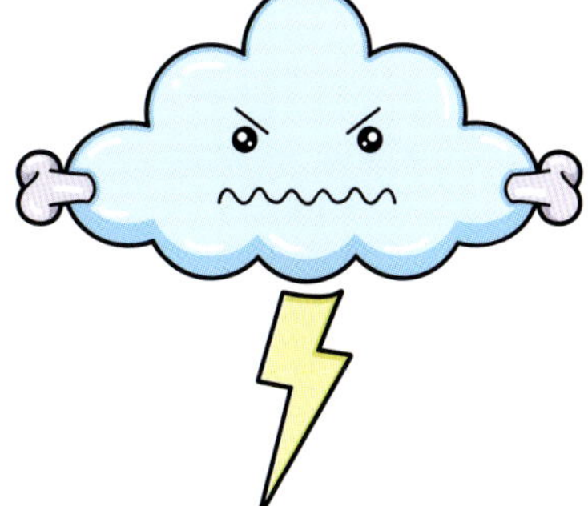

Color in your Angry Cloud!

MAD SUN

1. 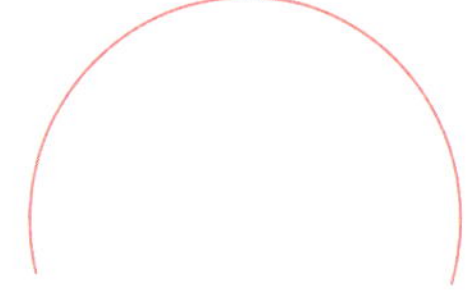

Start by drawing a little more than half of a circle. Leave the bottom open.

2. 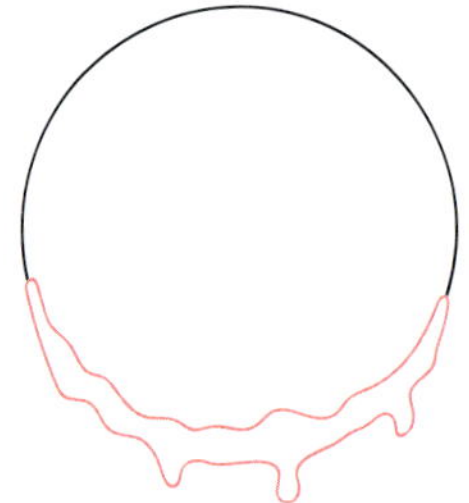

Add a wiggly line and drips at the bottom.

3. 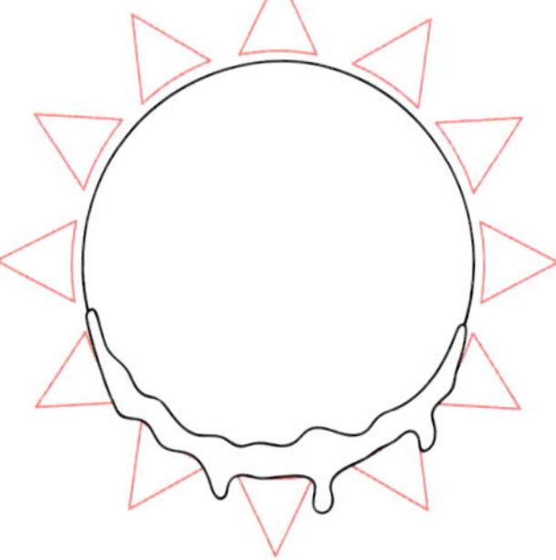

Draw triangles around the circle.

4. 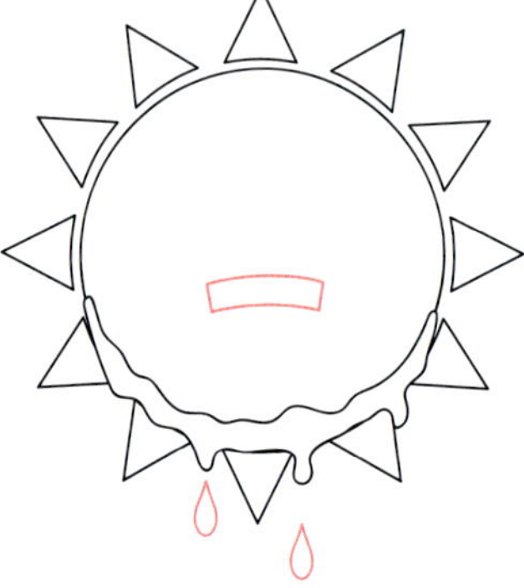

Add two teardrop drips under sun, and draw a curved rectangle for the mouth.

5. 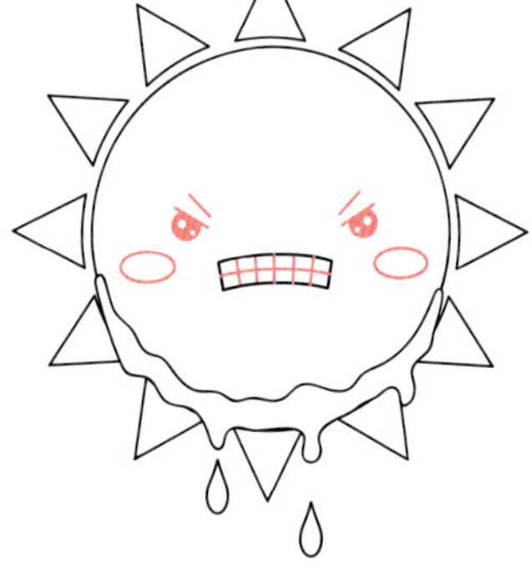

Draw slanted, shaded angry eyes; slanted eyebrows; and oval cheeks. Add teeth to the mouth.

6. 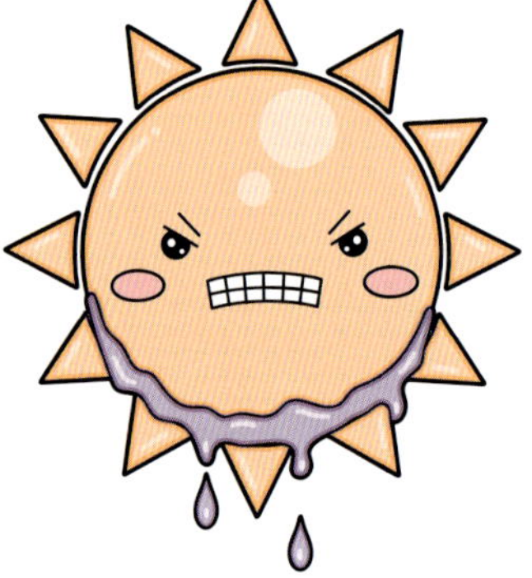

Color in your Mad Sun!

VAMPIRE MOON

1. 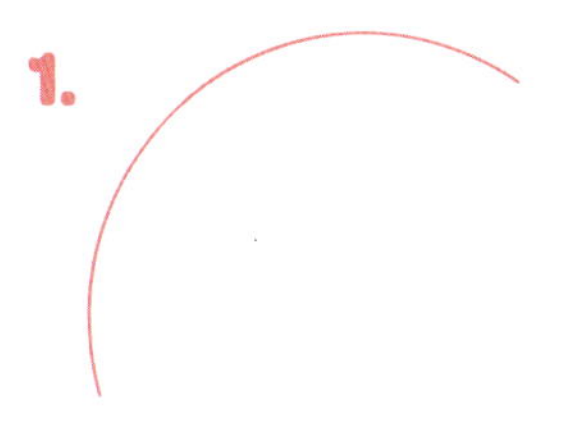

Start by drawing a curved line—about one-third of a circle—in the upper left.

2. 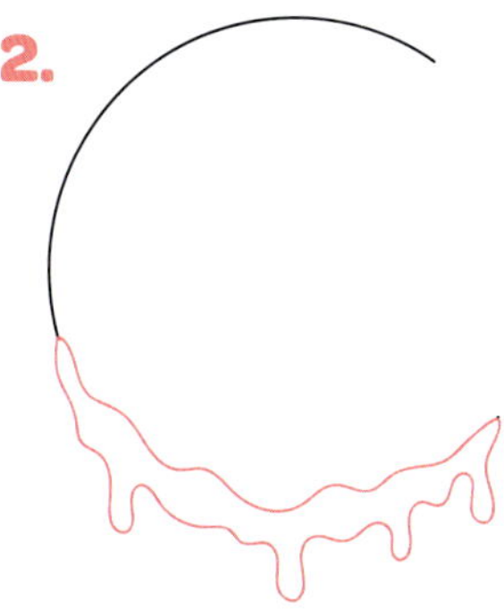

Add a wiggly line (about another one-third of a circle) to the bottom. Add drips below it.

3. 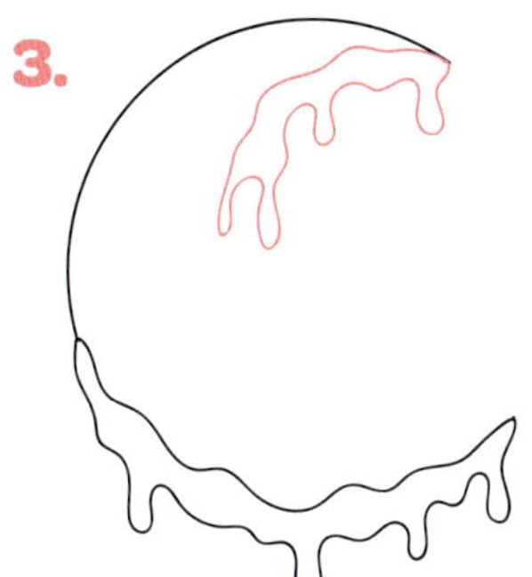

Inside the top of the curve, draw a wiggly line—about one-fourth of a smaller circle. Add drips below it.

4. 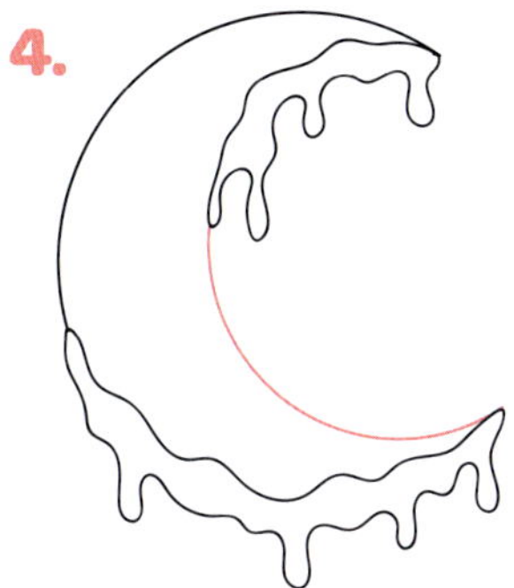

To complete the crescent moon shape, connect the top and bottom drips with a curved line.

5. 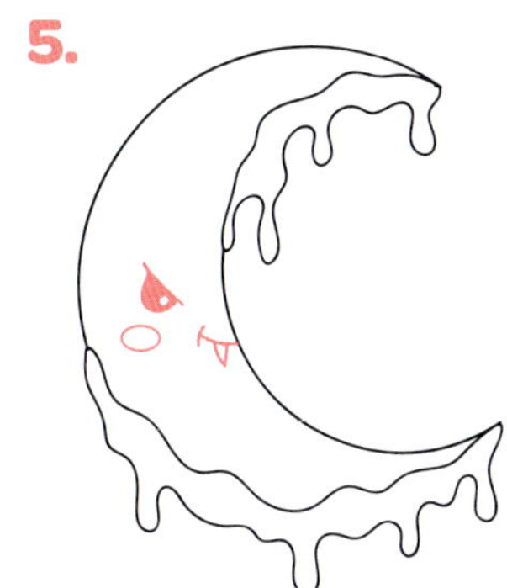

Add a slanted, shaded-in eye, an oval cheek, and an evil vampire grin.

6. 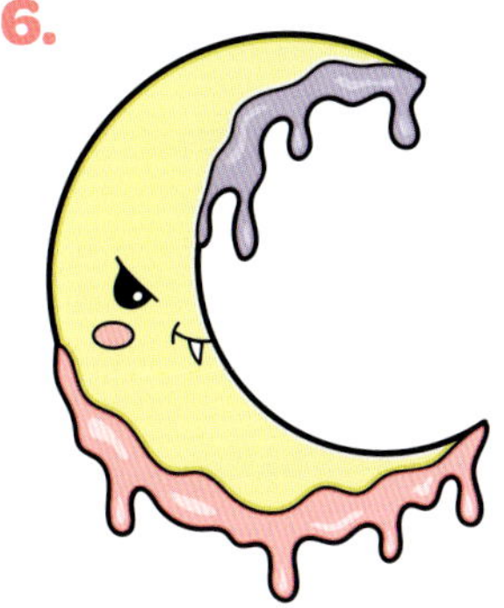

Color in your Vampire Moon!

GHOST BEE

1.

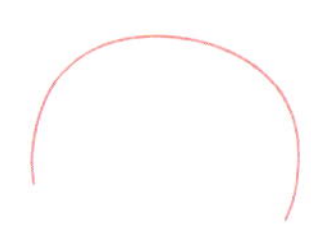

Start by drawing a curved line for the head.

2.

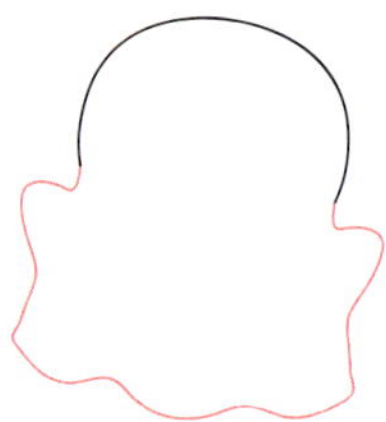

Add the ghost's arms and "sheet" with a wiggly line.

3.

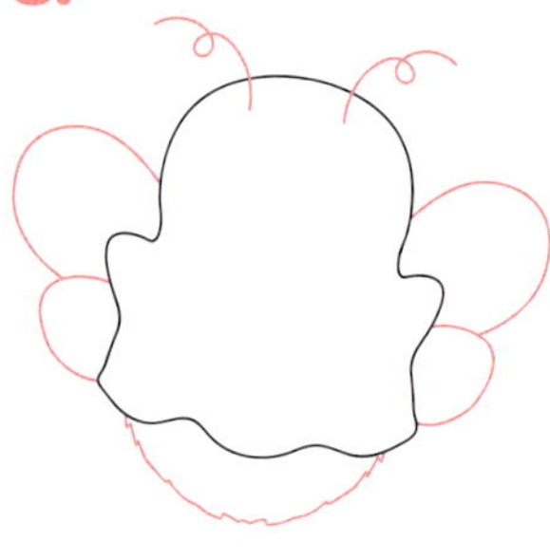

Draw two sets of oval wings—one larger and one smaller. Then add two curly antennae. Draw the bee's bottom as a curved, furry line under the ghost sheet.

4.

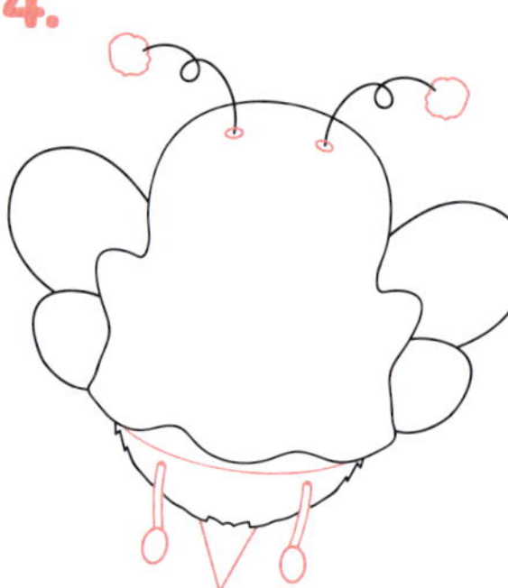

Add a triangle for the stinger. Draw the bee's legs as two curved sticks with ovals at the bottom. Add a puffy circle to the end of each antenna and a stripe along the body. Draw holes for the antennae.

5.

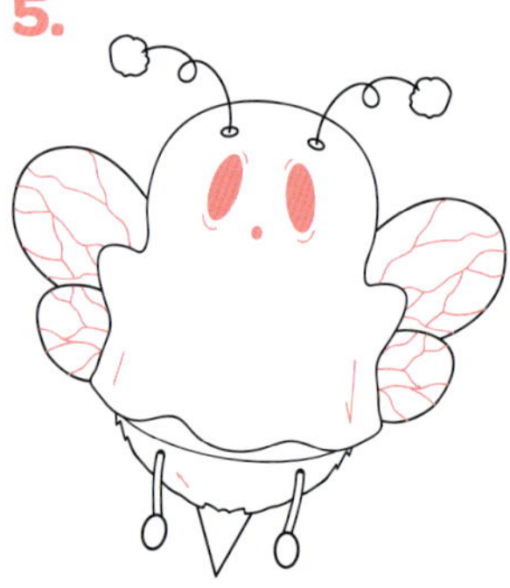

Add some wiggly lines inside the wings. Draw two big filled ovals for eyes and a small filled circle for the mouth. Add some little detail lines.

6.

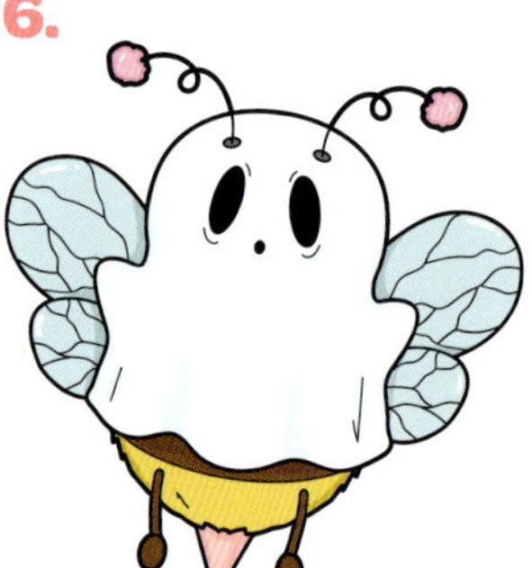

Color in your Ghost Bee!

GHOST BLUEBELLS

1.

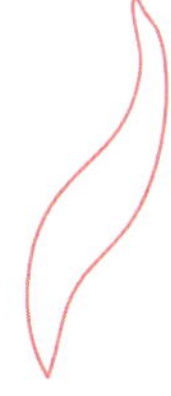

Start by drawing a curved leaf shape.

2.

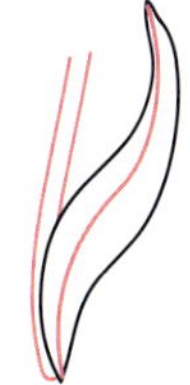

Add two curved lines to the left of the leaf for the stalk, and add a line to the middle of the leaf.

3.

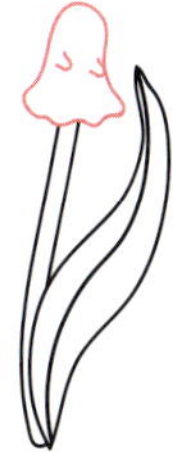

On top of the stalk, draw a bell-shaped ghost with a wiggly bottom line and two little arms.

4.

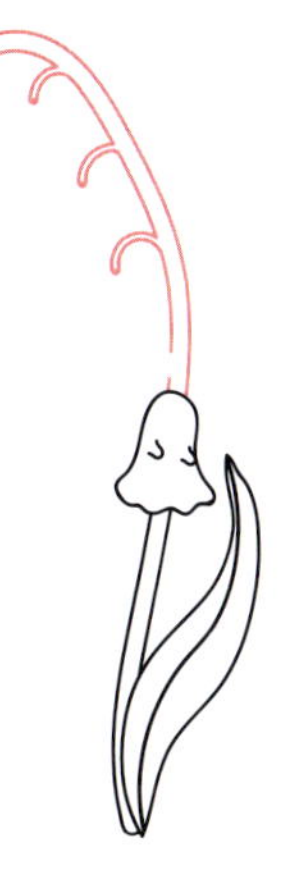

With a curved, double line, extend the stalk above the ghost. Draw three small curved double lines (stems) coming out from the left of the stalk.

5.

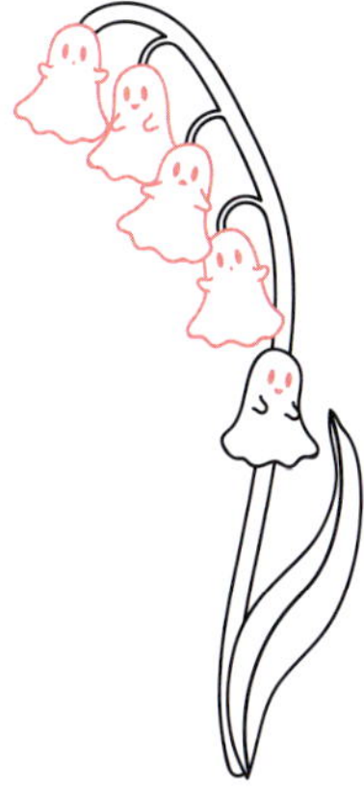

Add four more bell-shaped ghosts along the stalk, and draw on spooky little faces.

6.

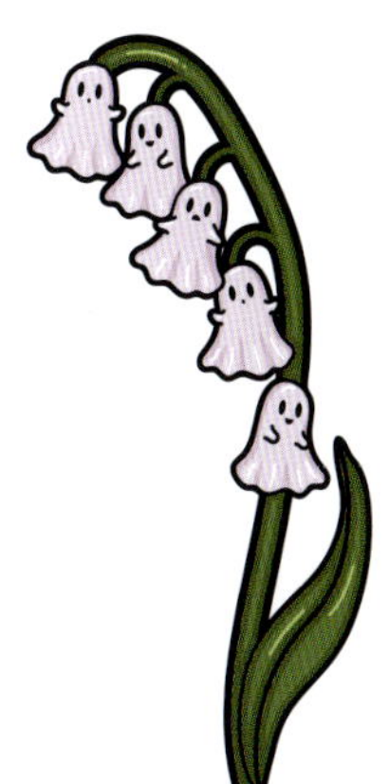

Color in your Ghost Bluebells!

MOUTHY ROSE

1.

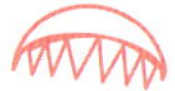

Start by drawing the top of the mouth as a crescent moon. Add upside-down triangles for teeth.

2.

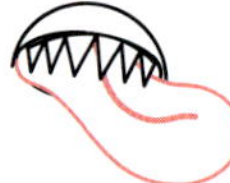

Under the teeth, add a wavy tongue with a line down the middle.

3.

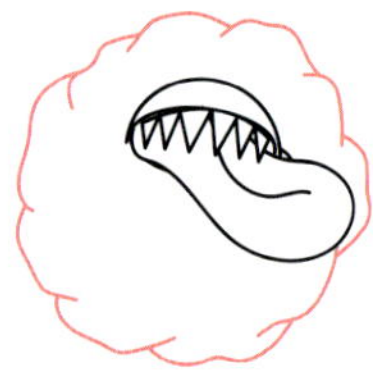

Around the mouth, draw the outline of the rose blossom.

4.

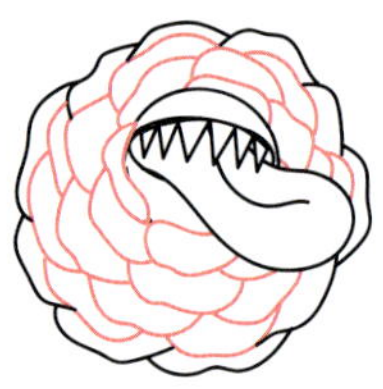

Fill the rose blossom with petals, and add a leaf shape underneath.

5.

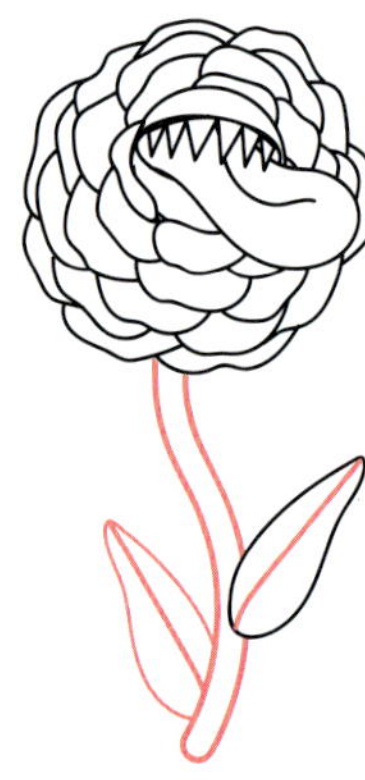

Add a curved double line for the stalk, then add another leaf near the bottom. Draw a line down the middle of each leaf.

6.

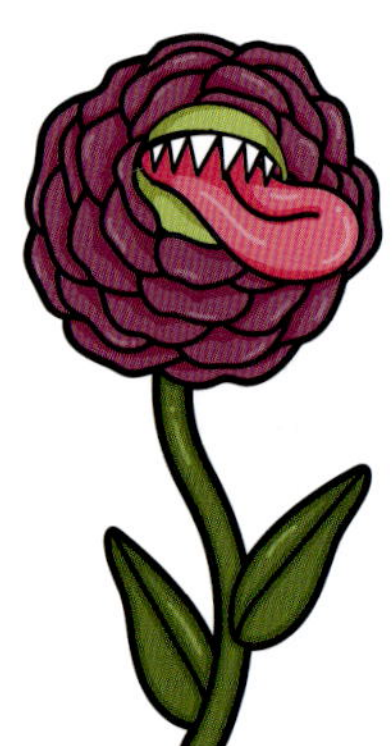

Color in your Mouthy Rose!

OUIJA MOTH

1. 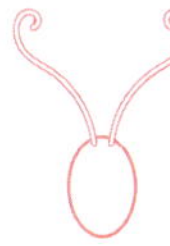

Start by drawing the moth's head as an oval with two curly antennae at the top.

2. 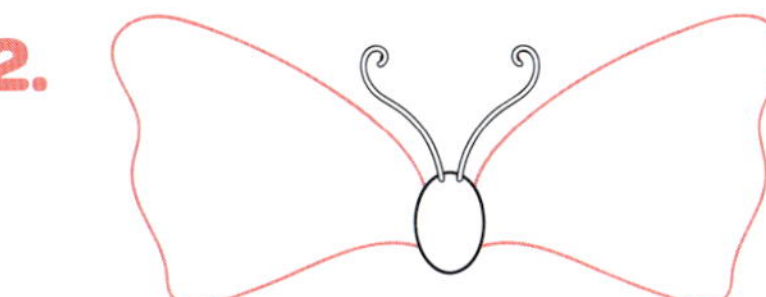

For the top wings, add a wavy triangular shape to each side.

3. 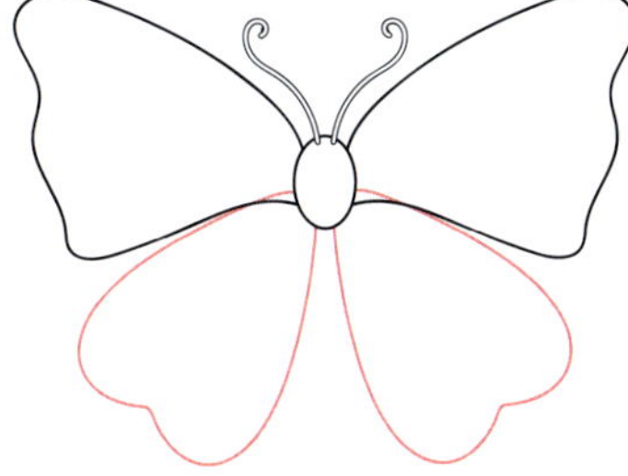

Draw the bottom wings as upside-down hearts on each side.

4. 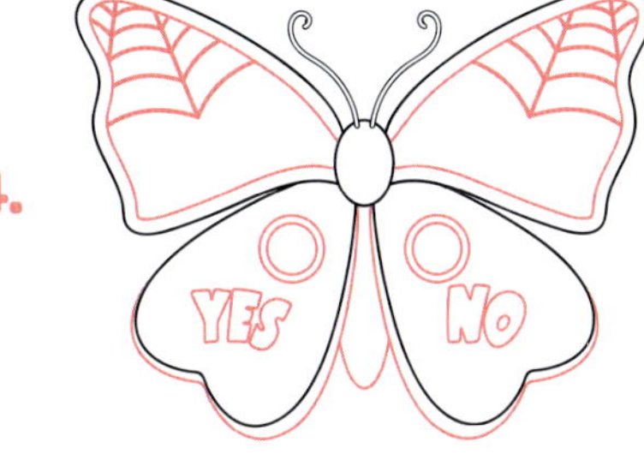

Draw the inside lines of the top wings, and add cobwebs to the corners. Add outlines to the bottom wings. Add a double circle to each bottom wing, and write "YES" and "NO" underneath. Add a curved line for the body of the moth.

5. 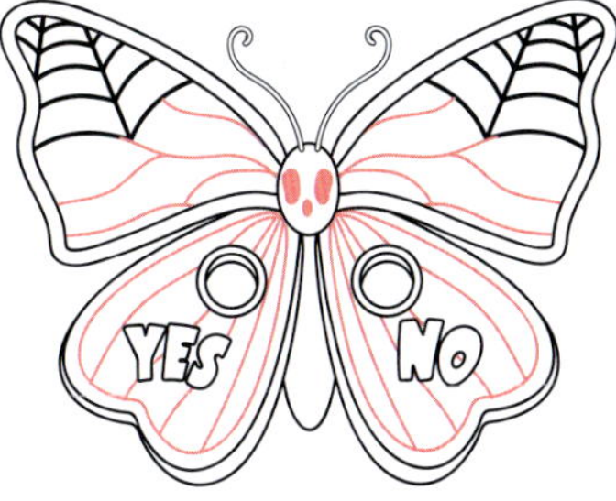

Add inside lines to the bottom wings, and add some detail lines to both sets of wings. Give the moth a creepy face.

6. 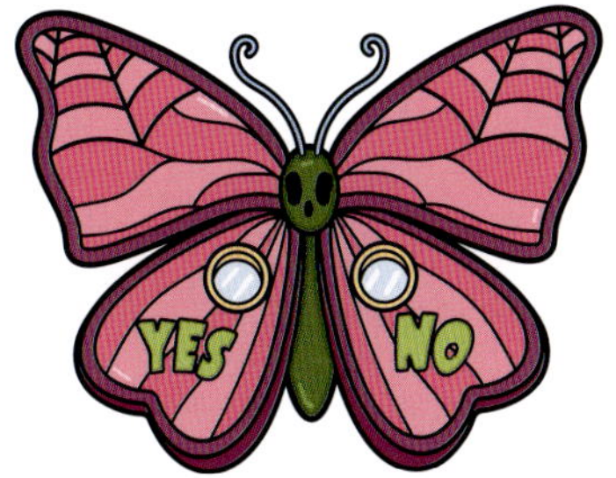

Color in your Ouija Moth!

SKULL DAISY

1.

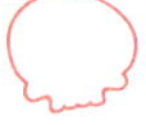

Start by drawing a skull shape: a circle with a squared-off, scalloped bottom.

2.

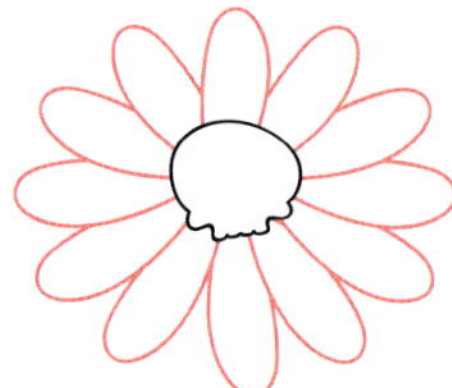

Draw oval petals around the skull.

3.

With a double line, draw a curved stalk under the flower. Add a line to the middle of each petal. Draw some little lines on the skull for teeth.

4.

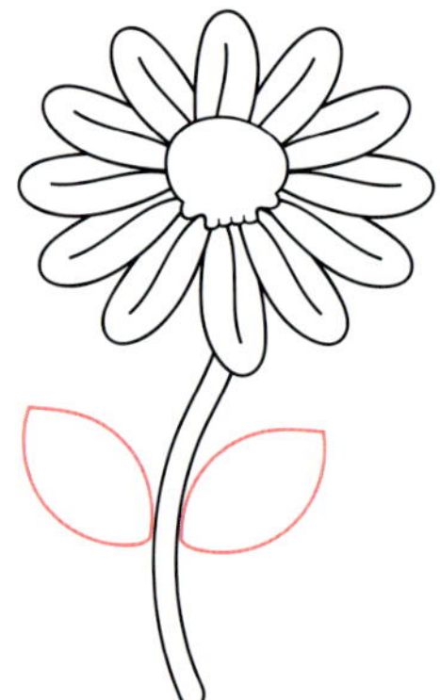

Add leaf shapes to either side of the stalk.

5.

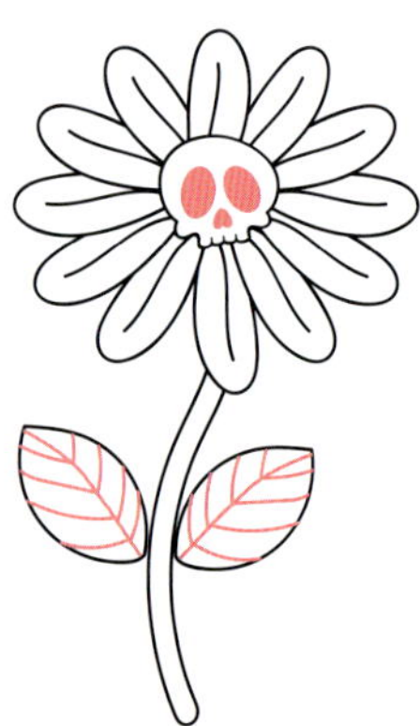

Add and fill in two big ovals for eye sockets and an upside-down heart for the nose. Then add curved lines to the leaves.

6.

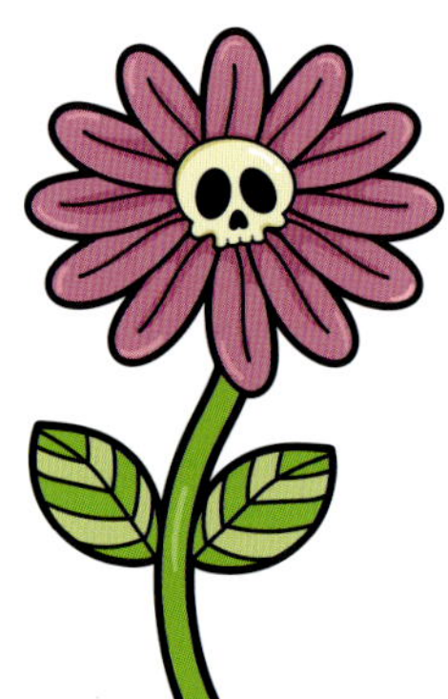

Color in your Skull Daisy!

SNAKE AND SKULL

1.

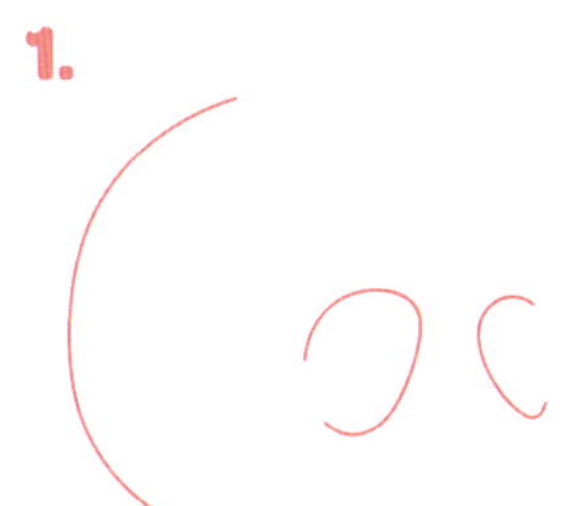

Start by drawing a curved line for the back of the skull and two round eye sockets with gaps at the far left and right.

2.

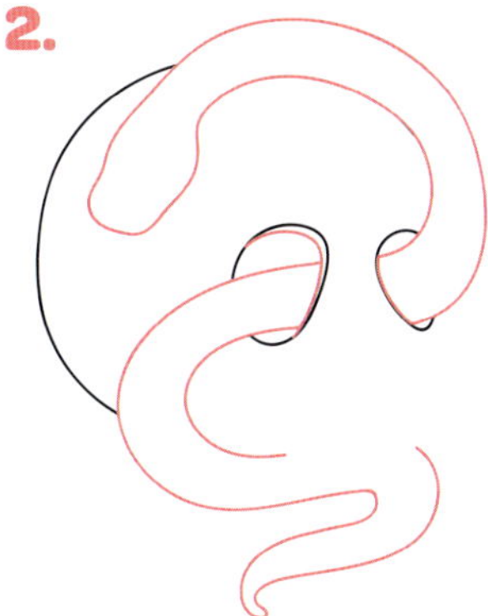

Add a rounded rectangle for the snake's head and curly lines for the body. Leave a gap in the body where it will touch the bottom of the skull.

3.

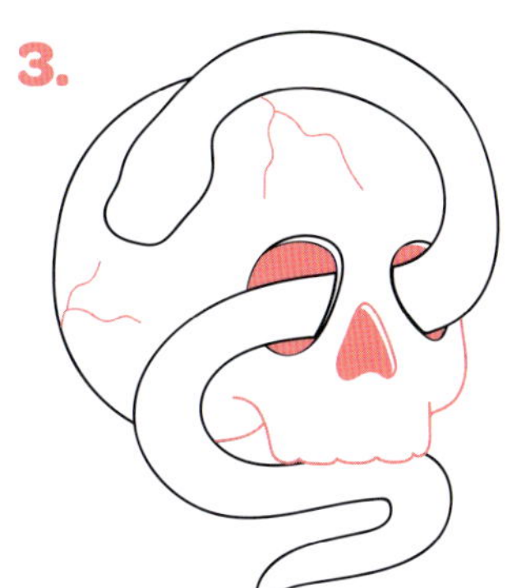

Fill in the eye sockets and add a shaded-in upside-down heart for the nose. Then draw a square jaw shape and add some cracks to the skull.

4.

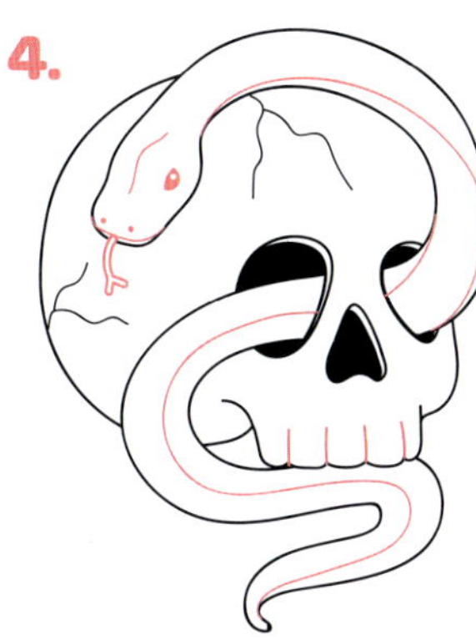

Draw the snake's tongue as an upside-down Y shape and add a line for the mouth. Give the snake an eye, two dots for a nose, and curved line details along the head and outlining its underside. Add teeth to skull.

5.

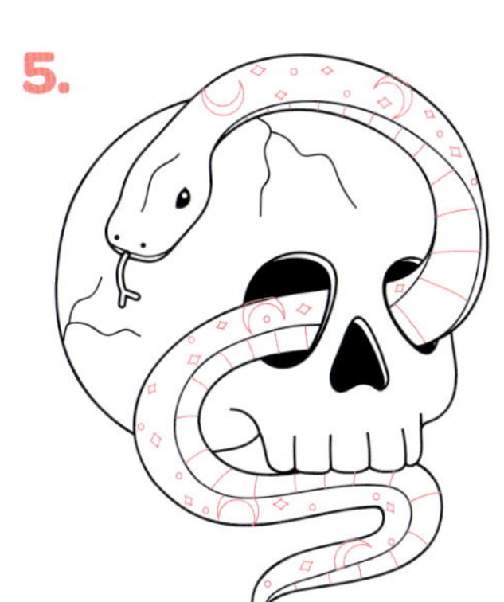

Add moon and star shapes to the snake's body, and draw stripes along the underside.

6.

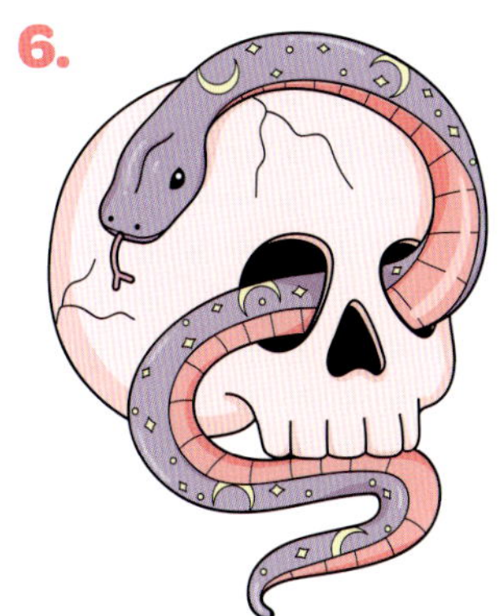

Color in your Snake and Skull!

SKULL SNAIL

1.

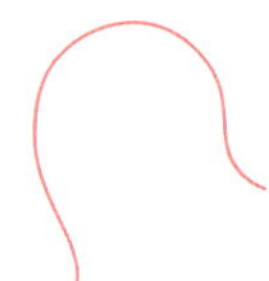

Start by drawing the head of the snail as a rounded line.

2.

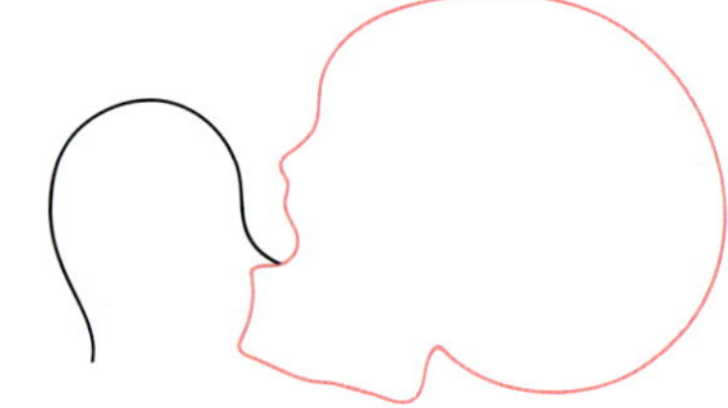

Add a sideways skull shape: a circle with a squared-off jaw.

3.

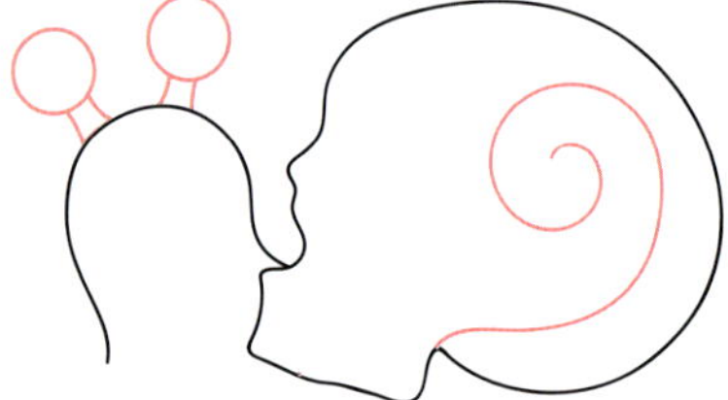

Add two circles for snail eyes and connect them to the head with stalks. Then add a swirly line to the skull.

4.

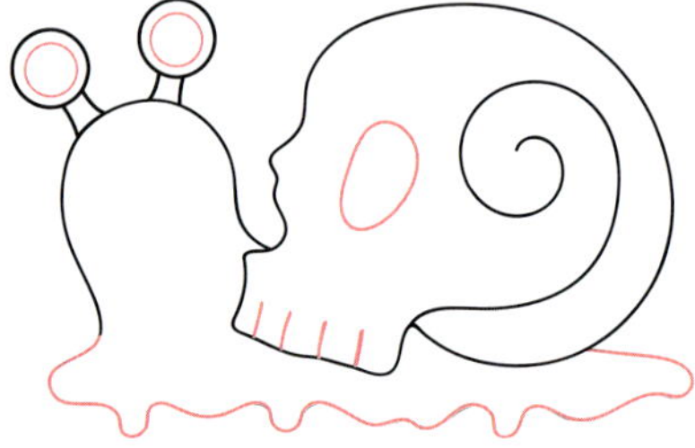

Draw a wiggly line for the snail's body. Then add an oval to the skull for the eye socket, and add some lines for teeth. Draw circles inside the snail's eyeballs.

5.

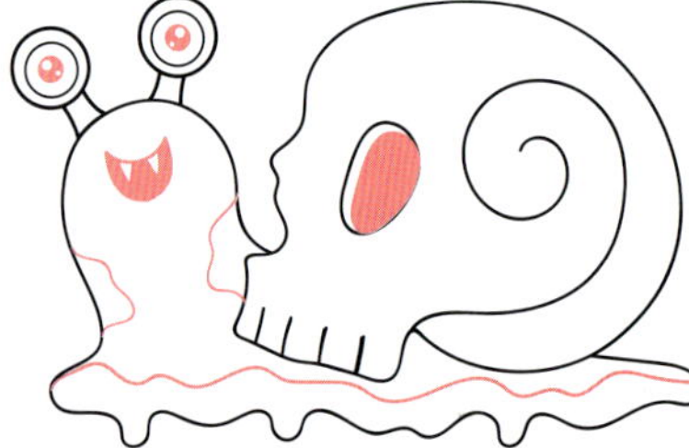

Give the snail a creepy smile with sharp teeth. Then add the pupils in its eyeballs. Shade in the eye socket on the skull. Add some curvy detail lines to the snail.

6.

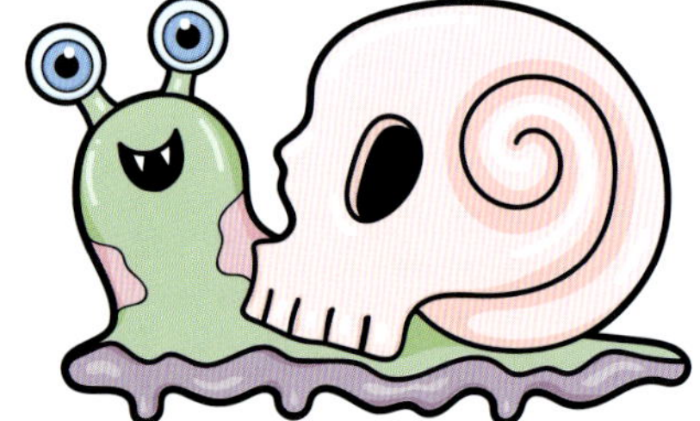

Color in your Skull Snail!

WIZARD FROG

1.

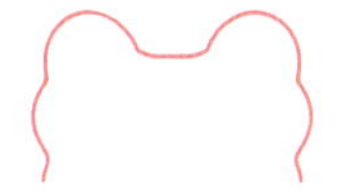

Start by drawing the frog's head. Put two half-circle eyes on top and a smaller half-circle cheek on each side.

2.

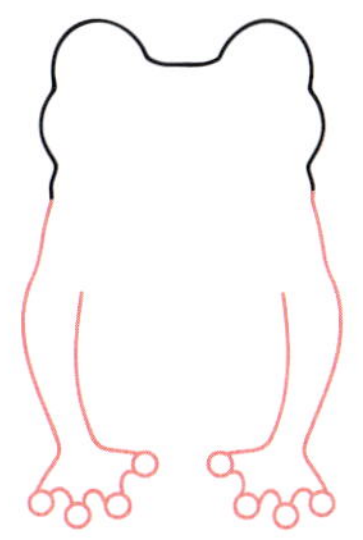

Extend the ends of the head line down to draw two front legs. Make webbed feet, and add circles for toes. Leave a little space between the feet.

3.

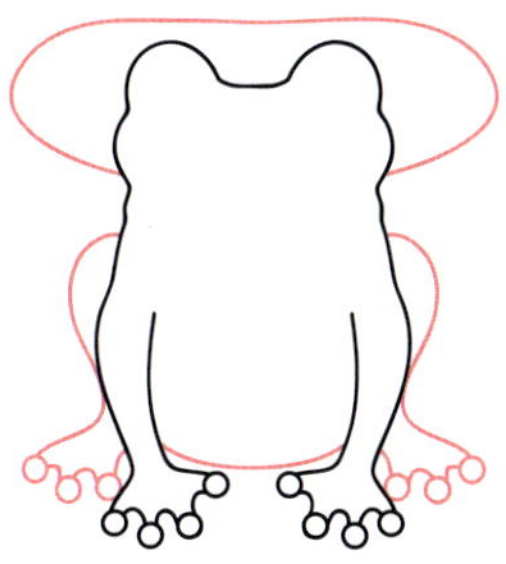

Draw the back legs with webbed feet at the bottom and little circles for toes. Draw a curved line between the front feet. Add a squished oval shape around the head.

4.

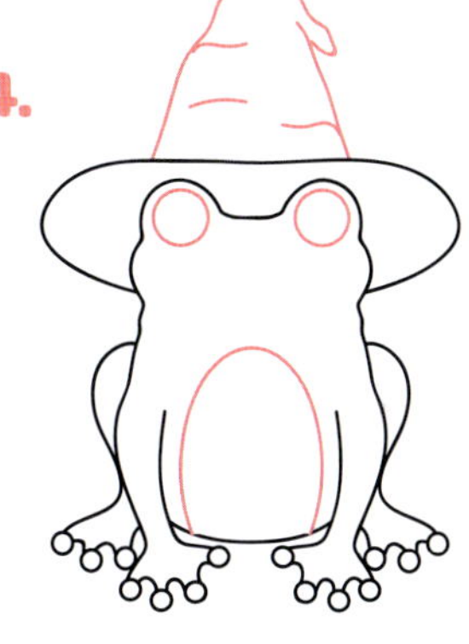

Finish the hat outline with a triangular shape and detail lines. Add a circle in each eye and an oval for the stomach.

5.

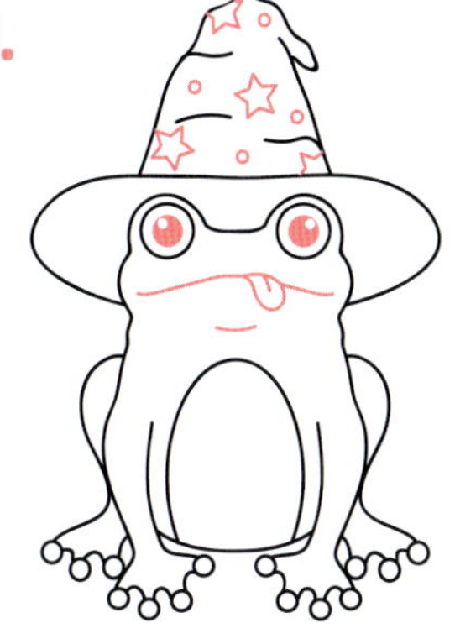

Add a wide mouth with a flopping tongue and a curved line underneath for the chin. Add shaded pupils to the eyes and stars and circles to the hat.

6.

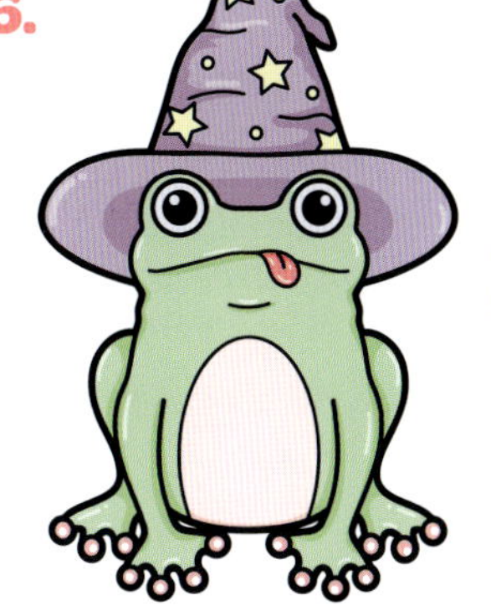

Color in your Wizard Frog!

ANGRY LADYBUG

1.

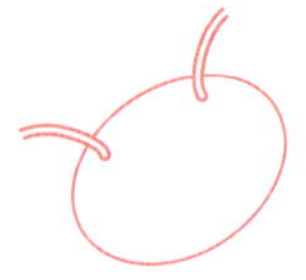

Start by drawing the head as an oval shape with two curved antennae on top.

2.

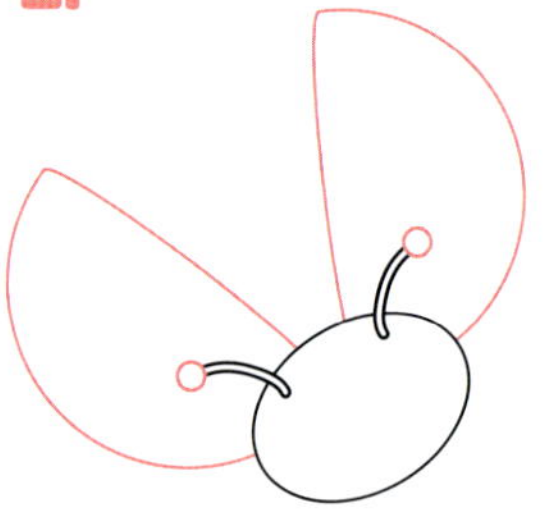

Draw circles at the ends of the antennae. Then add two half circles for the outer wings.

3.

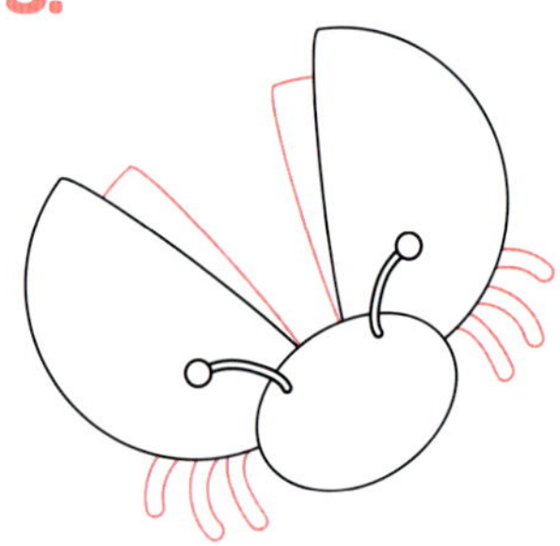

Draw inner wings. Then add three legs peeking out from behind each outer wing.

4.

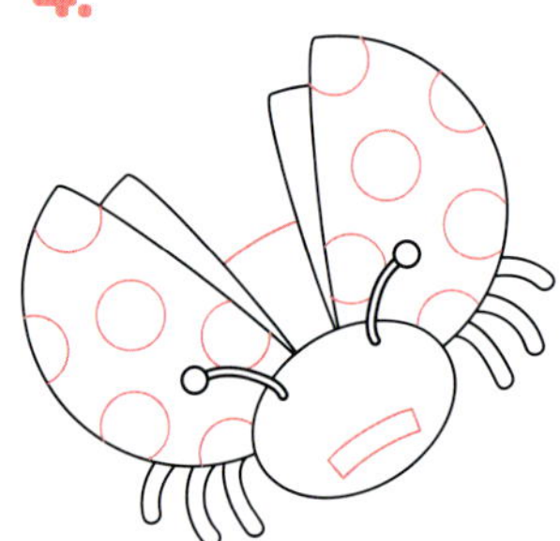

Add spots to the outer wings and a curved line for the body. Draw a curved rectangle for the mouth.

5.

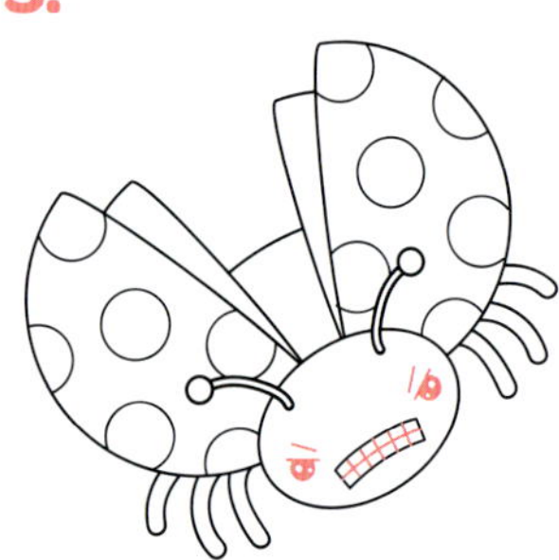

Add slanted, shaded angry eyes and some lines for teeth.

6.

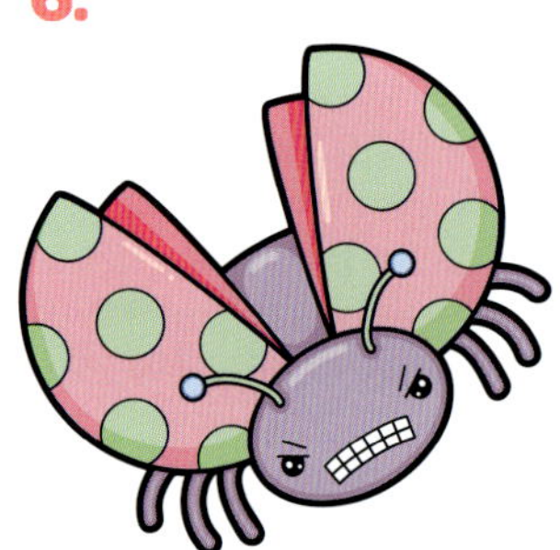

Color in your Angry Ladybug!

MUSHROOM KITTEN

1.

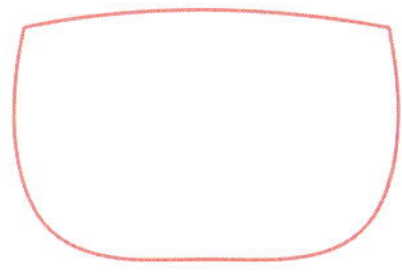

Start by drawing a rectangular shape with a rounded bottom.

2.

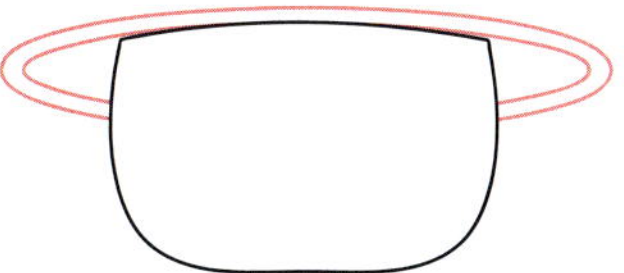

Add two oval shapes to the top.

3.

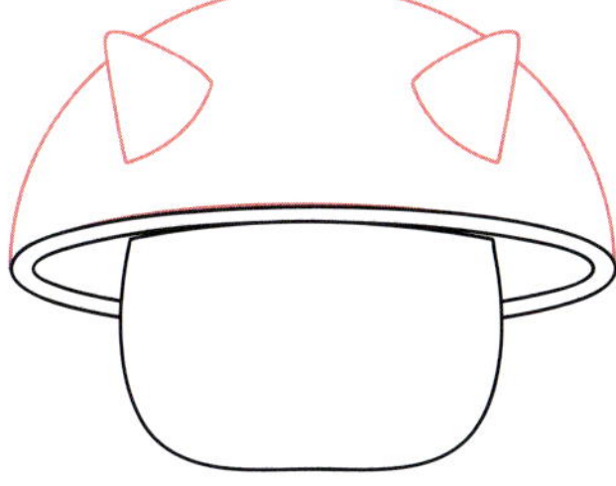

On top, draw a half circle (the mushroom cap) with two triangular ears.

4.

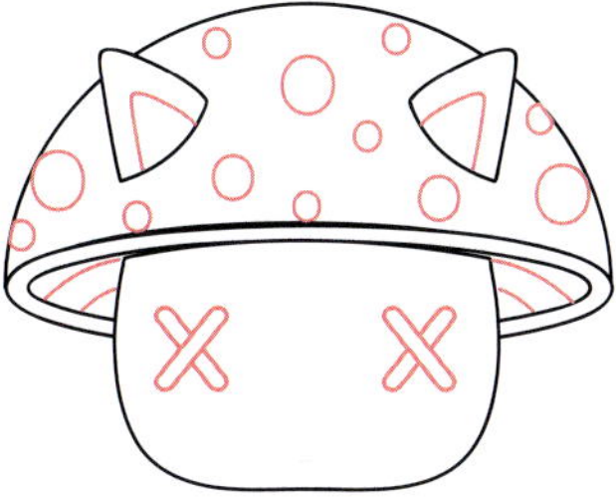

Add inner triangles to the ears, and add two X shapes for eyes. Add spots to the top of the mushroom cap and curved stripes to the inside.

5.

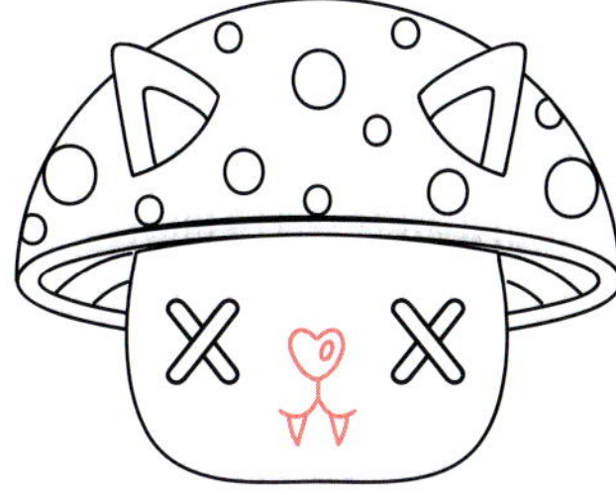

Add a heart-shaped nose, a little smile, and pointy teeth.

6.

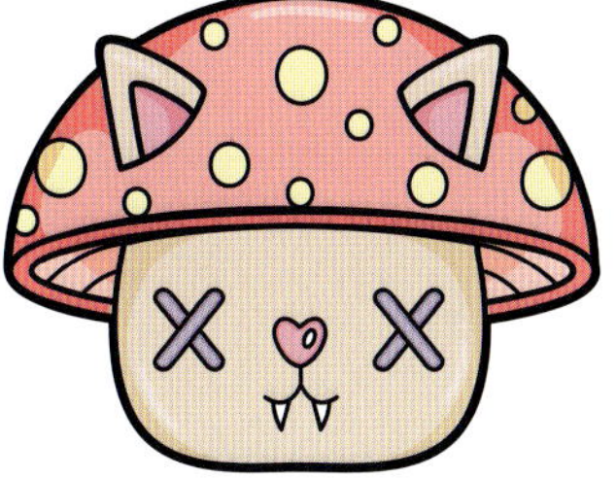

Color in your Mushroom Kitten!

BONEY BROCCOLI

1.

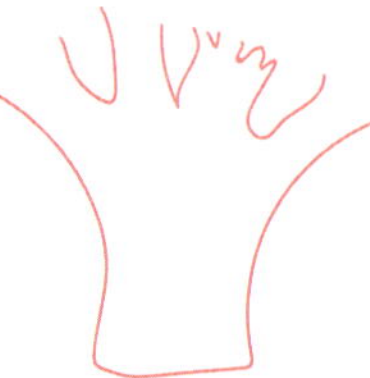

Start by drawing a tree trunk shape with branches, leaving the top part open.

2.

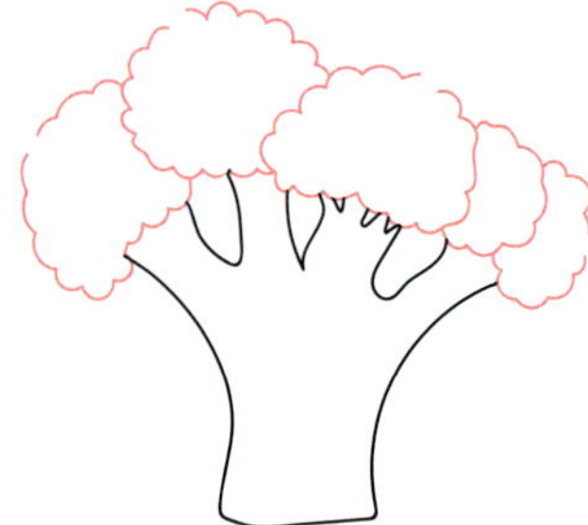

Draw cloud shapes above the branches, leaving some open spaces for the bones.

3.

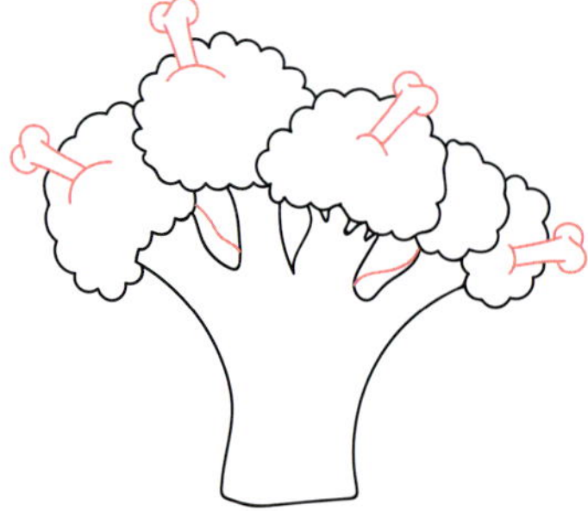

Draw bone shapes with curved lines at the bottom. Add branch detail lines.

4.

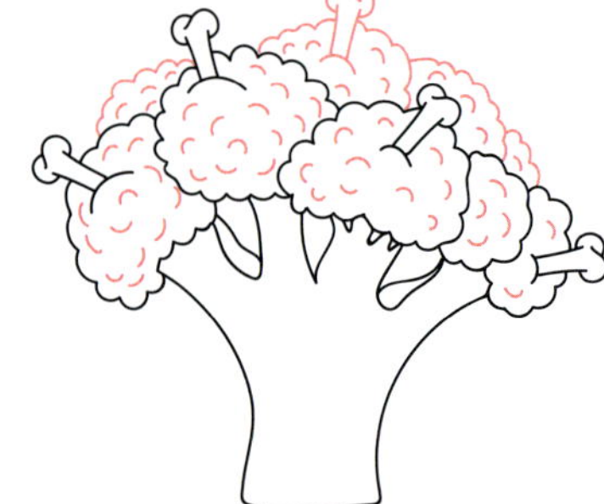

Add more cloud shapes on top. Add a bone to the middle, then add curved lines for texture.

5.

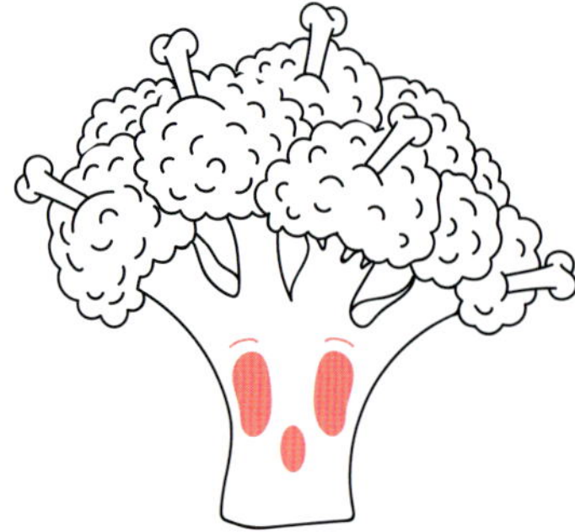

Add two big filled-in ovals with eyebrows for eyes and a smaller filled-in oval for the mouth.

6.

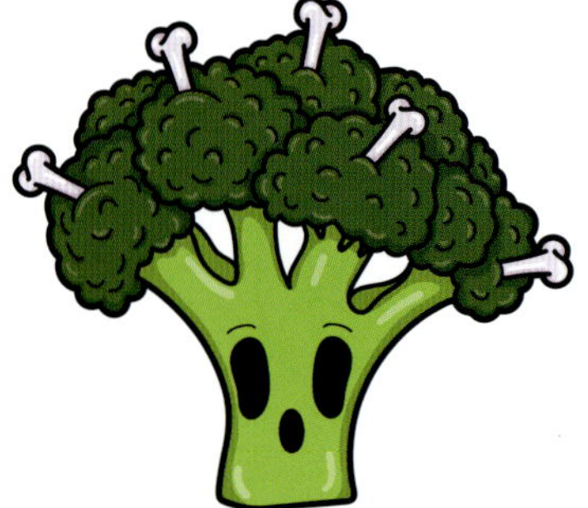

Color in your Boney Broccoli!

EYEBALL PEAS

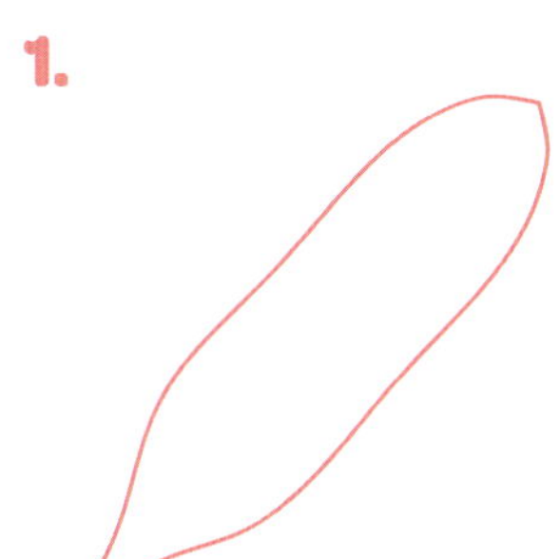

1. Start by drawing the outline of a pea pod.

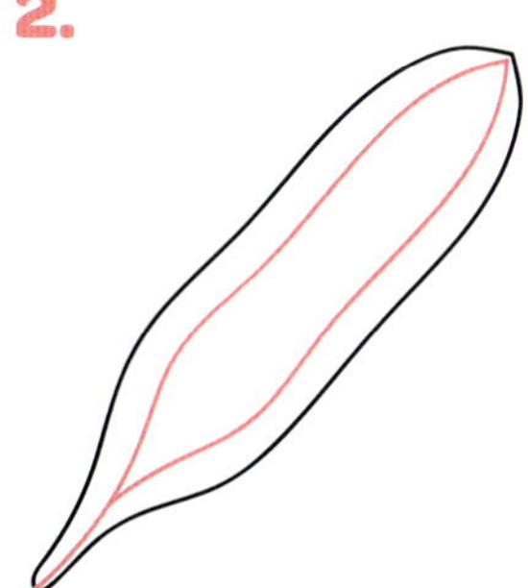

2. Draw the inside curved lines of the pod.

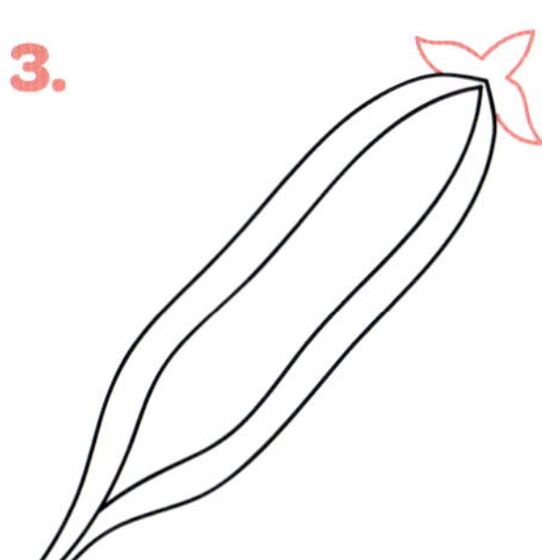

3. Add a three-lobed leaf to the top of the pod.

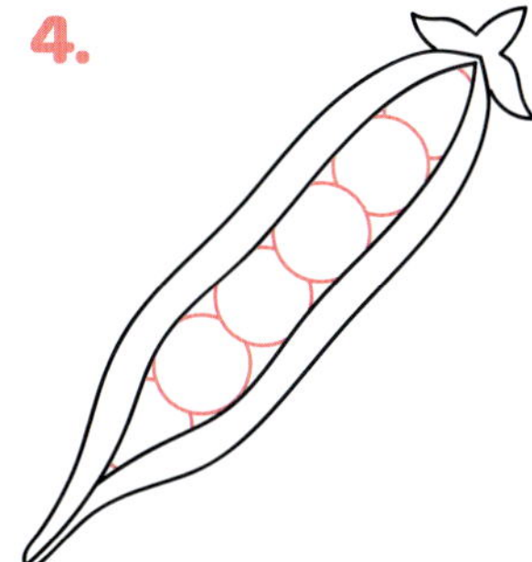

4. Draw six circles inside the pod.

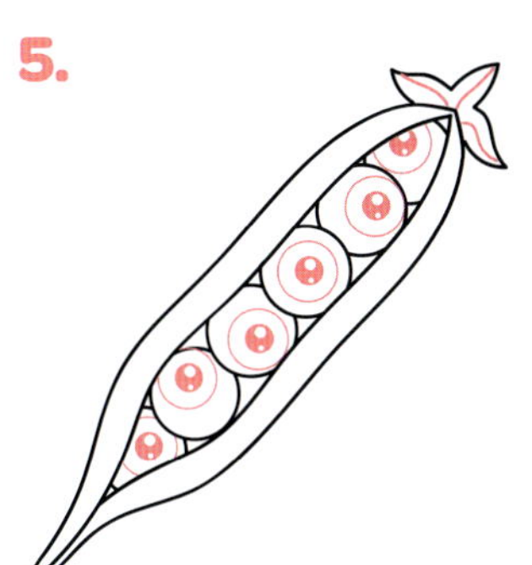

5. Add inner circles for irises and shade in pupils. Draw curved lines inside the leaf lobes.

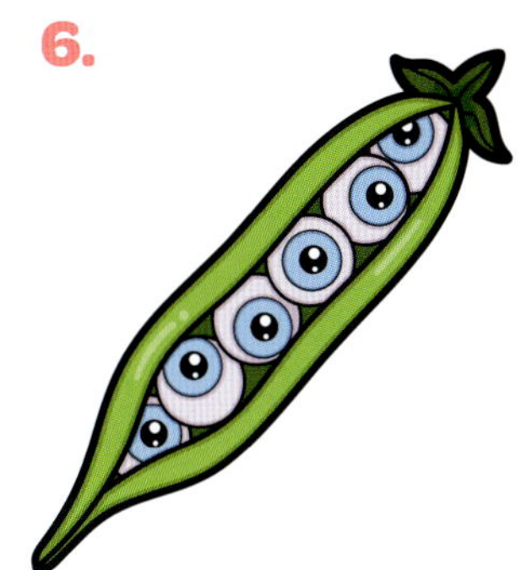

6. Color in your Eyeball Peas!

FRANKEN-PEPPER

1.

Start by drawing the bottom of the pepper: a line that curves upward on both sides, with four broad scallops along the bottom.

2.

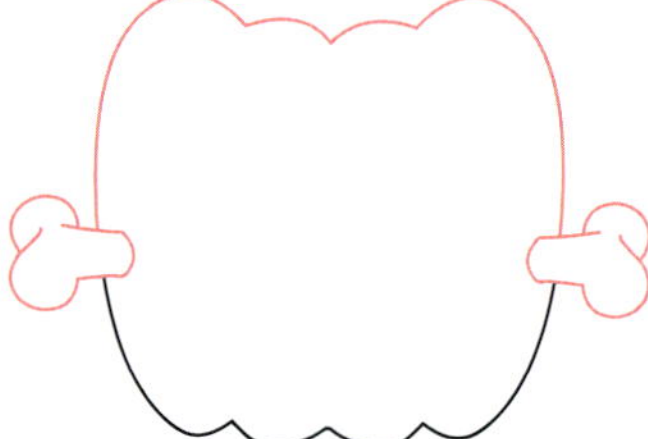

Add a bone shape to either side. Then draw the top of the pepper. Like on the bottom, make four broad scallops, but make the outer two a bit taller than the middle ones.

3.

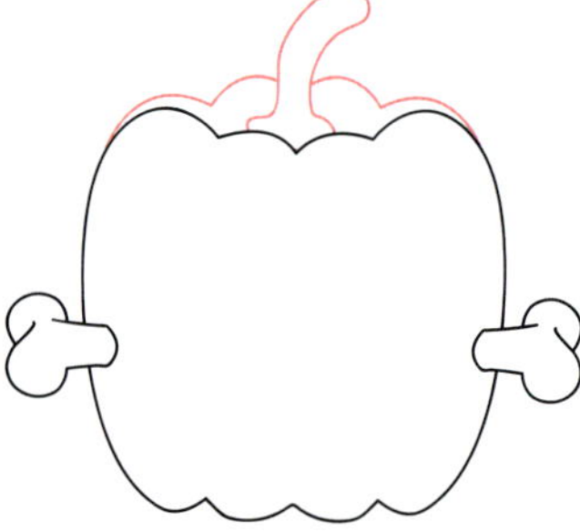

Add a stem to the top, and add two scallops on either side (the back of the pepper).

4.

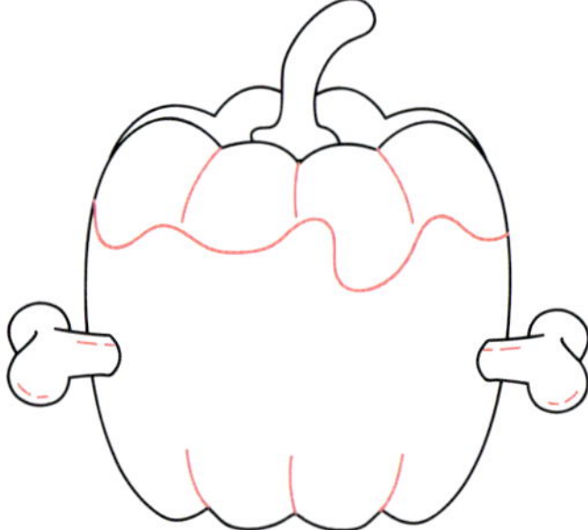

Draw a wavy line across the pepper near the top. Add some curved vertical lines to the top and bottom of the pepper, and add some little lines to the bones.

5.

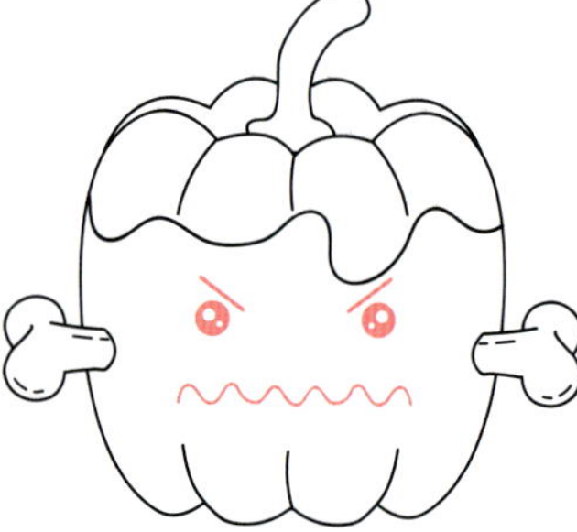

Add a long wiggly line for the mouth, two shaded circles for eyes, and some slanted eyebrows.

6.

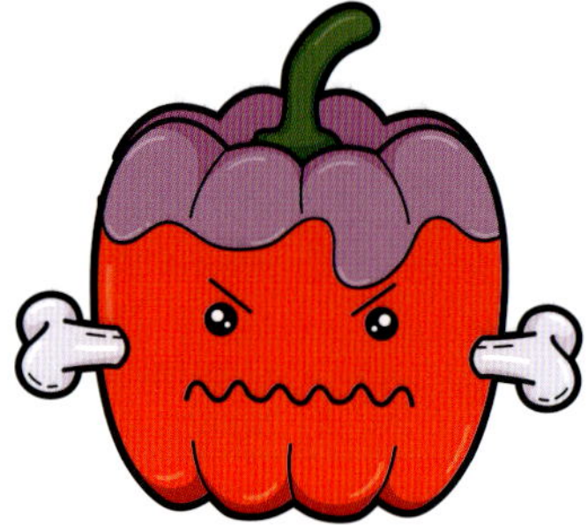

Color in your Franken-Pepper!

GHOST DRUMSTICK

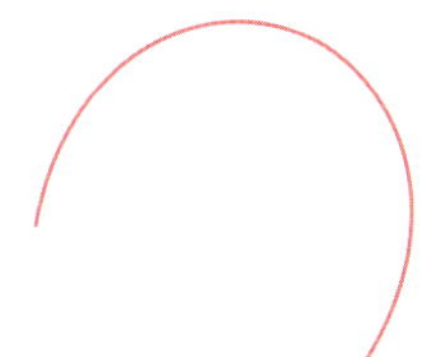

1.

Start by drawing the top of the drumstick as a half oval.

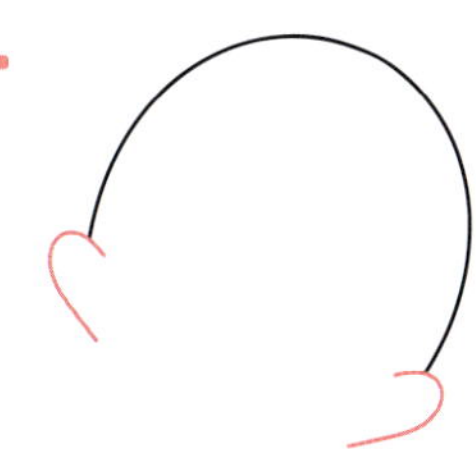

2.

Add two curved lines for the arms.

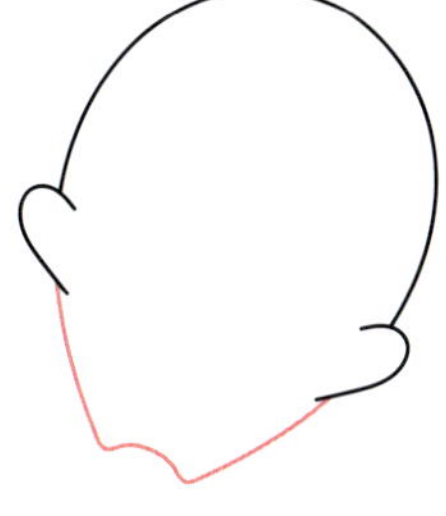

3.

Add the bottom of the drumstick as two slightly curved lines and another curved line at the bottom.

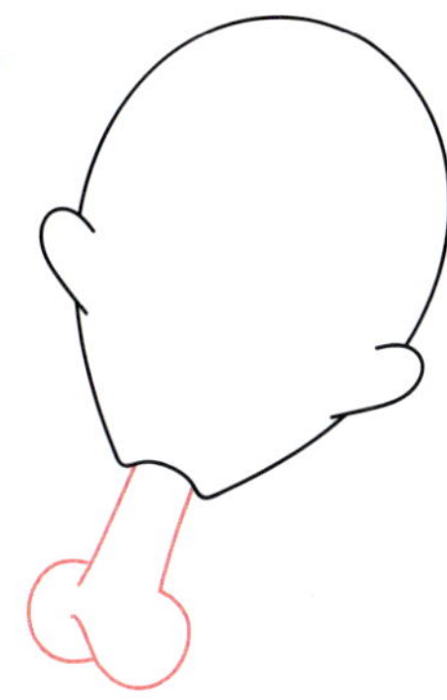

4.

Add a half bone shape at the bottom: an upside-down heart with two parallel lines connected to the top of the drumstick.

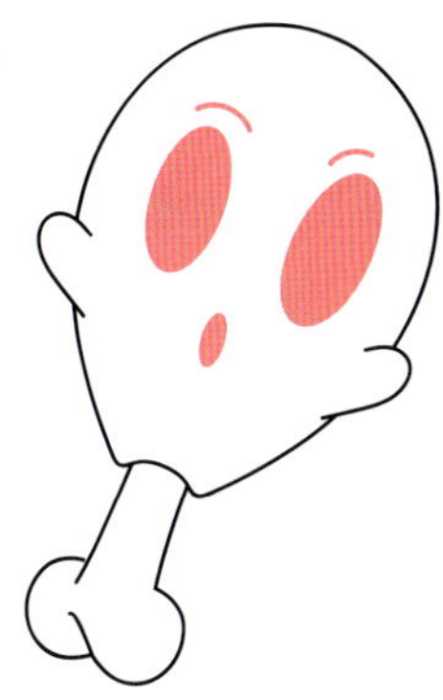

5.

Add two big filled-in ovals for the eyes, curved eyebrows, and a small filled-in oval for the mouth.

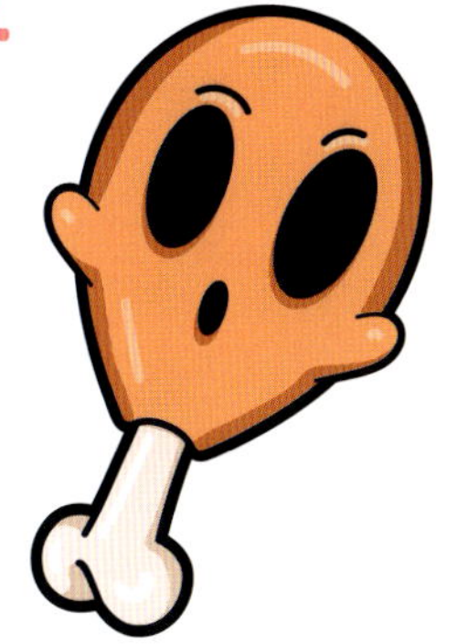

6.

Color in your Ghost Drumstick!

SKULL FRIES

1.

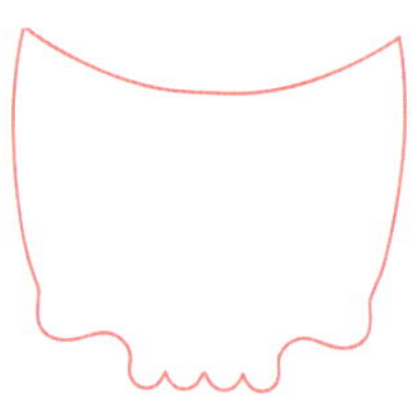

Start by drawing the outline of the skull: a curved square, a scalloped line for teeth, and a curved top.

2.

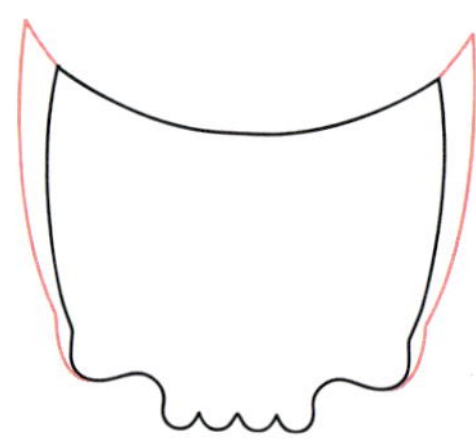

Add the side sections and slant them upward.

3.

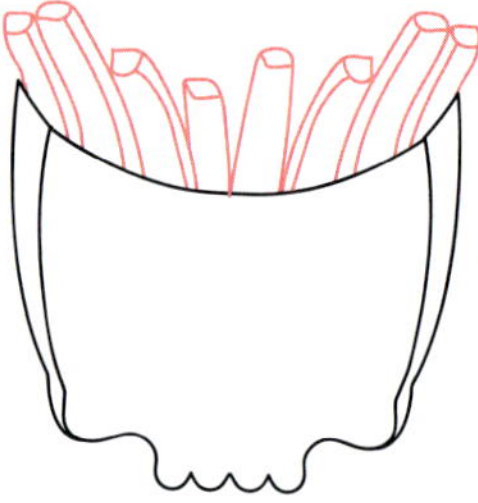

Add the front row of fries as slightly curved cuboid shapes.

4.

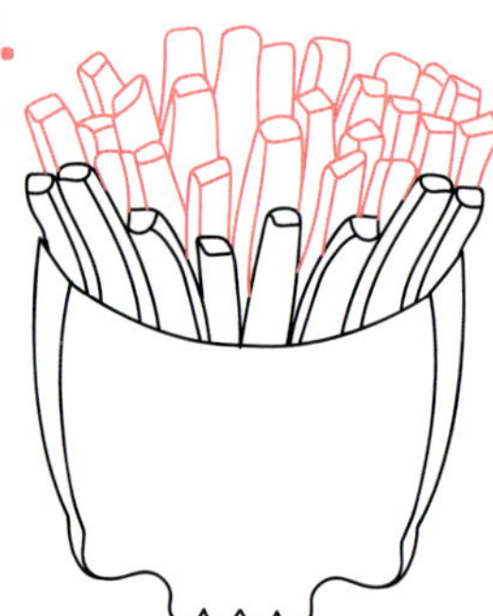

Add more fry shapes behind the front row.

5.

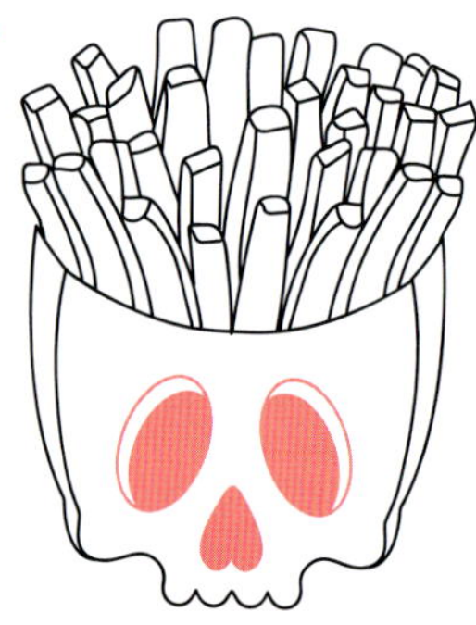

Add two slanted, shaded-in ovals for eye sockets and a filled-in, upside-down heart for the nose.

6.

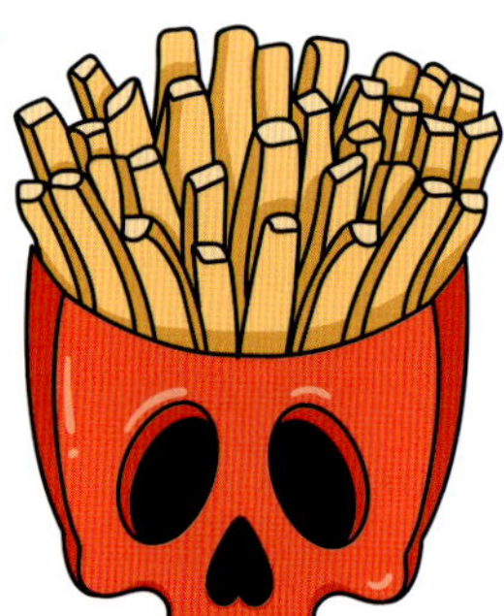

Color in your Skull Fries!

EYEBALL PIZZA

1.

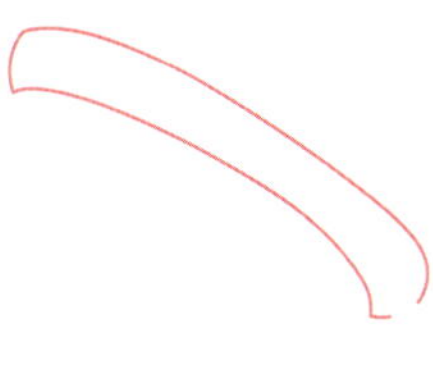

Start by drawing the pizza crust as a narrow, curved rectangle. Leave the right side of the rectangle open.

2.

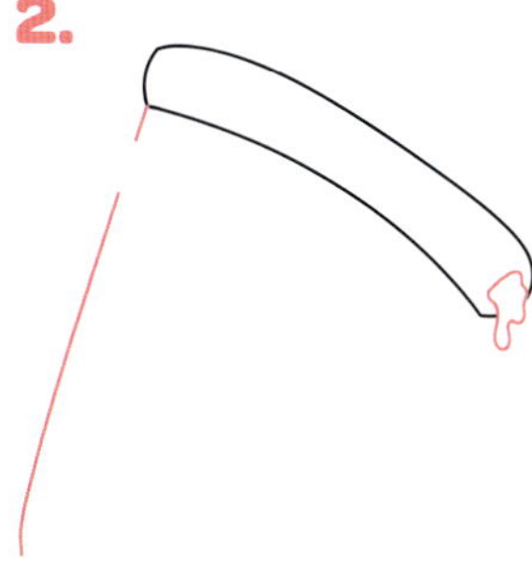

Add a slanted line on the left to start a triangle. Leave a small open space near the top. Then draw a dripping shape on the right side of the crust.

3.

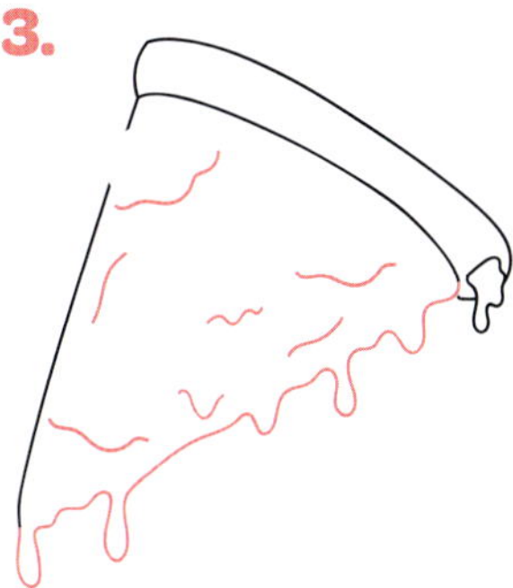

Add a dripping line to complete the triangle. Then draw some wavy lines for gooey cheese.

4.

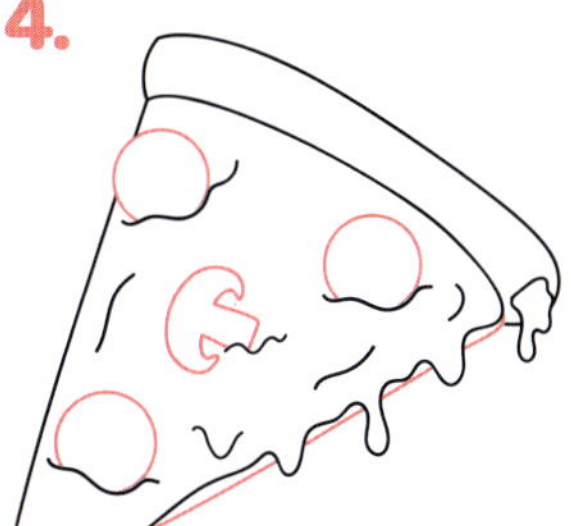

Add three eyeballs (circles) and a mushroom shape (a half circle with a stalk), placing each near a wavy line. Draw the straight edge of the crust below the dripping line.

5.

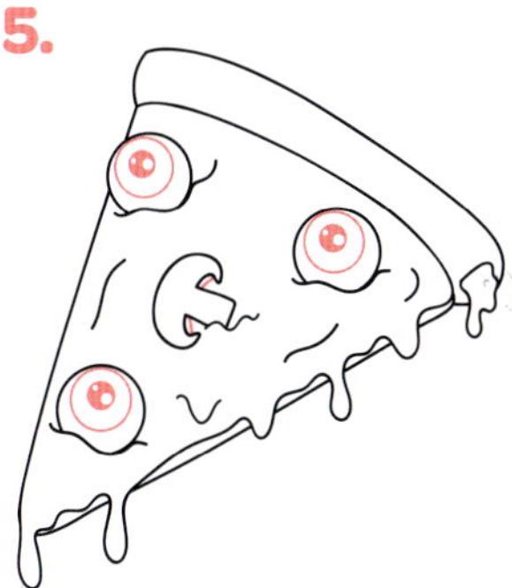

Add circles for irises, and shade in pupils. Add two lines to the mushroom for depth.

6.

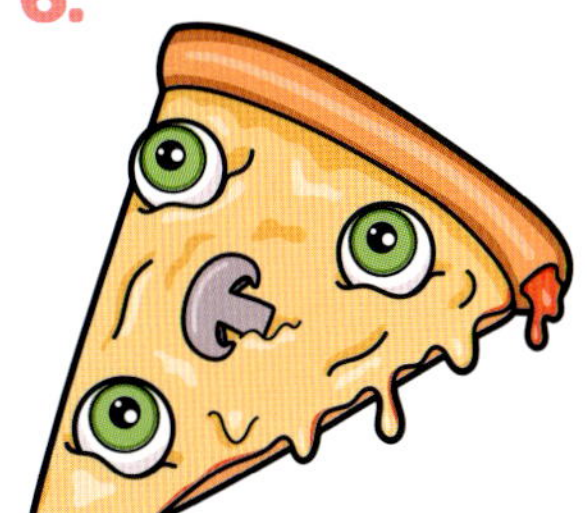

Color in your Eyeball Pizza!

EYEBALL ICE CREAM

1.

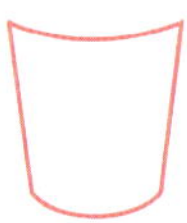

Start by drawing the bottom of the ice cream cone as a cylinder shape with slanted sides.

2.

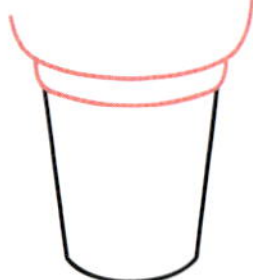

Draw the rest of the ice cream cone, leaving the top part open.

3.

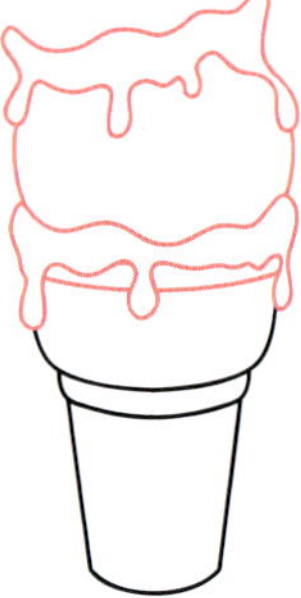

Add a dripping topping to the top of the cone, then draw the edge of the cone behind the drips. Add two curved lines for the sides of the first eyeball. Then add dripping topping on top of the eyeball.

4.

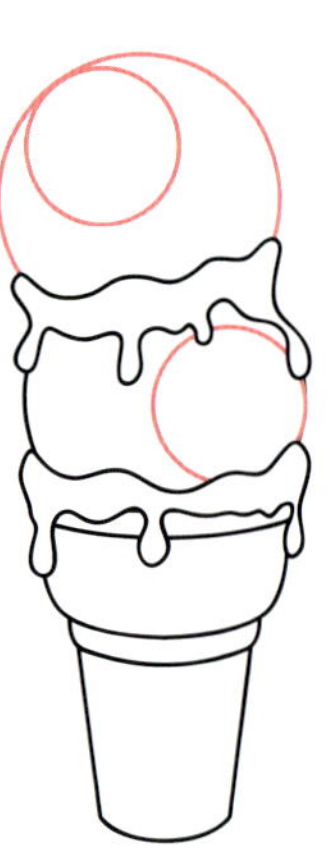

Draw a circle for the second eyeball. Then add circles inside both eyeballs for irises.

5.

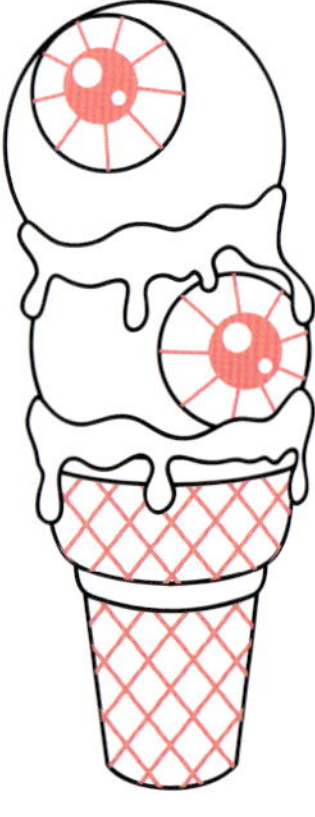

Add shaded pupils, and add lines to the irises. Then add cross-hatching to the cone for detail.

6.

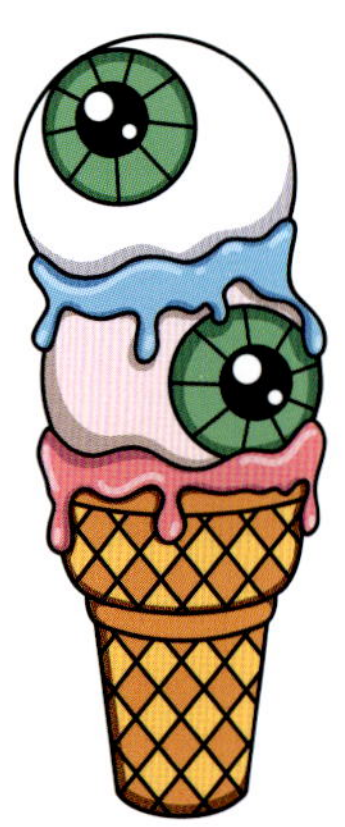

Color in your Eyeball Ice Cream!

SKULL ICE CREAM

1. 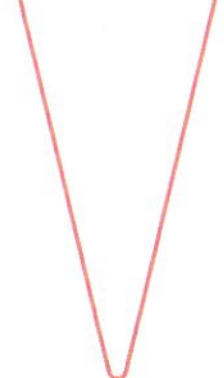

Start by drawing a cone shape, leaving the top open.

2. 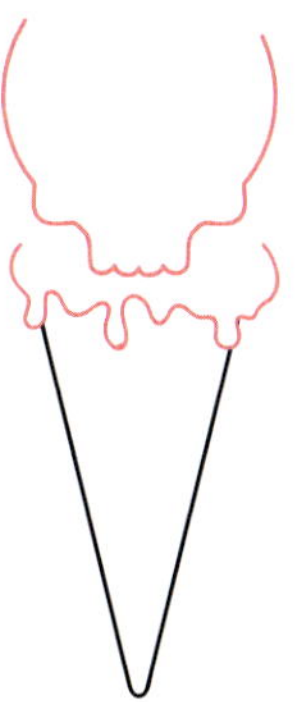

Add a dripping line to the top of the cone. Draw the skull as two curved lines and a square jaw with scallops for teeth. Leave the top open.

3. 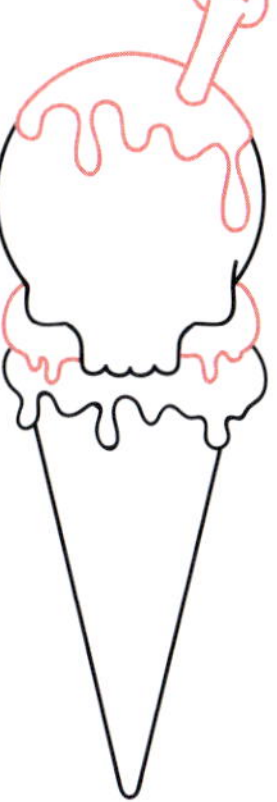

Draw dripping topping on the skull, and add a bone shape on the right. Add rounded dripping shapes on both sides of the bottom of the skull.

4. 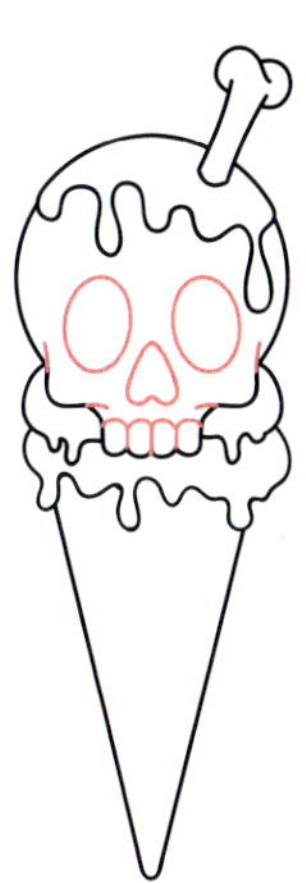

Add two big ovals for eye sockets, an upside-down heart for the nose, and rounded teeth. Then add little lines for the cheekbones.

5. 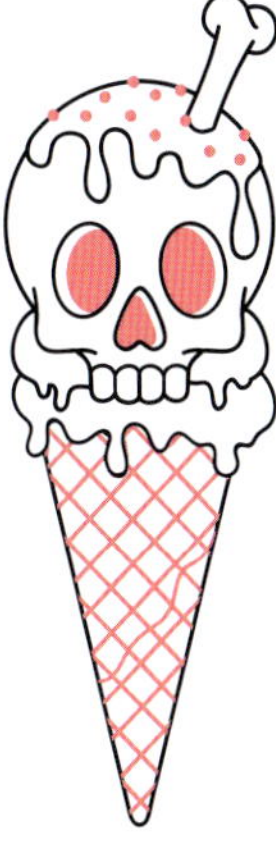

Add a wavy diagonal line across the cone. Shade in the eye sockets and nose. Add dots to the top for sprinkles and cross-hatching to the cone.

6. 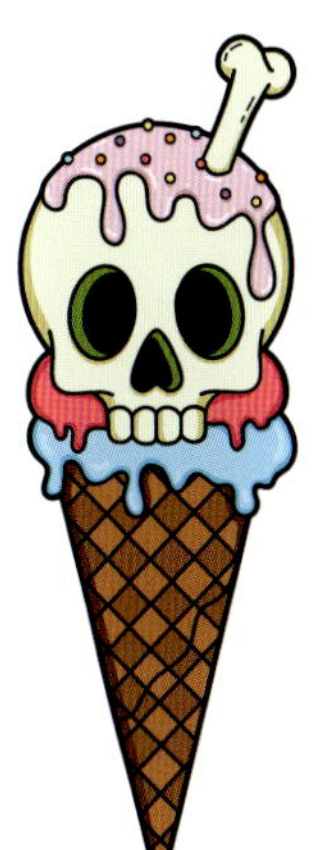

Color in your Skull Ice Cream!

BATWING POPSICLE

1.

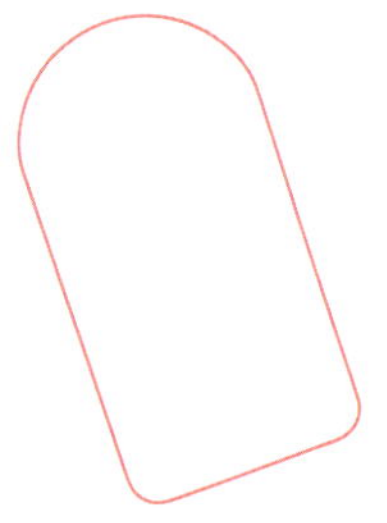

Start by drawing an arched shape for the Popsicle.

2.

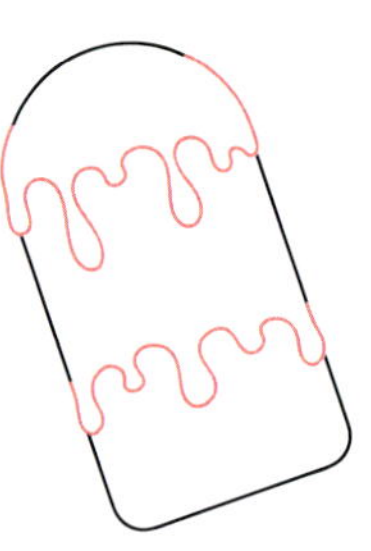

Add two wavy dripping horizontal lines to the Popsicle.

3.

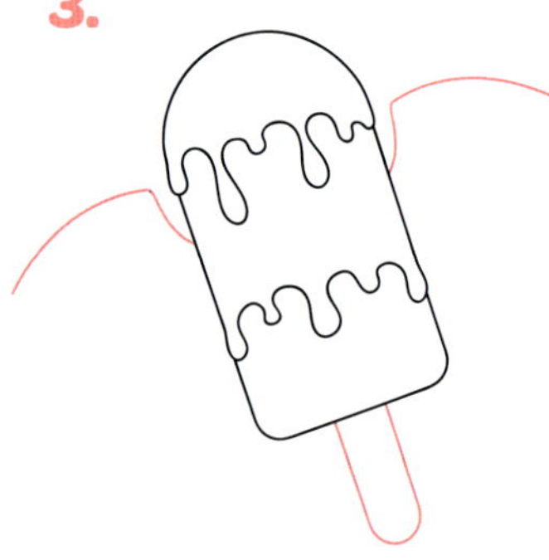

Draw a rounded stick at the bottom of the Popsicle. Then add the tops of the wings to both sides.

4.

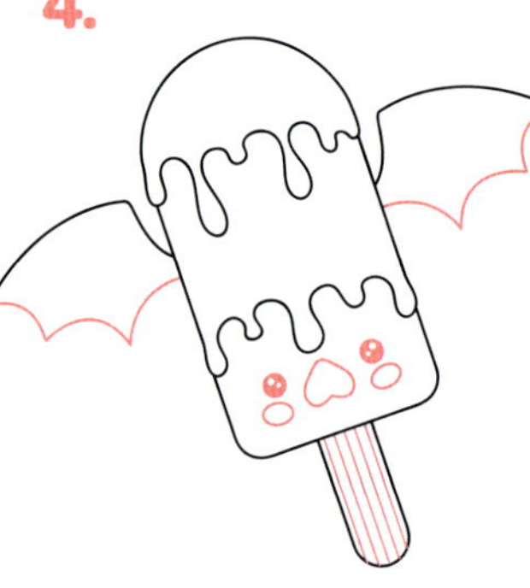

Draw three curved lines to form the bottom of each wing. Then draw an upside-down heart with two ovals and two shaded-in circles for the face. Add lines on the stick.

5.

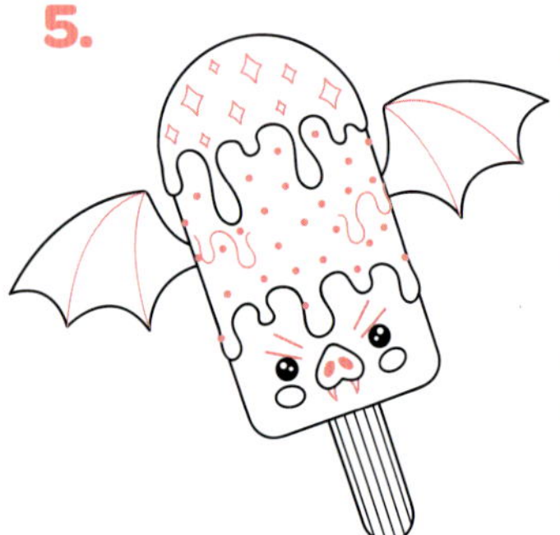

Add curved lines to the wings. Then add more dripping lines to the Popsicle. Draw in pointy teeth, angry eye lines, and filled-in ovals for nostrils. Add dots for sprinkles and diamonds inside the top section.

6.

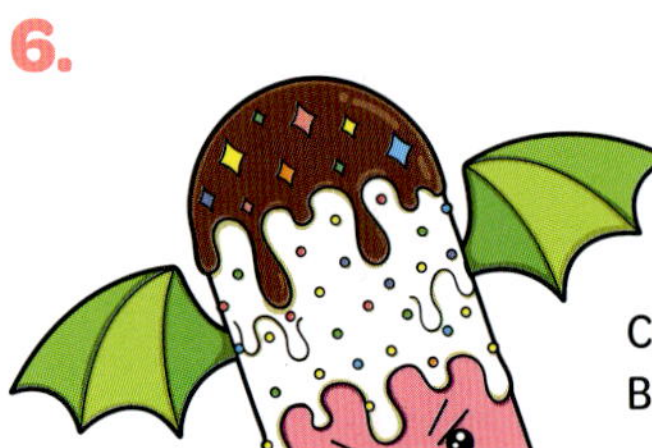

Color in your Batwing Popsicle!

EYEBALL PEARL

1.

Start by drawing a curved line for the bottom of the clamshell.

2.

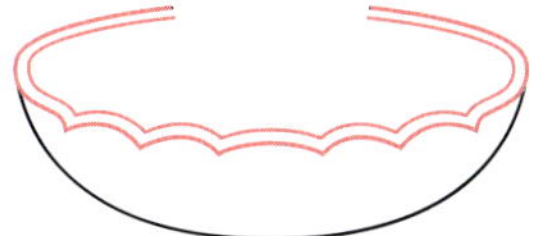

For the top rim of the bottom shell, use a double line to add an oval that's scalloped across the front. Leave the top section open.

3.

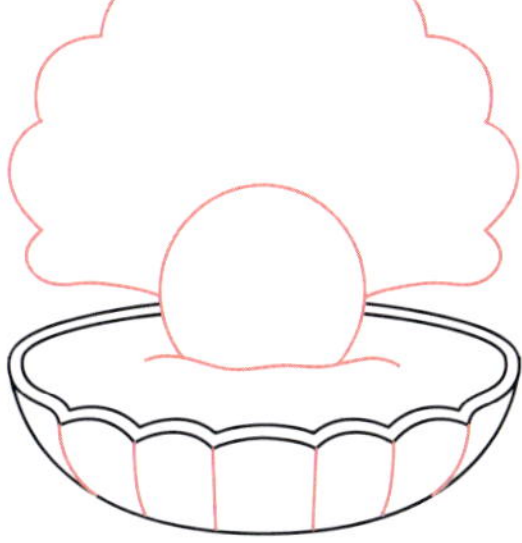

Draw a wavy line in the middle of the bottom shell and a circle above the wavy line. Then, for the top shell, add a scalloped fan shape. Add curved lines to the bottom shell.

4.

Add curved lines to the top shell. Then add a circle in the pearl eyeball.

5.

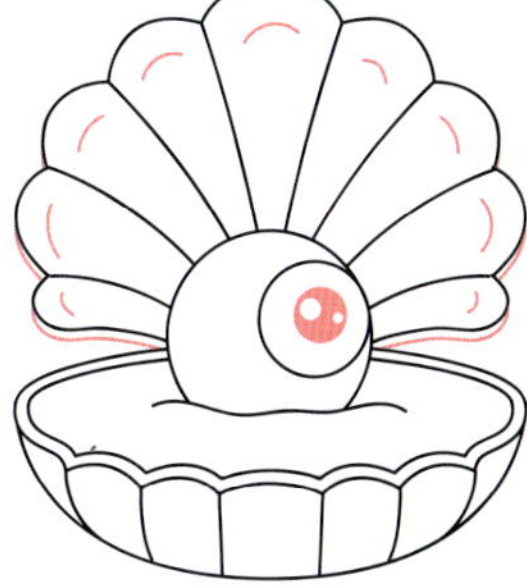

Add a shaded circle for the pupil. Then add some detail lines to the top shell.

6.

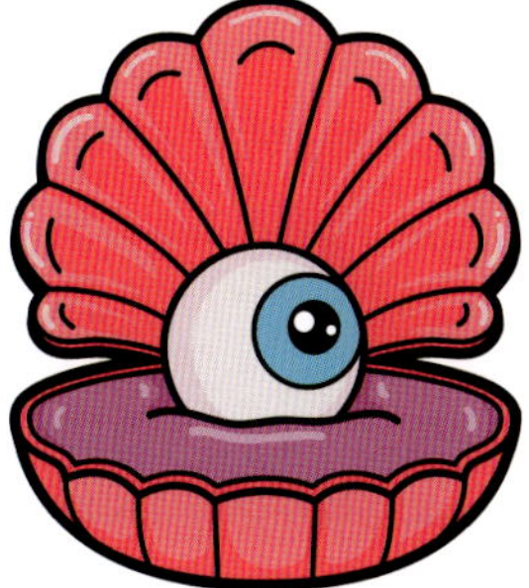

Color in your Eyeball Pearl!

SHARK WITH A SNACK

1.

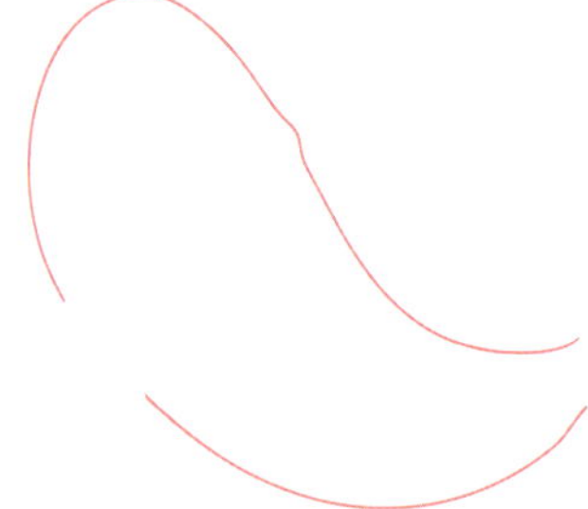

Start by drawing the long, curved body of the shark with gaps for the tail and the arm fin.

2.

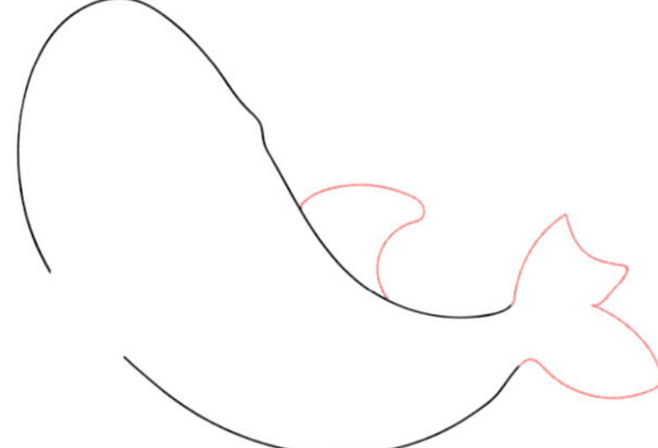

Add a tail shape with a bite taken from the top and a curved triangle for the dorsal fin.

3.

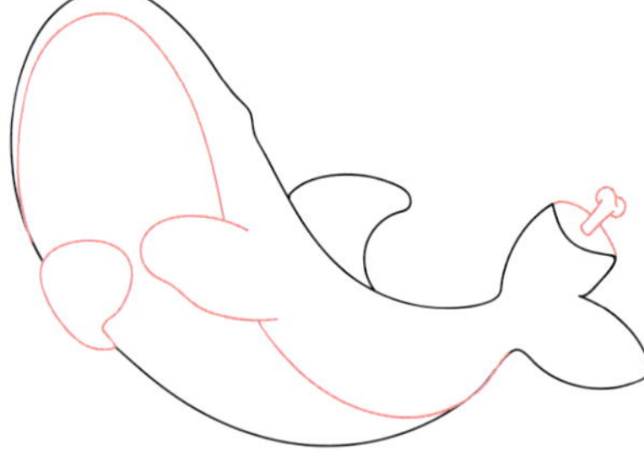

Draw the arm fins, then add a curved shape to the body. Draw a curved line to give depth to the tail, and add a bone shape sticking out.

4.

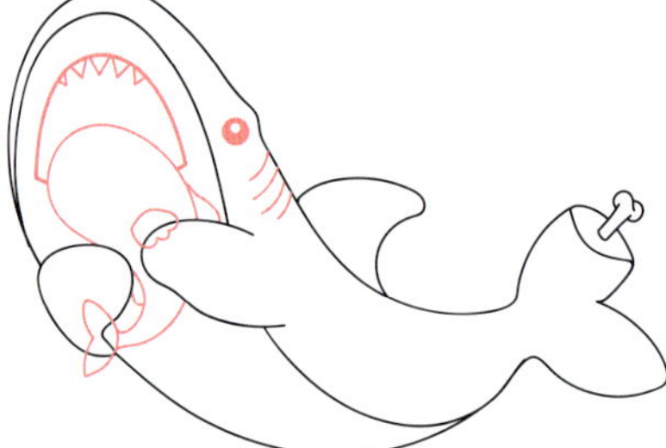

Add an arch for the mouth, and give it pointy teeth. Draw a fish snack between the arms. Add a shaded circle for the shark's eye, and add four curved lines for gills.

5.

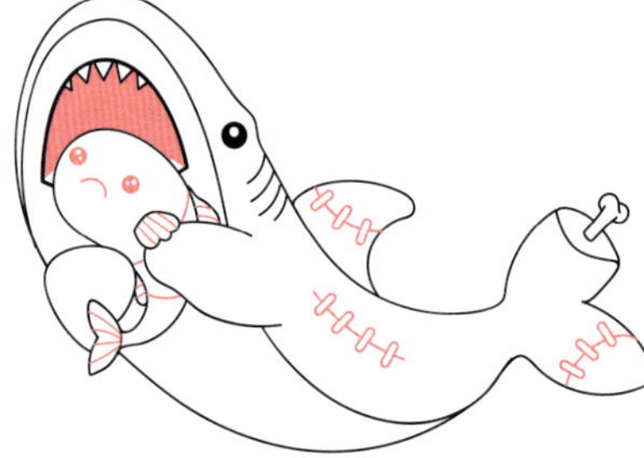

Add bottom teeth and fill in the shark's mouth. Add some curved lines and stiches to the body, tail, and dorsal fin. Add a frowny face to the snack. Add some lines to the fish's fins and tail for detail.

6.

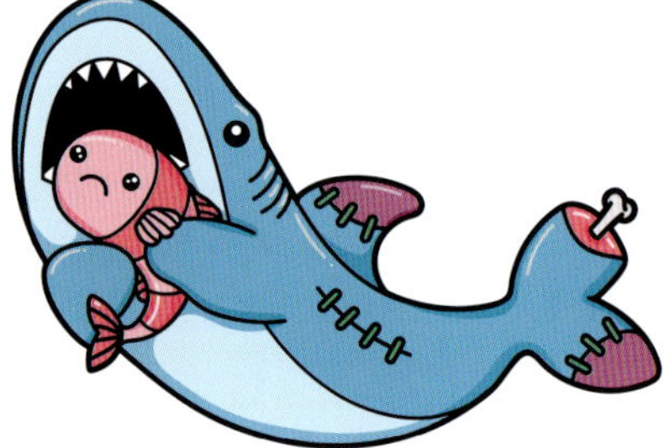

Color in your Shark with a Snack!

HAUNTED BEACH DOLL

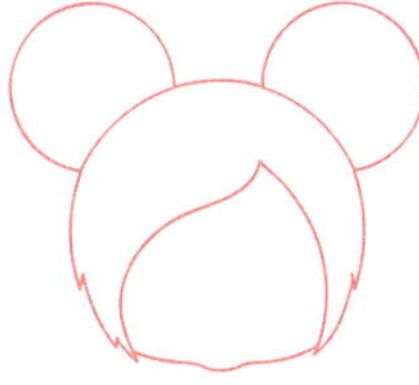

1. Start by drawing a circle for the head with smaller circles on top for the hair. Add some jagged lines for the texture of the hair.

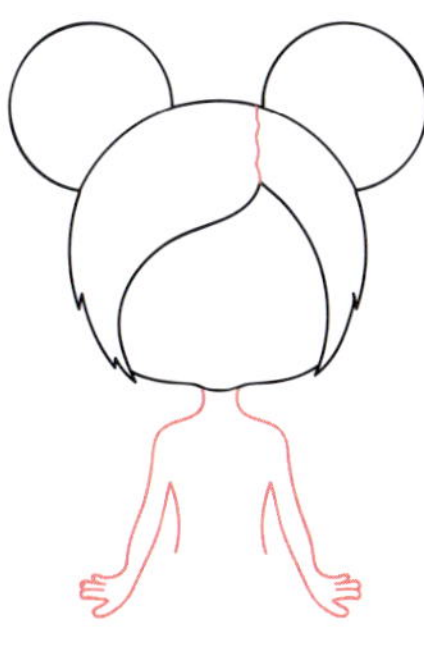

2. Draw a wiggly line for the hair part. Add the torso and arms.

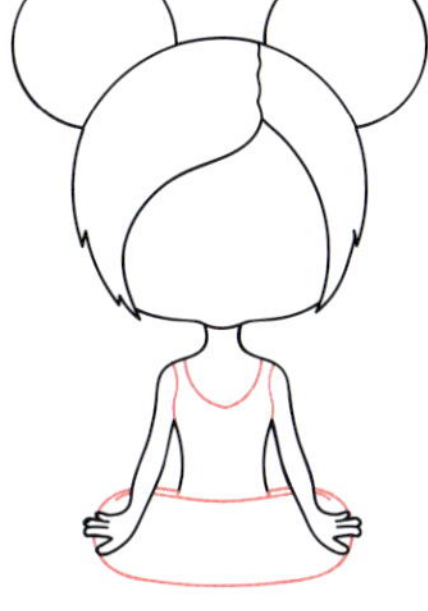

3. Add an oval for the swim tube, and draw in the shape of the swimsuit.

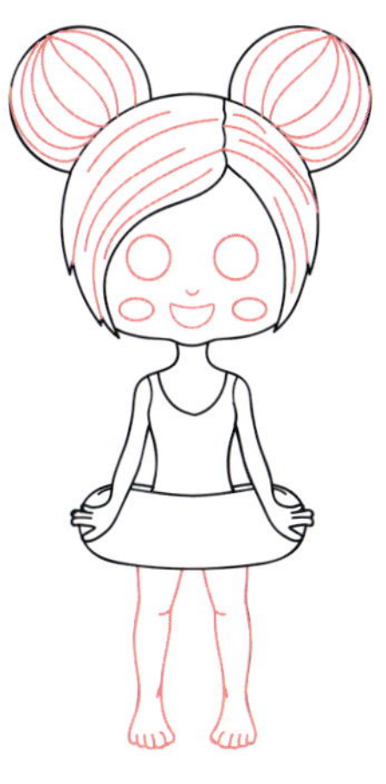

4. Add legs and feet. Draw two circles for eyes, ovals for cheeks, a curved half-circle mouth, and a little curved nose. Then add lines for the hair.

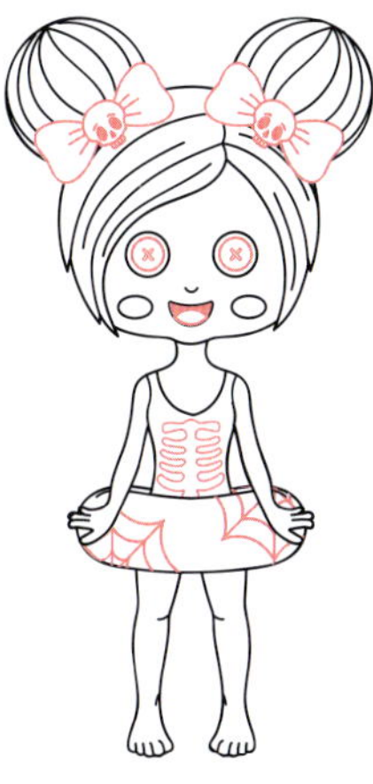

5. Add inner circles and X's to the eyes to make them look like buttons. Draw a tongue and fill in the mouth. Then add creepy cute bows in the hair, cobwebs on the swim tube, and a rib cage design on the swimsuit.

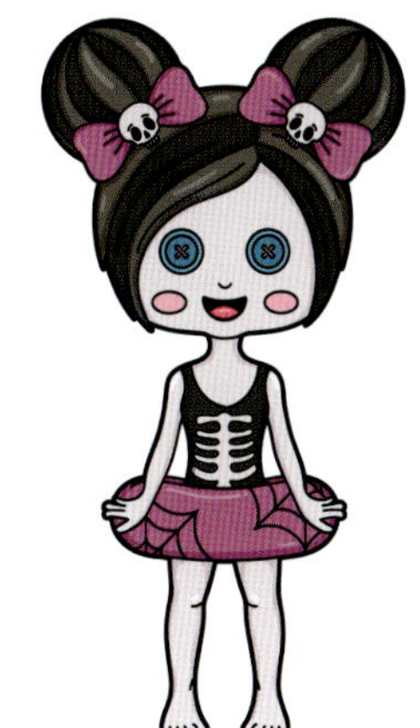

6. Color in your Haunted Beach Doll!

SKULL JELLYFISH

1.

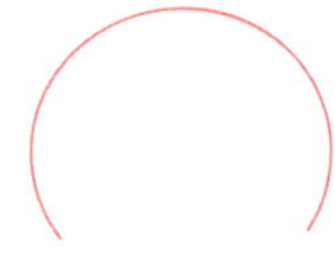

Start by drawing a circle, leaving the bottom open.

2.

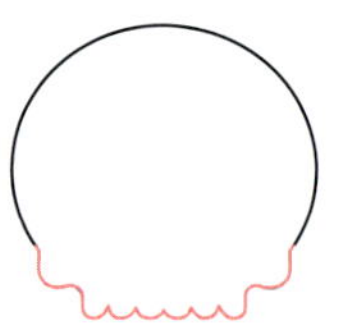

Add a square jaw and teeth to the skull.

3.

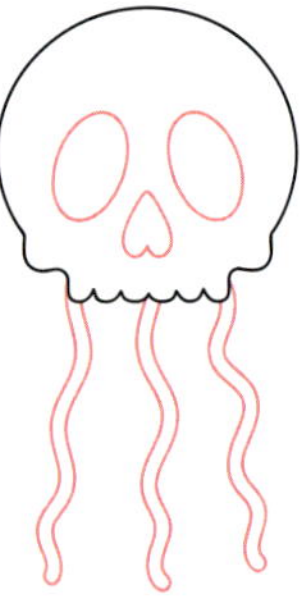

Draw three wiggly tentacles under the skull. Add two big ovals for eye sockets and an upside-down heart for the nose.

4.

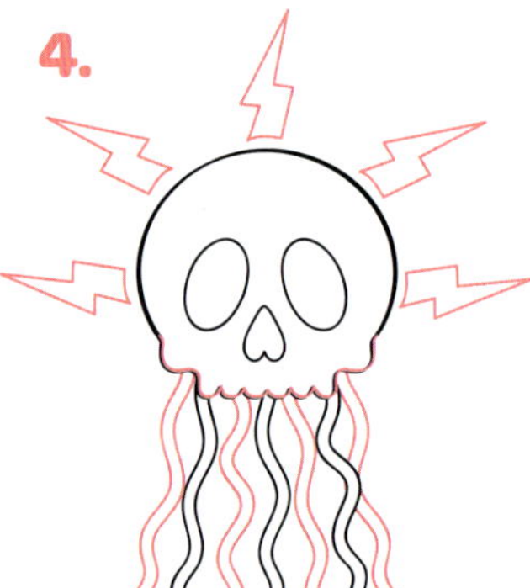

Add four more wiggly tentacles. Then add zigzag lightning bolts around the skull.

5.

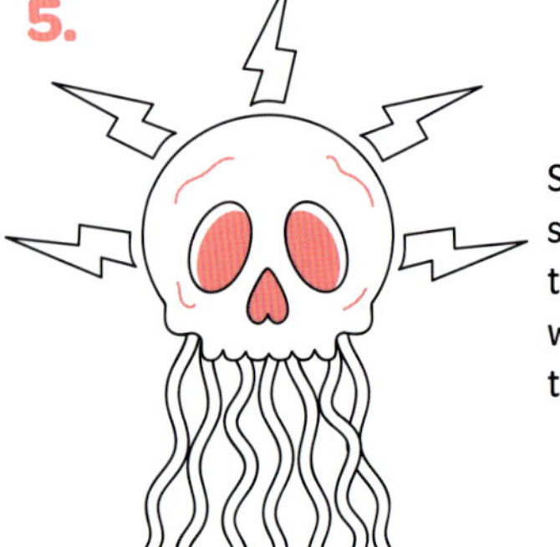

Shade in the eye sockets and fill in the nose. Add some wiggly lines for jelly texture.

6.

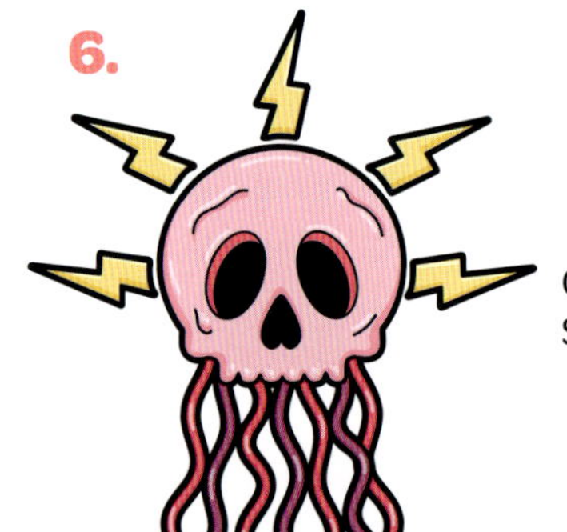

Color in your Skull Jellyfish!

BASEBALL GHOST

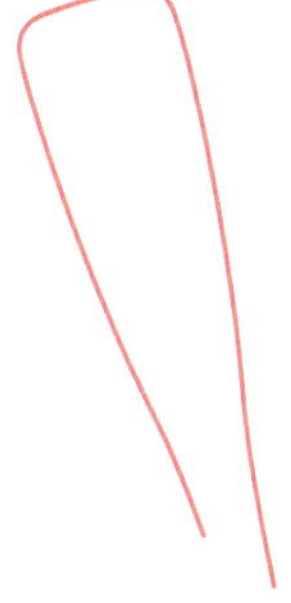

1. Start by drawing the top of the baseball bat.

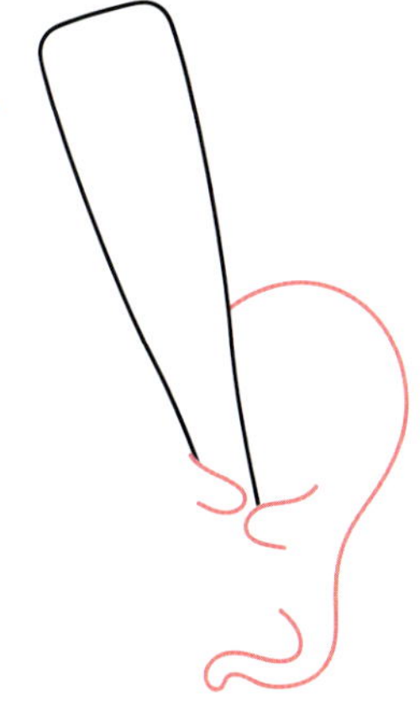

2. Add a curved teardrop shape to the bottom, and draw the arms of the ghost.

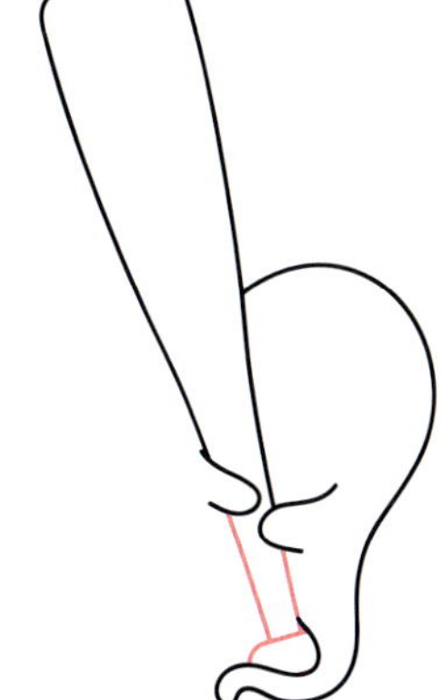

3. Add the bottom of the baseball bat.

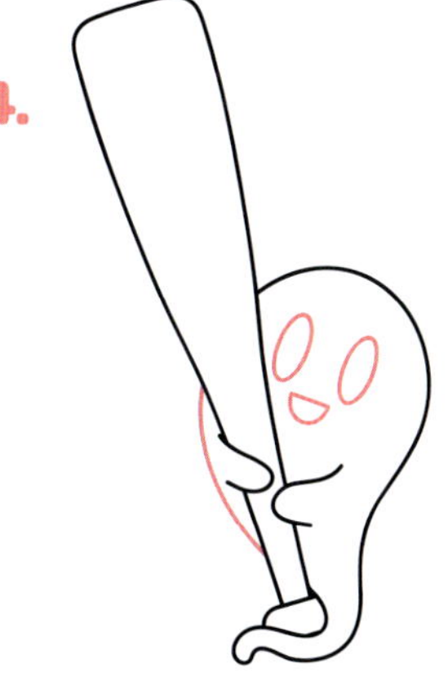

4. Add a curved line to the side to finish the ghost shape. Draw two large ovals for eyes and a half circle for the mouth.

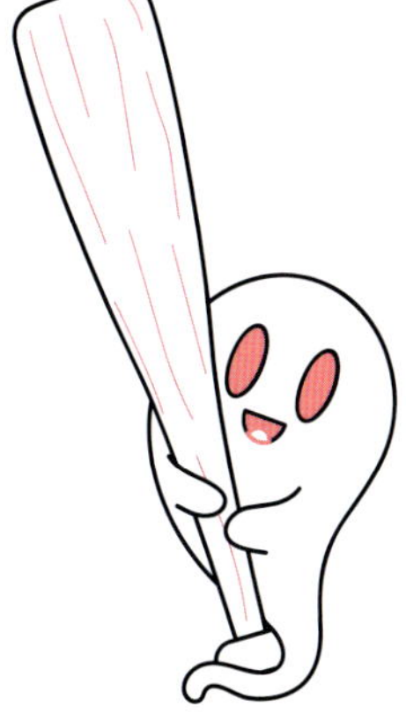

5. Add a tongue, fill in the mouth and eyes, and add lines to the bat for texture.

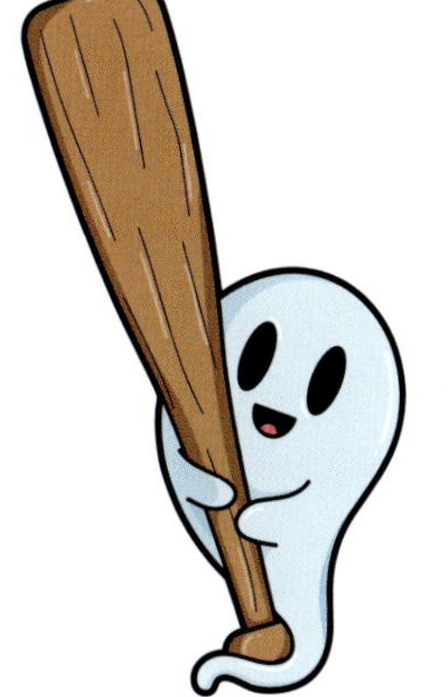

6. Color in your Baseball Ghost!

MUMMY VOLLEYBALL

1.

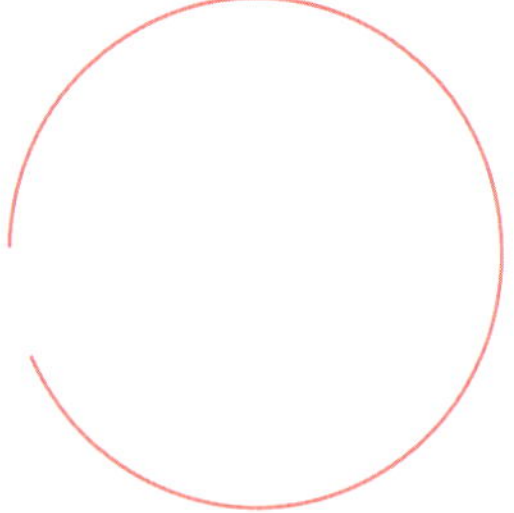

Start by drawing a circle, leaving an open space on the left side.

2.

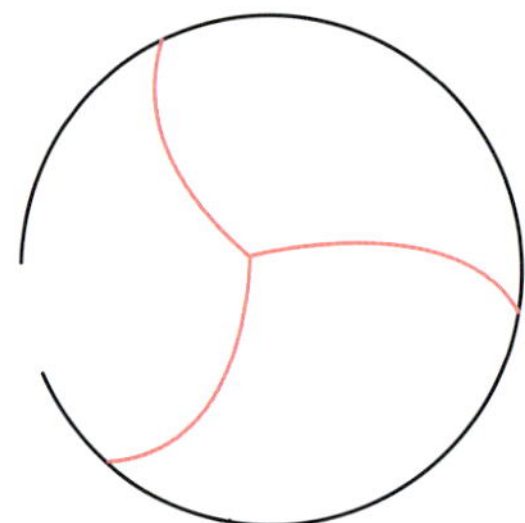

Add three curved lines to the circle, joining them slightly off-center.

3.

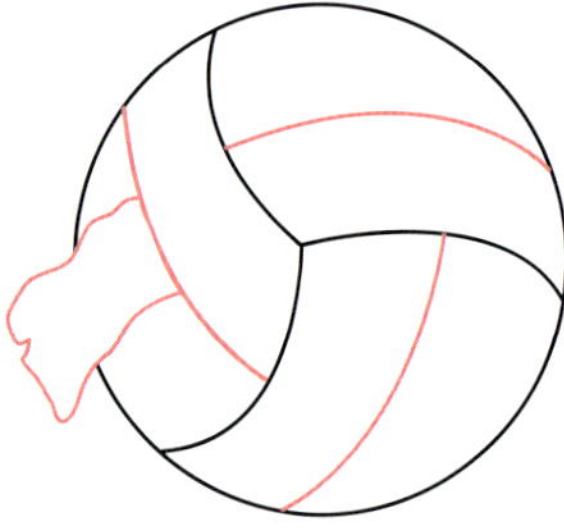

Add three more curved lines parallel to the first set, and draw a wavy rectangle through the gap on the left.

4.

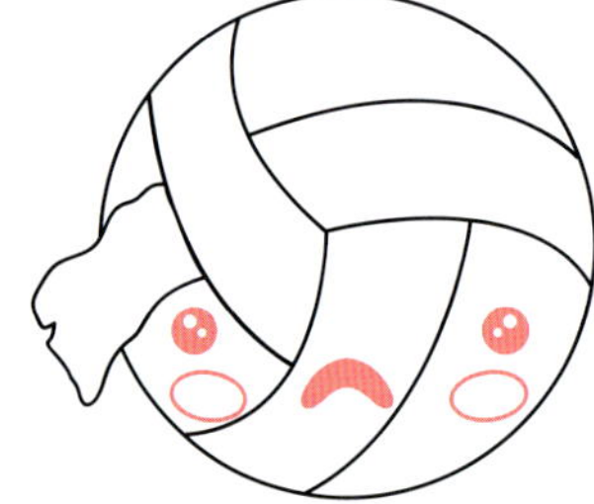

Draw two shaded circles for eyes; a filled-in, rounded crescent-moon mouth; and two ovals for the cheeks.

5.

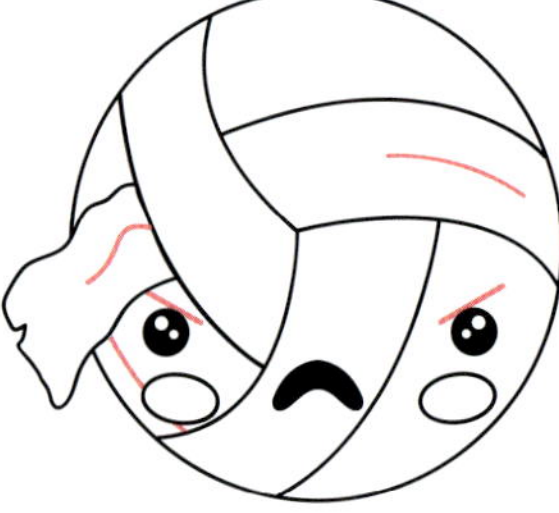

Add slanted lines above the eyes to make them look angry. Then add curved lines for the texture of the bandages.

6.

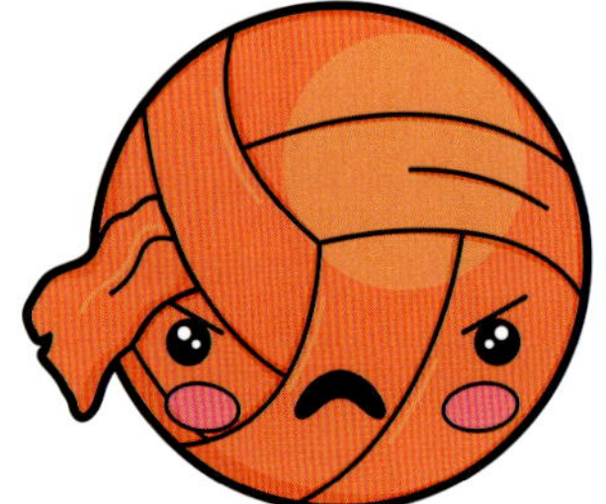

Color in your Mummy Volleyball!

VAMPIRE TENNIS BALL

1.

Start by drawing a circle.

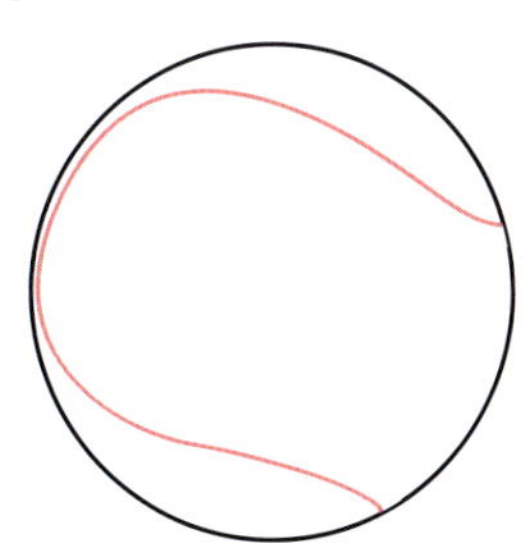

2.

Add a slanted U shape inside the circle.

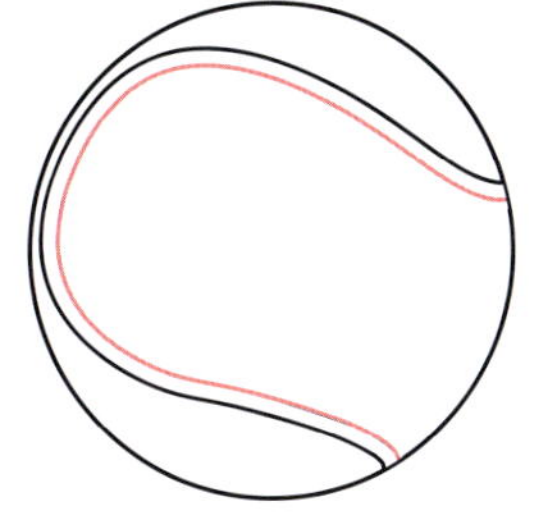

3.

Draw an inner U shape close to the first.

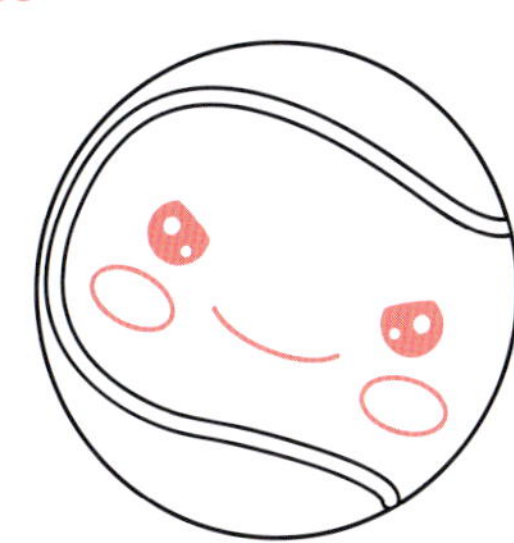

4.

Add a smile to the middle and two ovals for cheeks. Draw two shaded, slanted eyes.

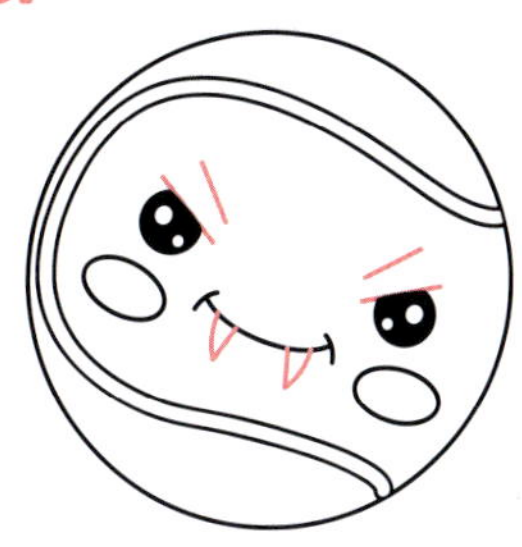

5.

Draw pointed teeth, and add slanted lines above the eyes to make them look evil.

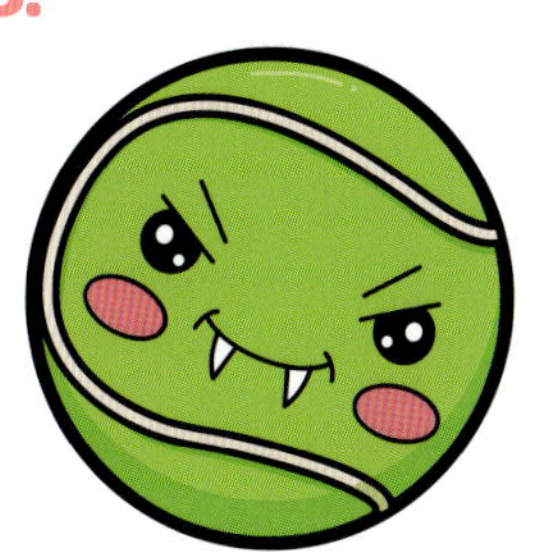

6.

Color in your Vampire Tennis Ball!

HAUNTED CAMPFIRE

1.

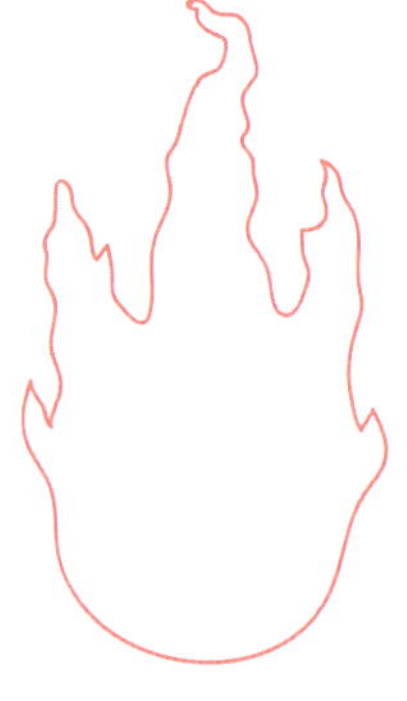

Start by drawing the shape of the flames.

2.

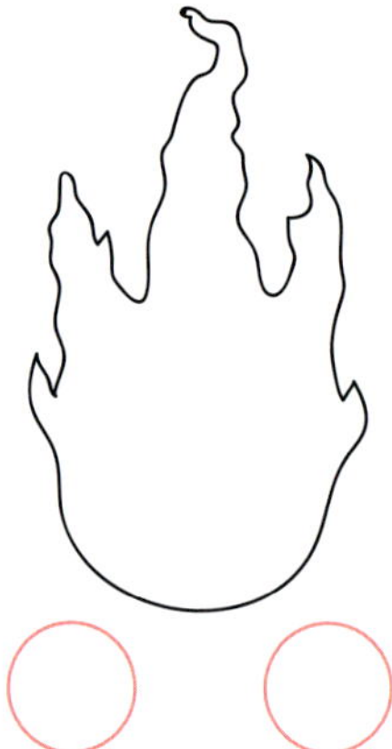

Add two circles (the ends of the logs) under the flames.

3.

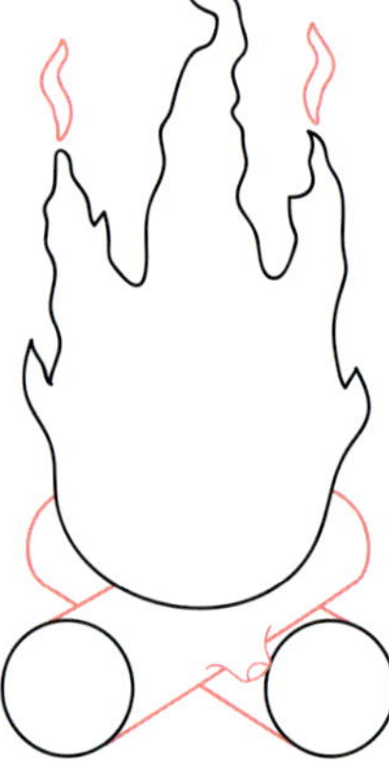

Draw two crossed cylinders for the logs. Add smaller flame shapes at the top of the fire.

4.

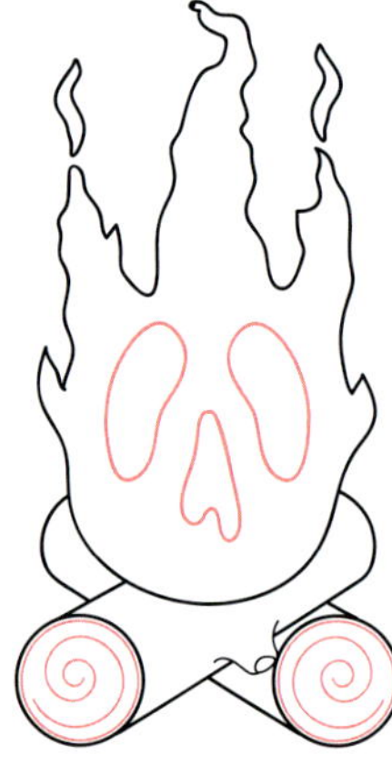

Add an inner circle to each log and a spiral inside. Then draw ovals inside the flame for eyes and an upside-down heart for the nose.

5.

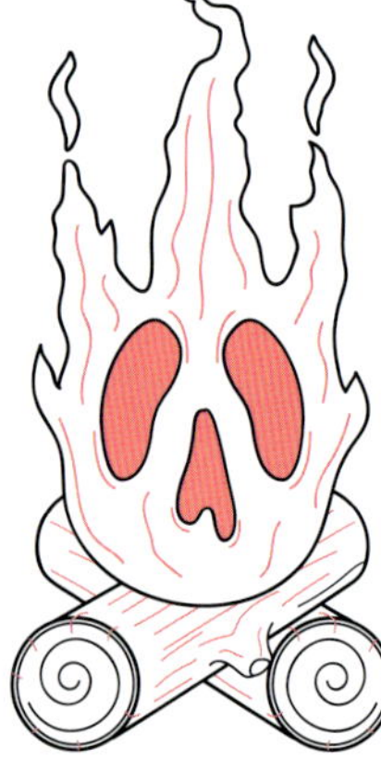

Add some wiggly detail lines to the logs and the flames. Then fill in the eyes and nose.

6.

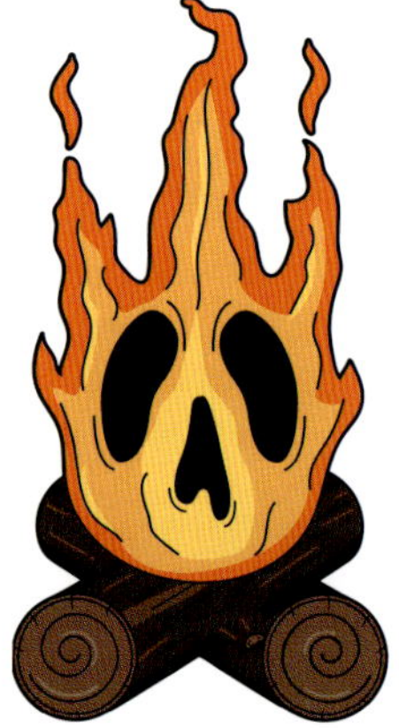

Color in your Haunted Campfire!

VAMPIRE CHOCOLATE BAR

1.

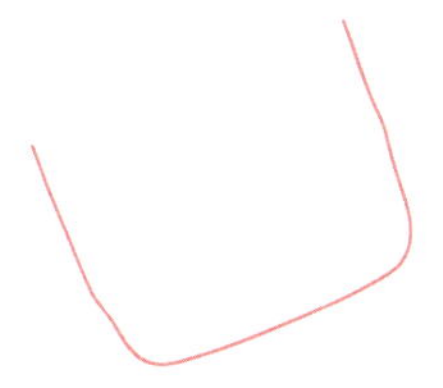

Start by drawing the bottom half of the chocolate bar as a rectangle with rounded edges. Leave the top open.

2.

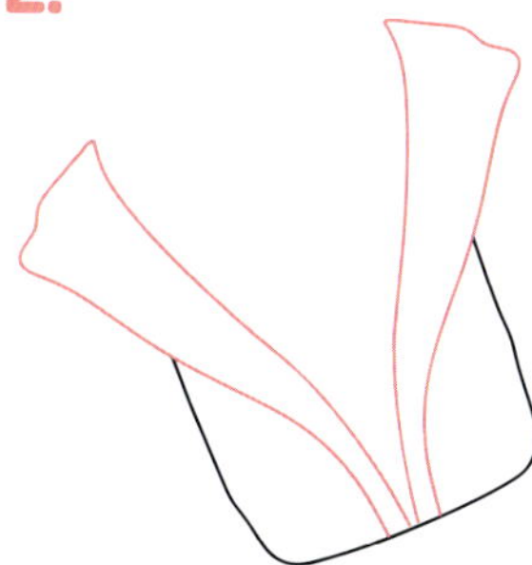

Add curved triangles to both sides.

3.

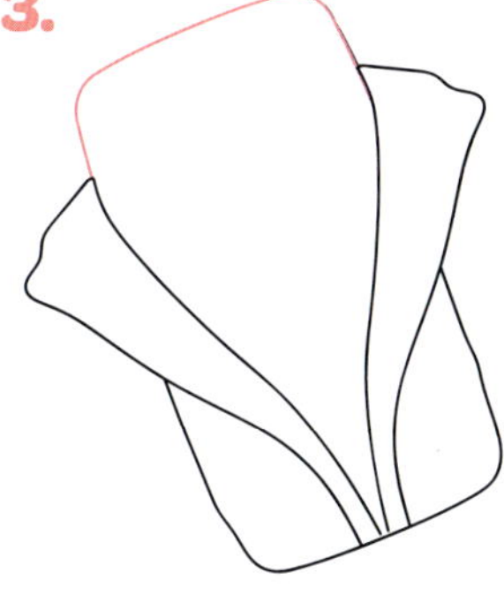

Draw the top part of the chocolate bar as another curved rectangle.

4.

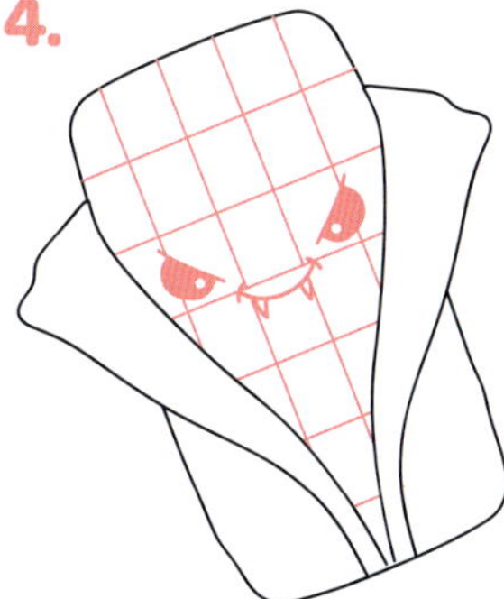

Add a grid of straight lines inside the chocolate bar and a creepy cute face with fangs.

5.

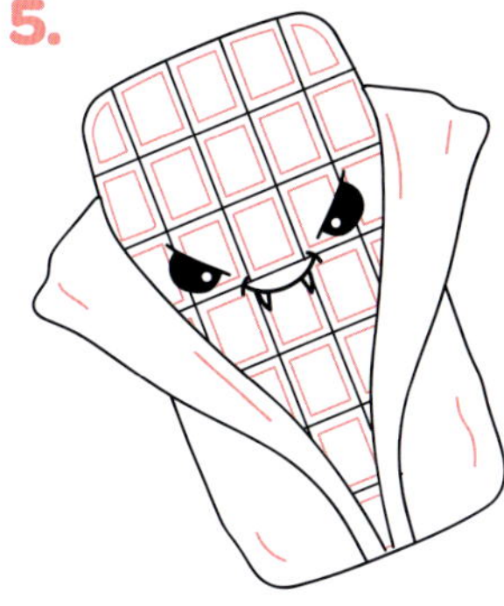

Draw a smaller rectangle inside each chocolate piece. Then add lines for the texture of the wrapper.

6.

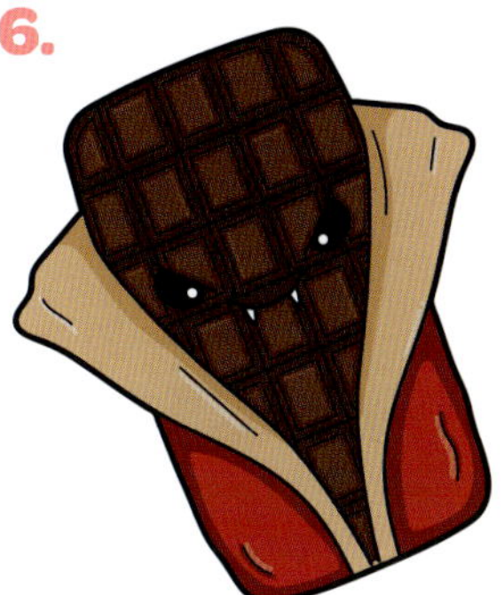

Color in your Vampire Chocolate Bar!

MONSTROUS S'MORE

1. 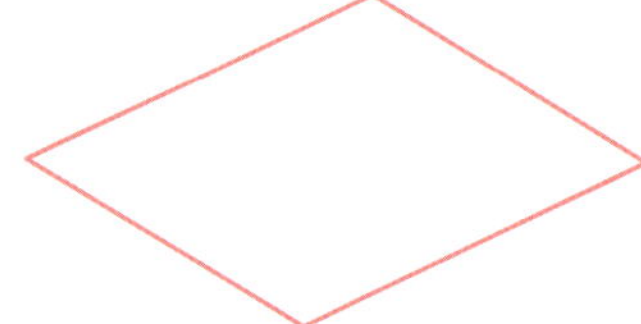

Start by drawing the top graham cracker as a slanted rectangle.

2. 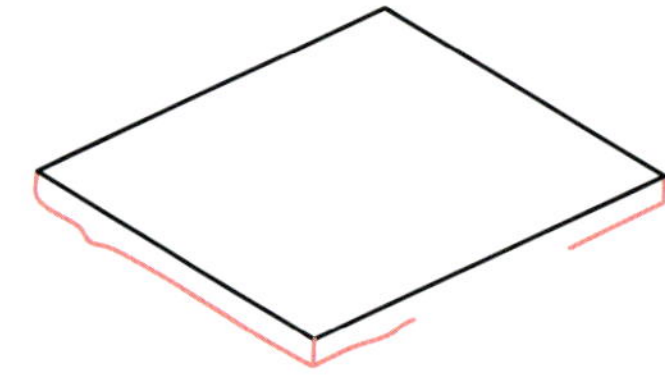

Draw the bottom edge of the graham cracker, leaving an open space on the right.

3. 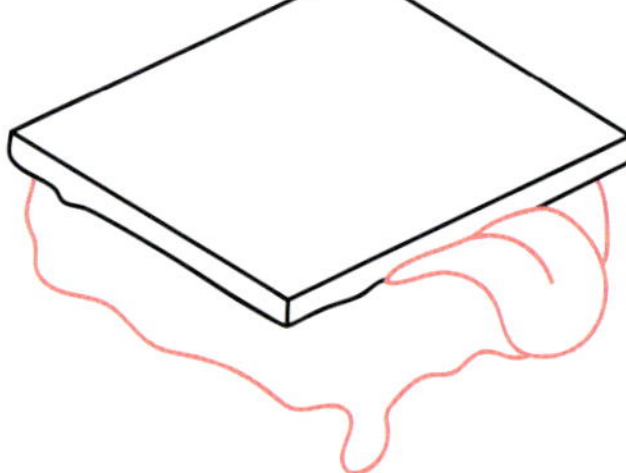

Add a tongue shape under the cracker, and then add wavy, drippy lines for the melty marshmallow.

4. 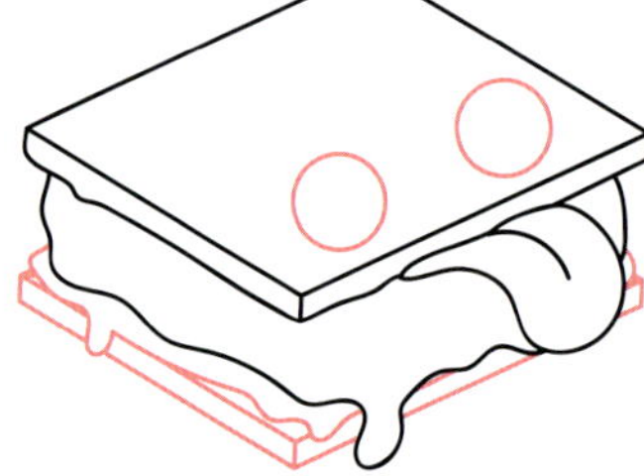

Draw two circles for eyes and another dripping wavy line under the first one for the melted chocolate. Then add the shape of the bottom graham cracker.

5. 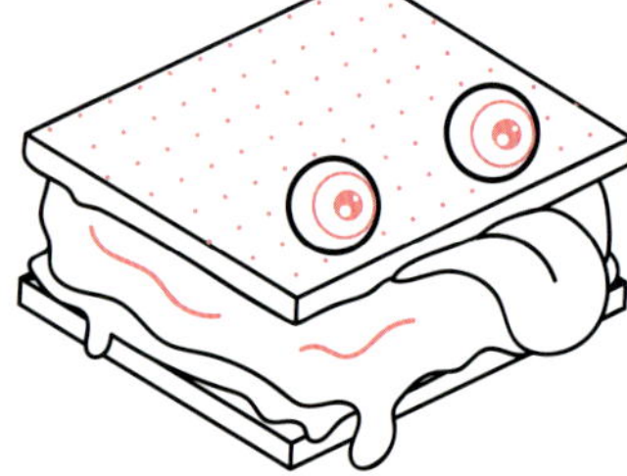

Inside the eyeballs, draw circles for irises and shaded circles for pupils. Add dots to the top graham cracker and some wavy lines to make the marshmallow look extra squidgy.

6. 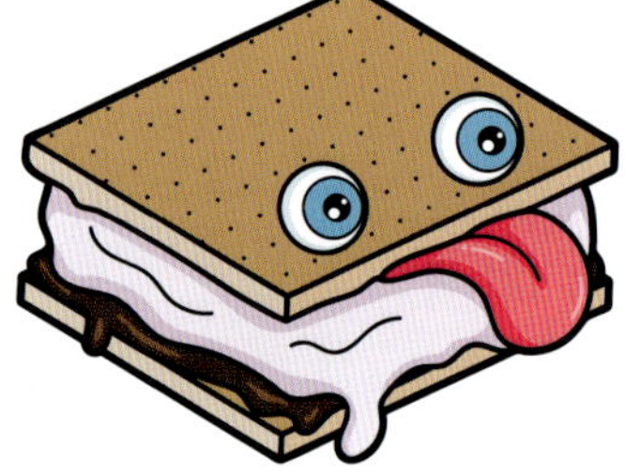

Color in your Monstrous S'more!

BONE AND EYEBALL COCOA

1.

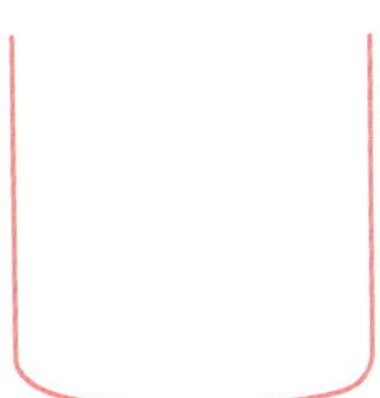

Start by drawing the bottom of the mug as a cylinder, leaving the top open.

2.

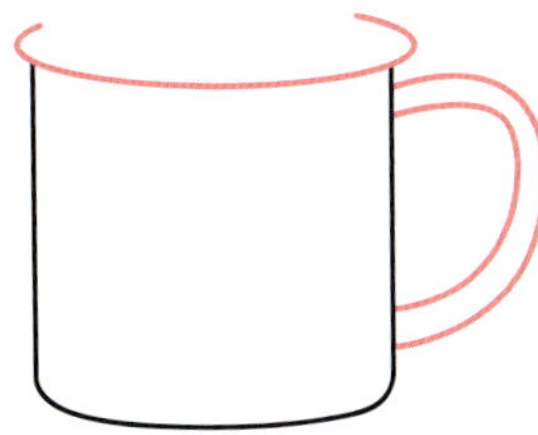

Add a flat, wide oval for the top of the mug, and draw the handle.

3.

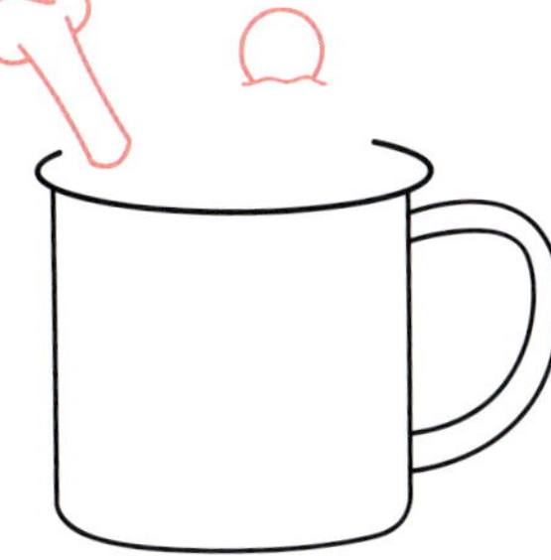

Draw a bone shape at the top and a circle with a wavy line for the eyeball.

4.

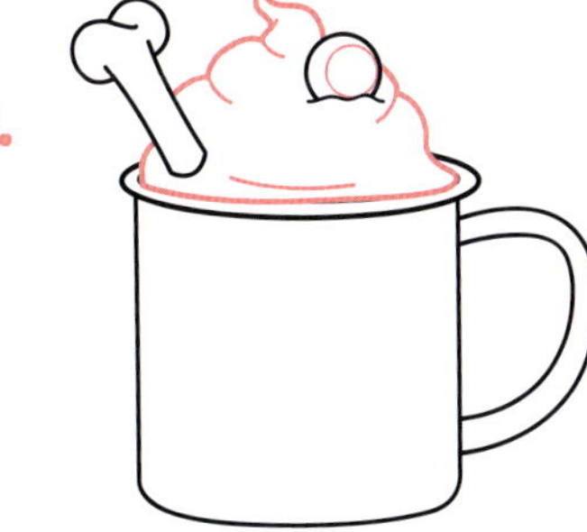

Add a swirly mound of whipped cream and a circle (iris) inside the eyeball.

5.

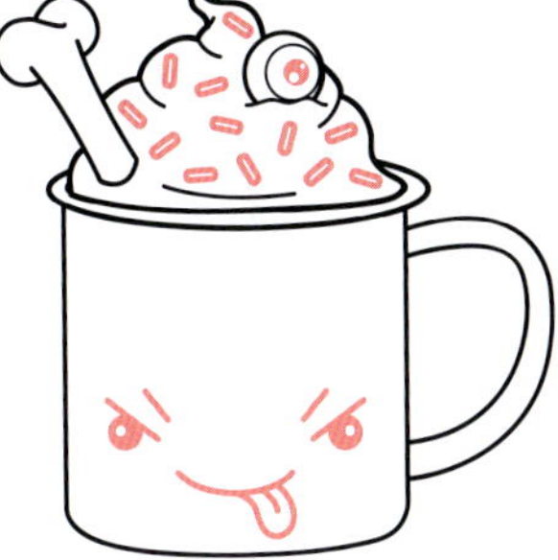

Draw little rectangles for sprinkles, and add a shaded circle inside the iris for the pupil. Add a creepy cute face to the mug.

6.

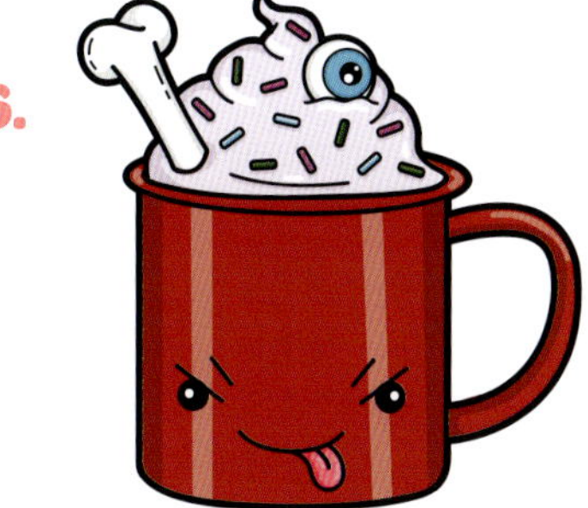

Color in your Bone and Eyeball Cocoa!

EYEBALL GRAPES

1.

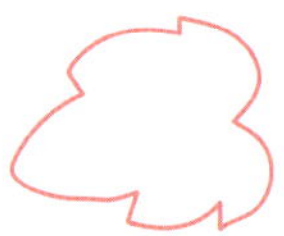

Start by drawing the outline of a five-pointed leaf.

2.

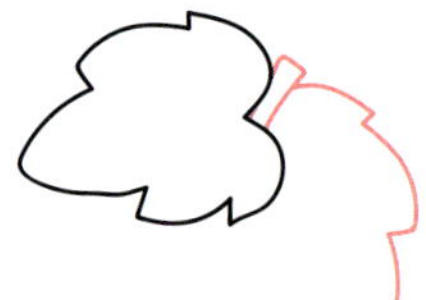

Add a stalk and the side of another leaf on the right.

3.

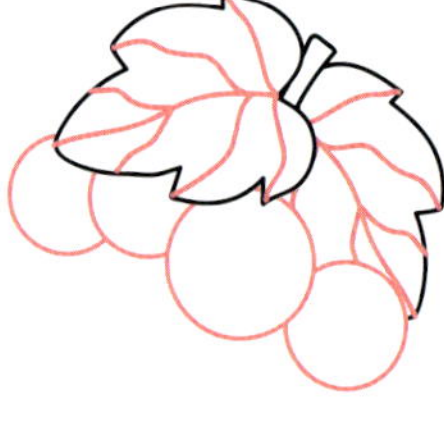

Draw four circles under the leaves. Then add veins to the leaves.

4.

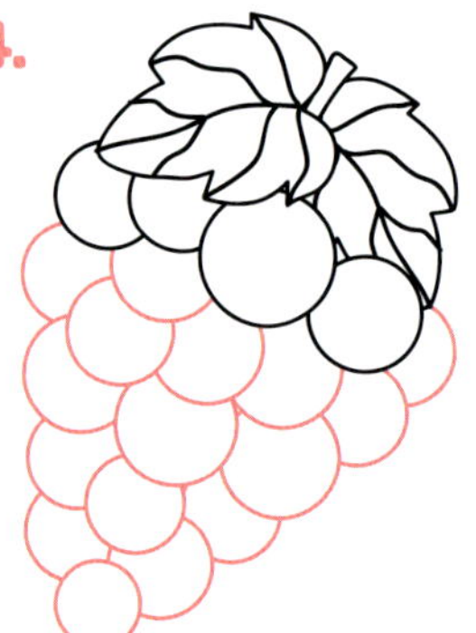

Add more circles in a triangular cluster.

5.

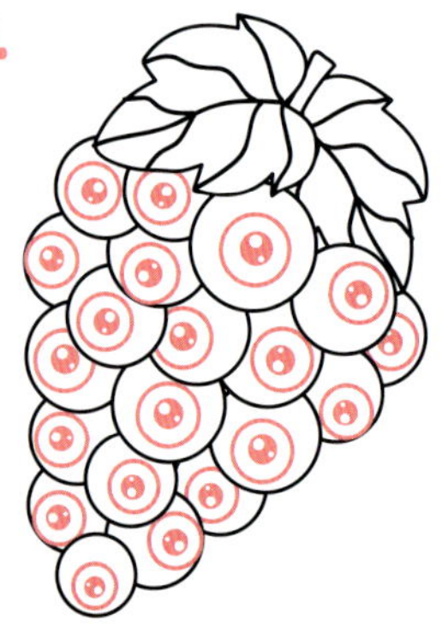

Add circles inside the eyeball grapes for irises, and add a shaded pupil in each.

6.

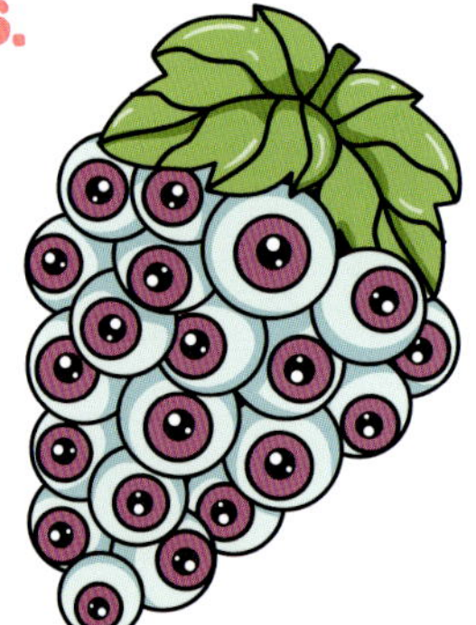

Color in your Eyeball Grapes!

GHOSTLY APPLE

1. 

Start by drawing the stem at the top of the apple.

2. 

On either side of the stem, add a leaf with a line down the middle.

3.

Draw the top of the apple—shaped like the top part of a heart.

4. 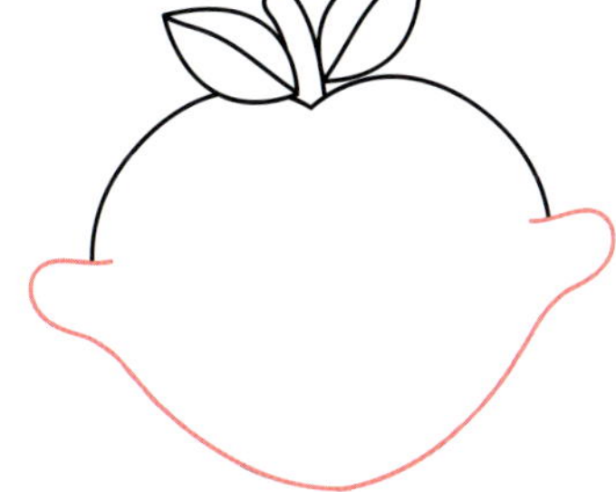

Draw two little arms and the rounded bottom of the apple.

5. 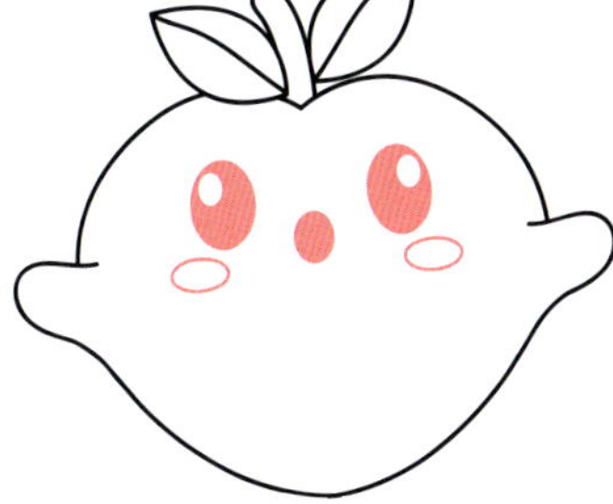

Add a spooky face: Draw two large, shaded ovals for eyes; a smaller, filled oval for the mouth; and ovals at either side for cheeks.

6. 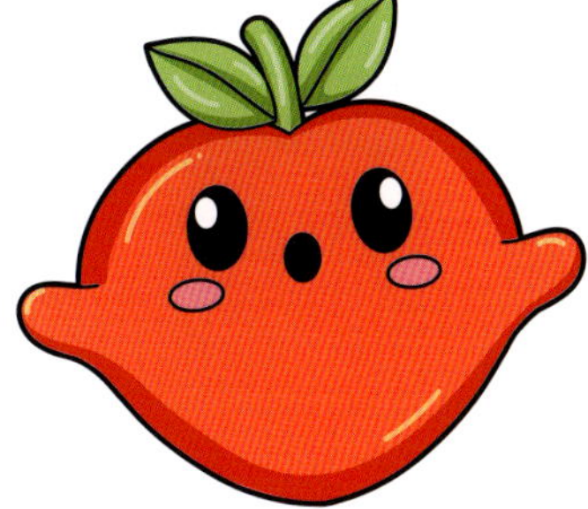

Color in your Ghostly Apple!

ANGRY LEMON

1.

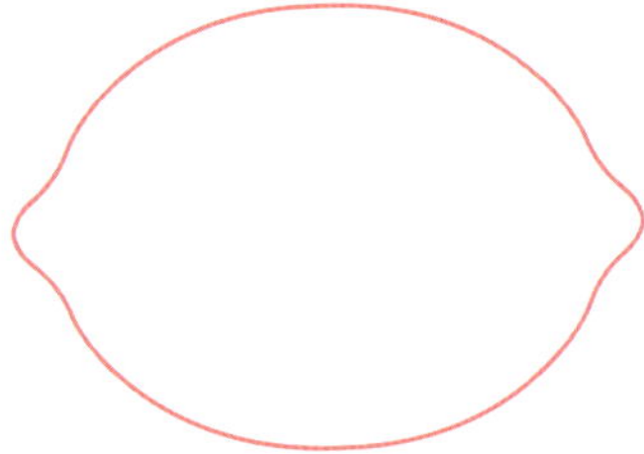

Start by drawing the outline of the lemon: an oval with a lump on either side.

2.

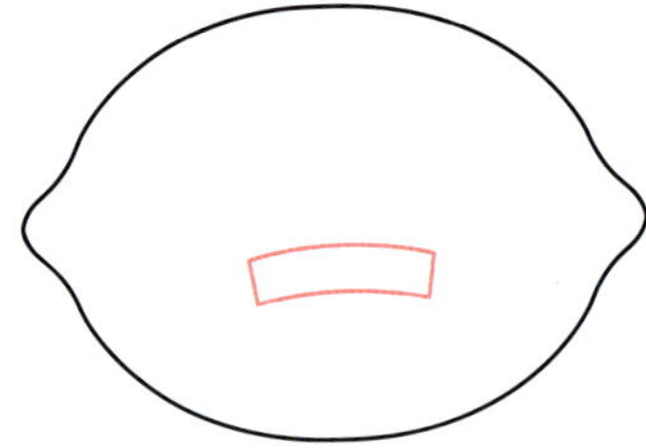

Add a curved rectangle (the angry mouth) slightly below the middle of the lemon.

3.

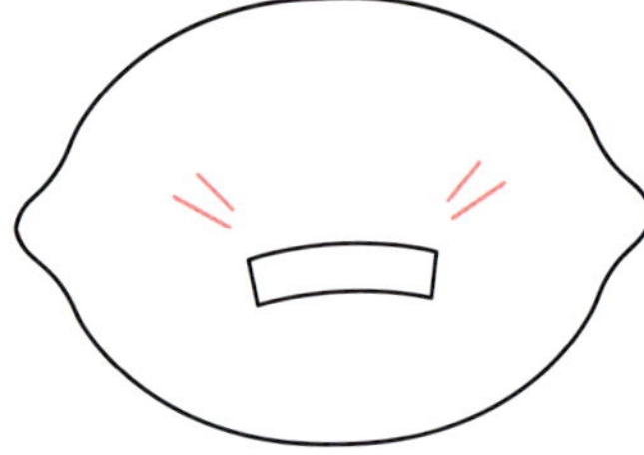

Add two slanted lines on each side of the rectangle.

4.

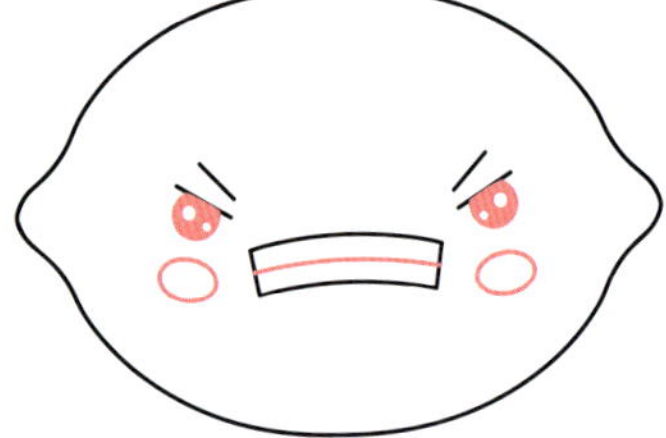

Draw a curved line through the middle of the mouth. Add two shaded circles for eyes and two ovals for cheeks.

5.

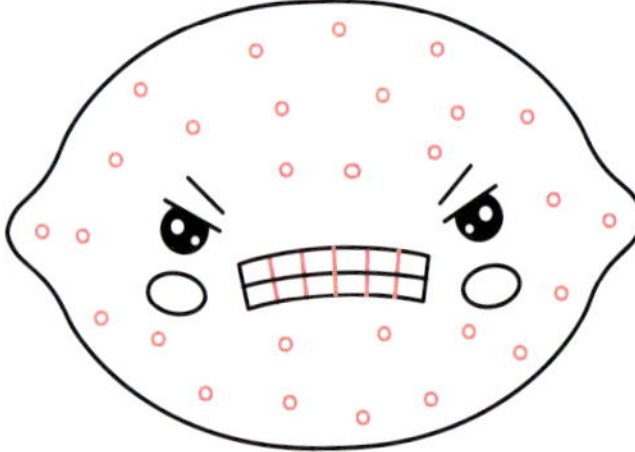

Add lines to the mouth for teeth, and add small dots for texture.

6.

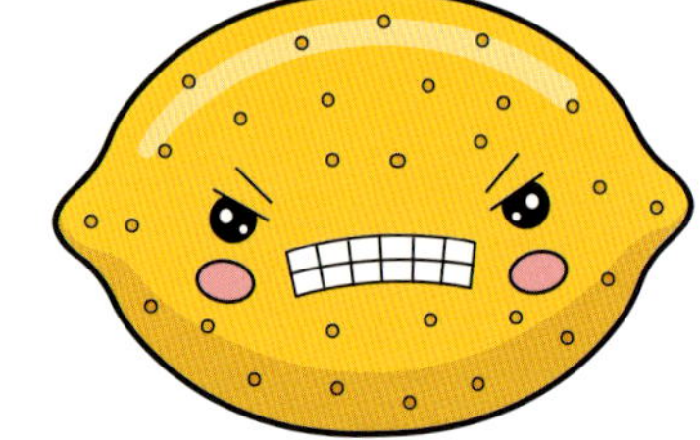

Color in your Angry Lemon!

EYEBALL SANDWICH

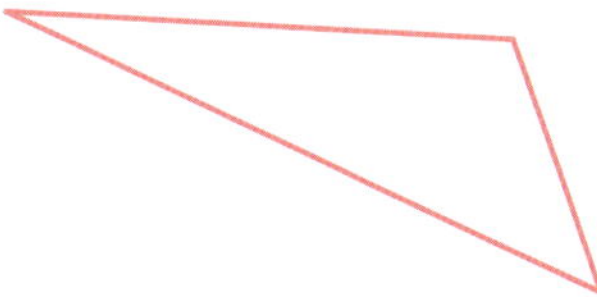

1. Start by drawing the top of the sandwich as a triangle.

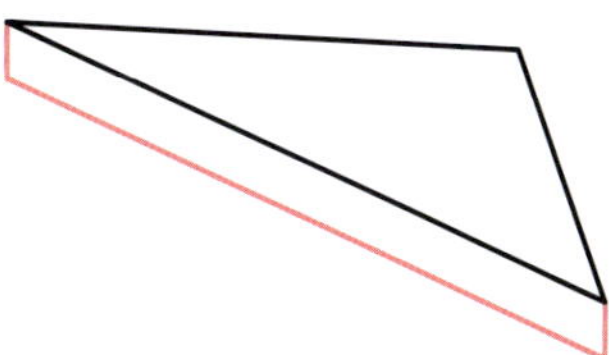

2. Add two small vertical lines to the corners, and join them up with a straight line.

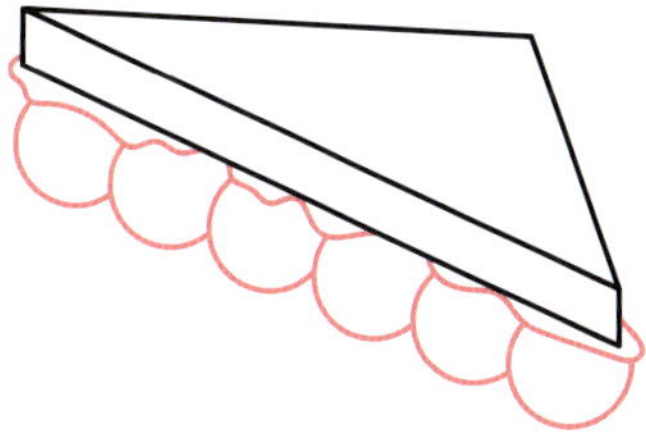

3. Add a wiggly line under the top section, then add six circles.

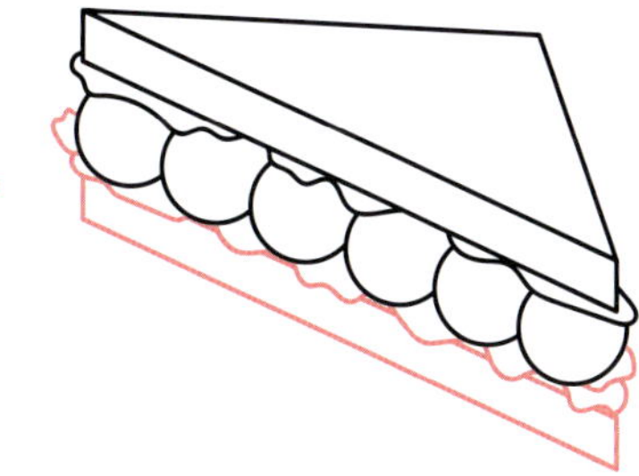

4. Add another wiggly line under the circles. Then draw a thin rectangle for the bottom of the sandwich.

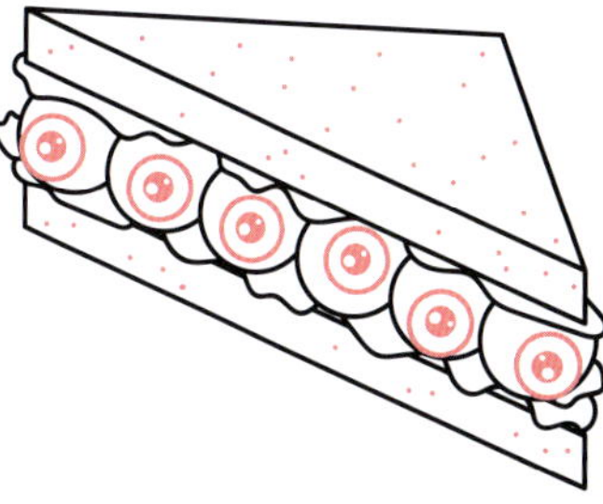

5. Add circles for the irises and shaded pupils. Then add little dots to the bread to make it look spongy.

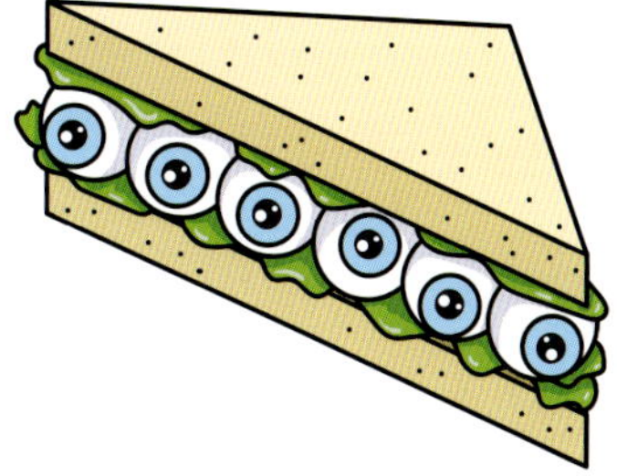

6. Color in your Eyeball Sandwich!

SKULL LEMONADE

1.

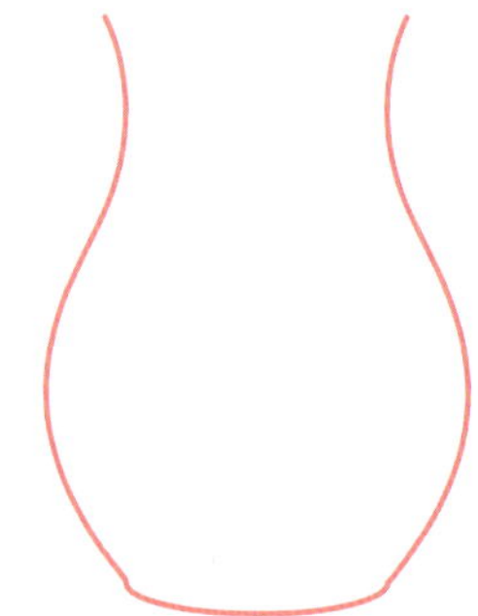

Start by drawing the curved outline of the jug, leaving the top open.

2.

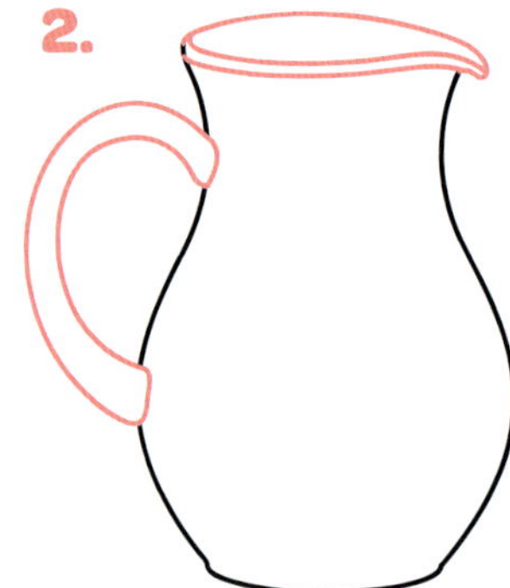

Add the top of the jug as a sideways, squished teardrop with a double line in front. Then add the handle.

3.

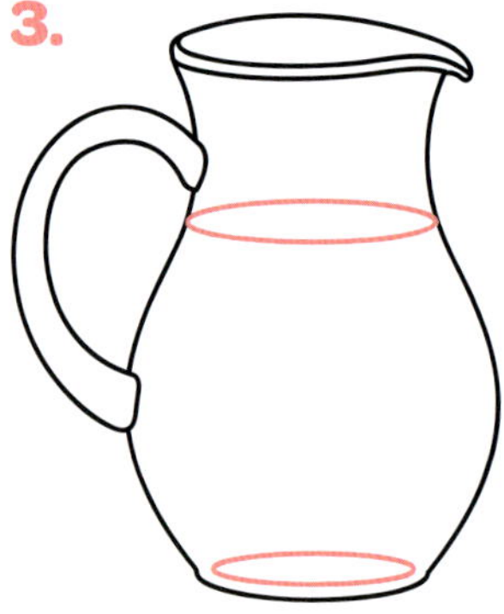

Add an oval to the bottom of the jug and another, larger oval near the top.

4.

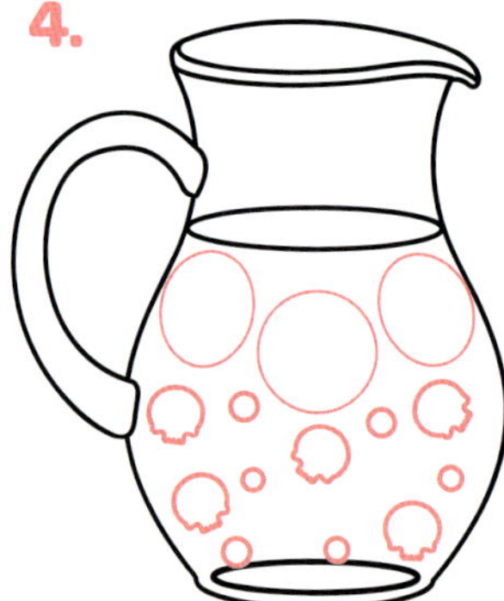

Add a large circle and two ovals. Then add some little skulls. Draw little circles for bubbles.

5.

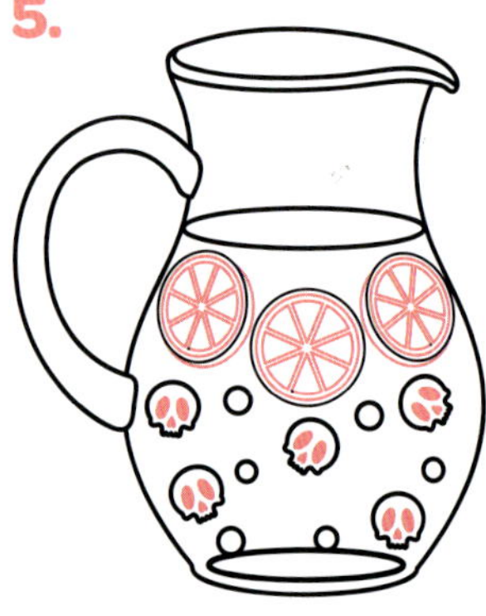

Draw the rind and sections of each lemon. Make filled-in eye sockets and noses on the skulls.

6.

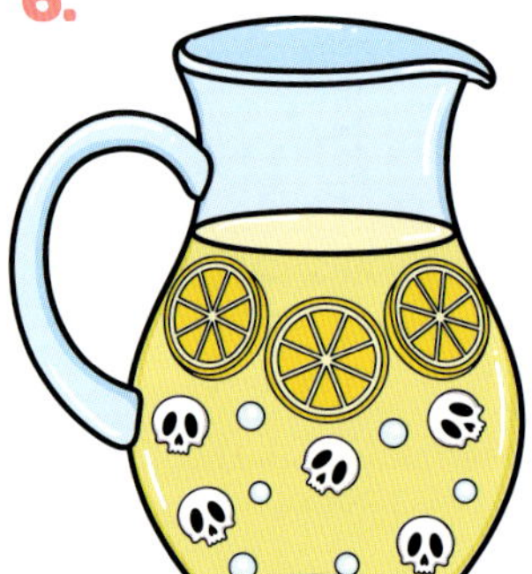

Color in your Skull Lemonade!

FANGED CAKE

1.

Start by drawing the bottom of the cake as a slanted line with two small vertical lines on either side.

2.

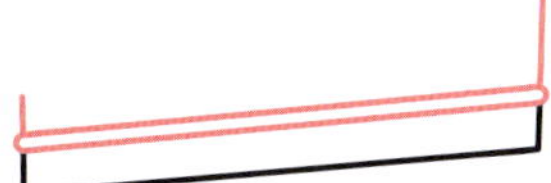

Add a thin, slanted rectangle for the filling, then two more small vertical lines for the next layer of cake.

3.

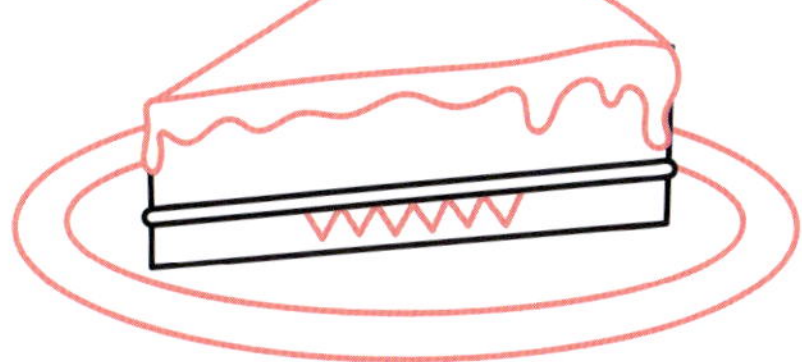

Draw a wiggly dripping line for the topping, then add the top triangle, leaving the top corner open. Draw two ovals for the plate, and add some pointy teeth to the cake.

4.

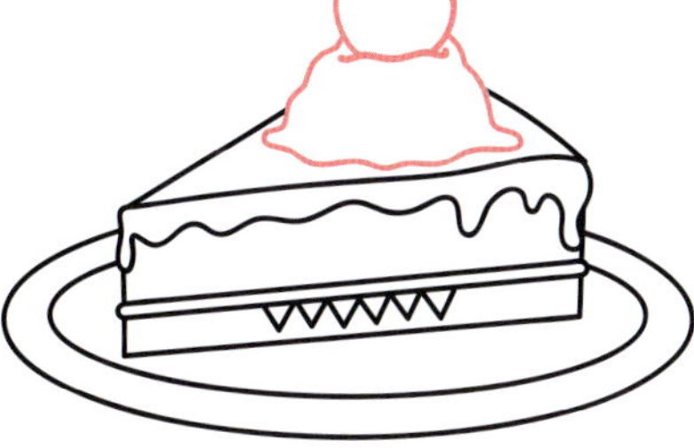

Add a dollop of cream with a heart-shaped cherry on top.

5.

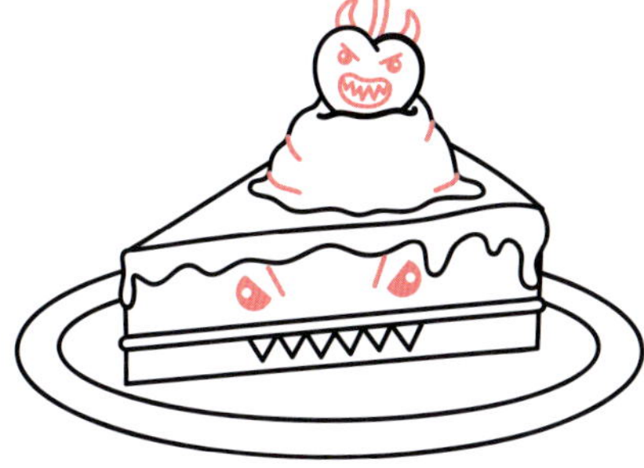

Add the cherry stem and two little triangular horns. Add a spooky face to the cherry. Draw slanted, shaded eyes and eyebrows on the cake, and add lines to the cream for texture.

6.

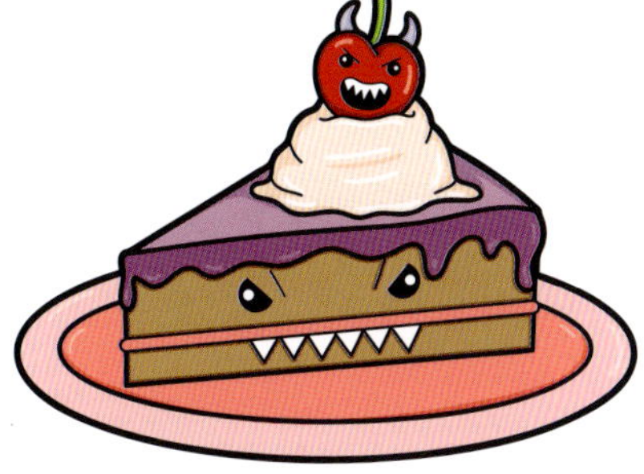

Color in your Fanged Cake!

BATWING SHADES

1. 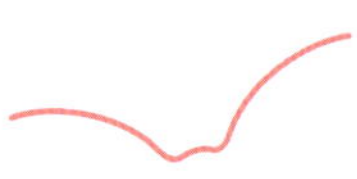

Start by drawing the top part of the shades.

2. 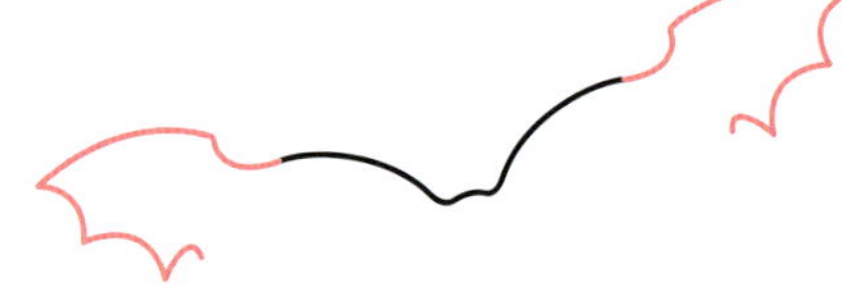

Add the wing shapes to either side.

3. 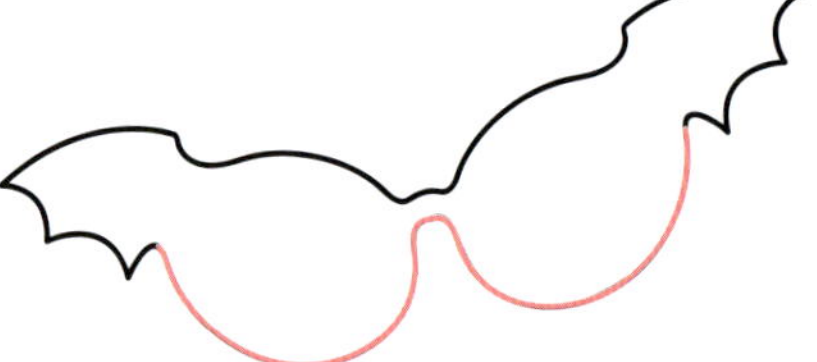

Continue the wing lines to draw the bottom of the shades.

4. 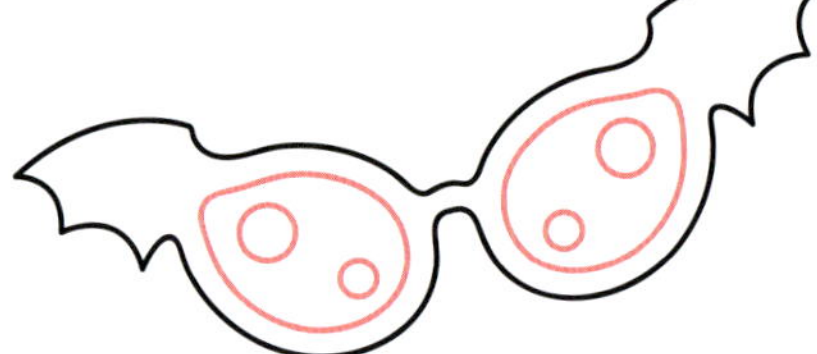

Add two ovals for the lenses, and add two circles inside each.

5. 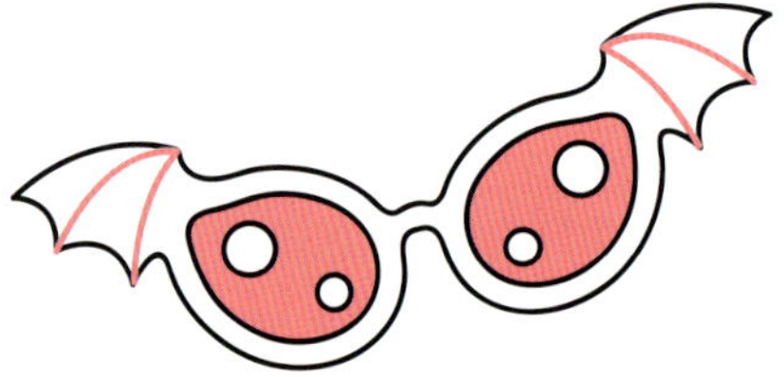

Fill in the lenses, and add curved lines to the wings.

6. 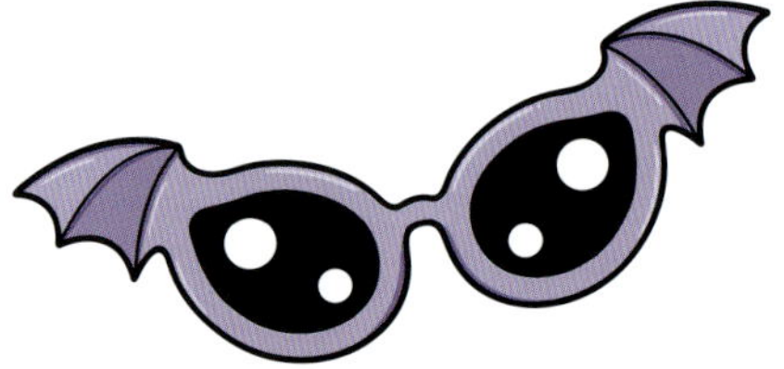

Color in your Batwing Shades!

SKELETON TRAIN

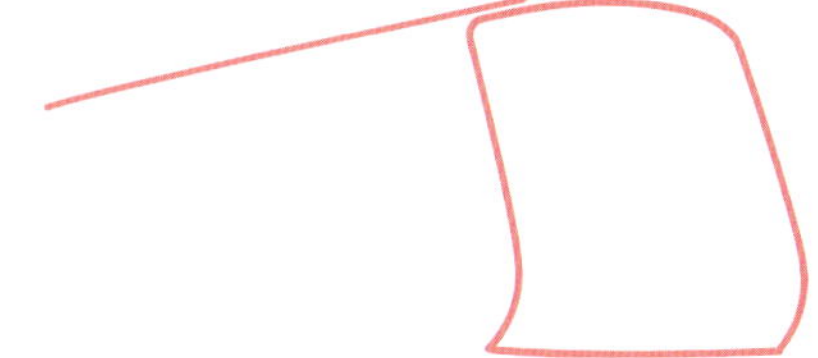

1. Start by drawing a slanted line for the top of the train and a curved rectangle for the front.

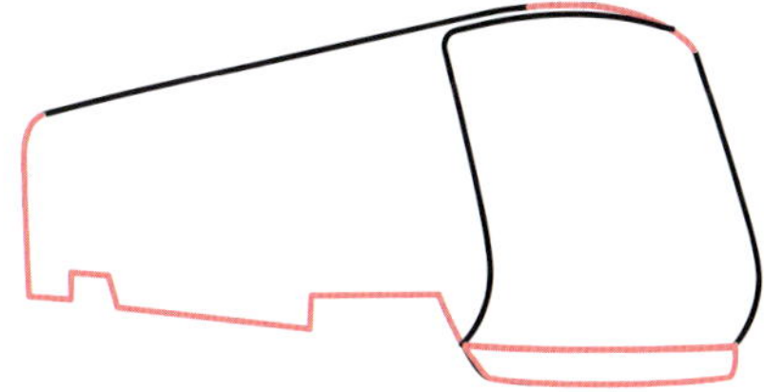

2. Draw the main body of the train and join up the top line with the curved rectangle.

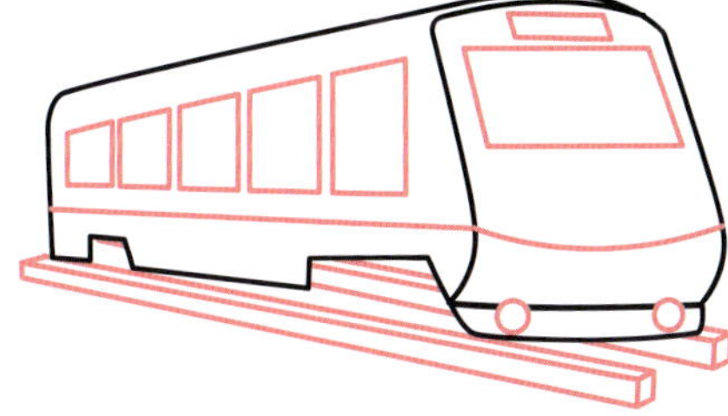

3. Draw cuboid shapes at the bottom for the train tracks. Add slanted squares for windows; a large, slanted rectangle for the windshield; and a smaller rectangle above. Add circles for the headlights.

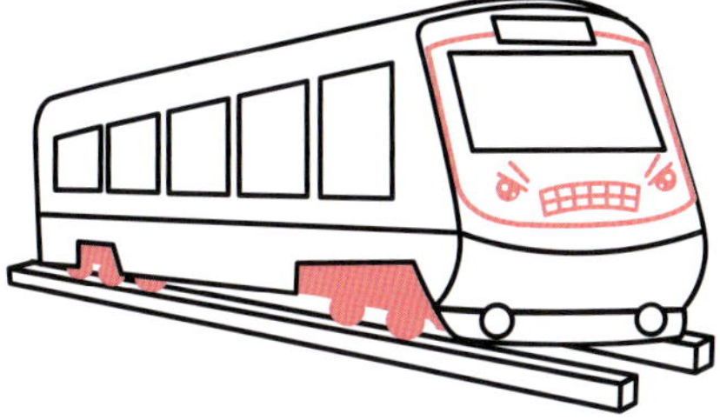

4. Add filled-in wheels to the side of the train. Draw a curved square around the windshield, and then add an angry face to the train.

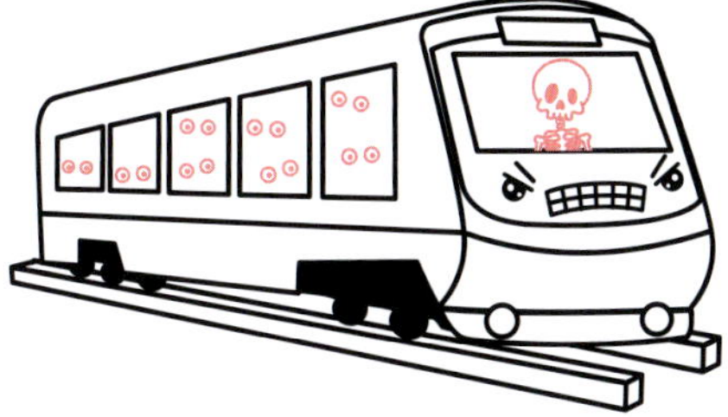

5. Add little eyeballs in the windows, and draw a simple skeleton (or ghost!) train driver.

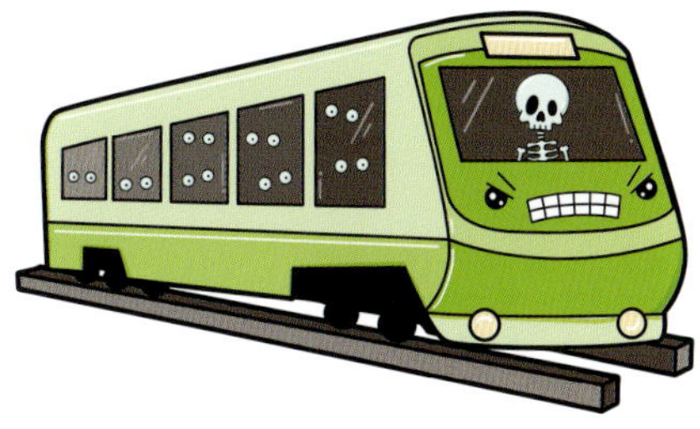

6. Color in your Skeleton Train!

GHOSTLY ROAD TRIP

1.

Start by drawing the top of the car as a rounded rectangle with a curved line at the bottom.

2.

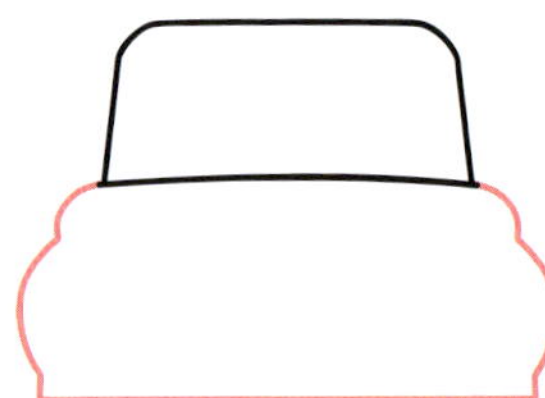

Add the car's curved sides and a straight line at the bottom.

3.

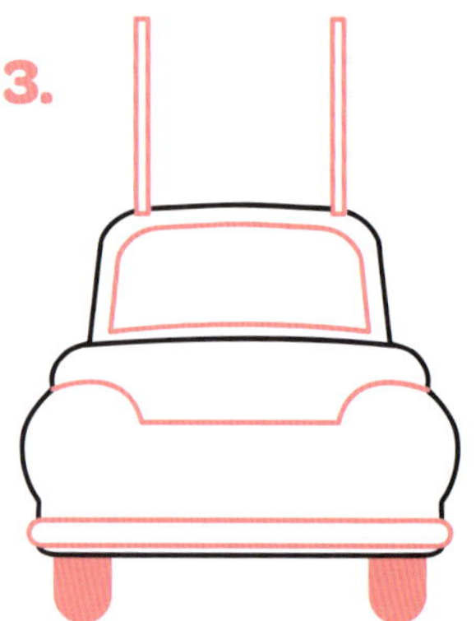

Add two thin rectangles at the top. Then, inside the front of the car, add curved lines that will surround the headlights. Join them with a straight line. Draw the windshield and bumper, and add filled-in wheels.

4.

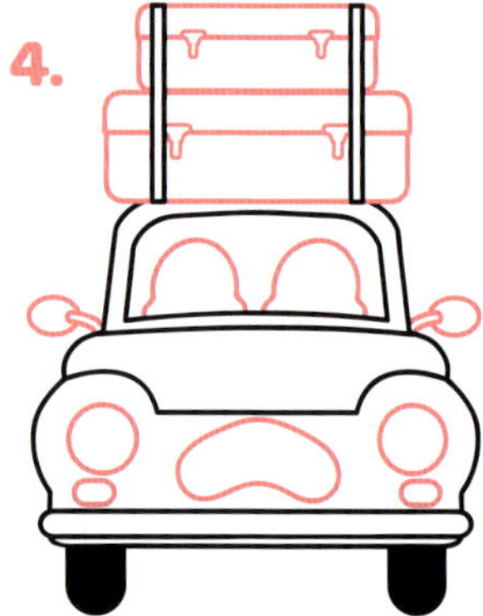

For the suitcases, add two rectangles with hinges. Draw ghost outlines in the windshield. Add two ovals on narrow stems for the wing mirrors. Give the car headlight eyes (circles), fog light cheeks (ovals), and a jellybean-shaped mouth.

5.

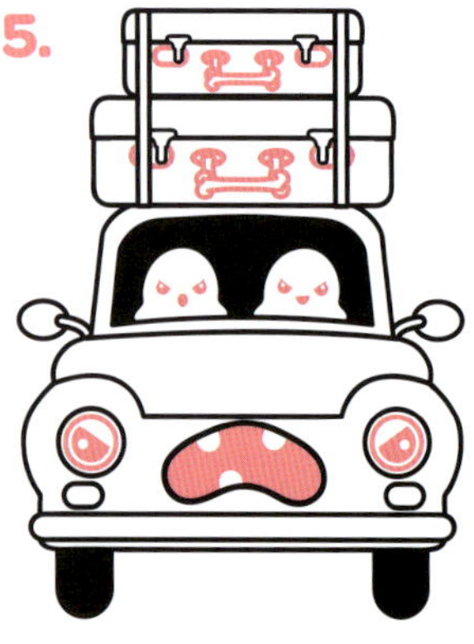

Add bone-shaped handles and locks to the suitcases. Give the ghosts creepy cute faces. For the face of the car, draw teeth, fill in the mouth, draw circles inside the headlights, and shade in slanted pupils.

6.

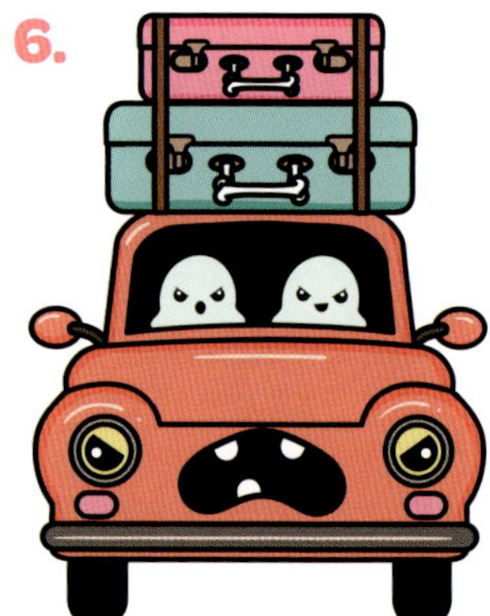

Color in your Ghostly Road Trip!

BATWING BOOM BOX

1.

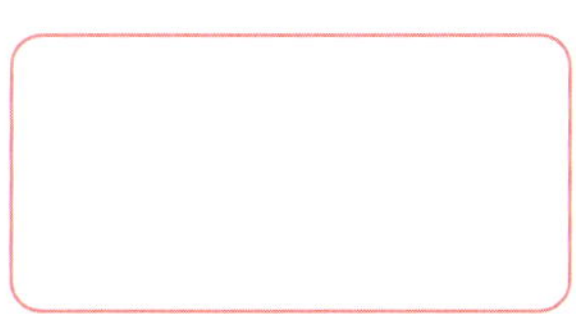

Start by drawing a rectangle with rounded corners.

2.

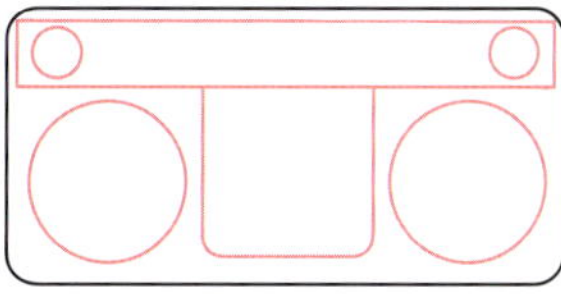

Inside the top of the outline, draw a thin rectangle with a circle at either side. Then add two large circles for the speakers and a square in the middle.

3.

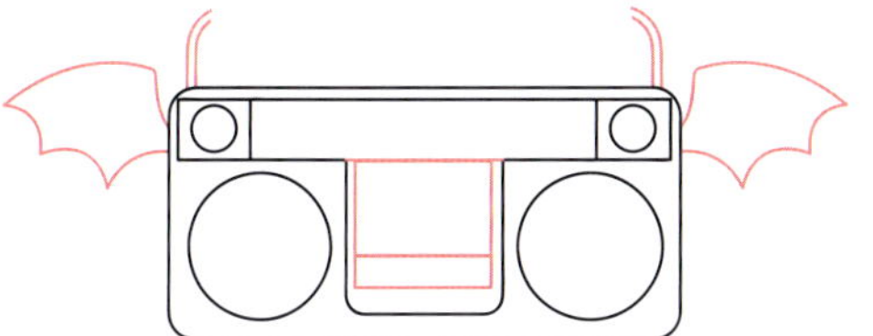

Add wing shapes to both sides. Then add a smaller square inside the middle square. Inside that, draw a half circle. Draw a horizontal line across the bottom third of the smaller square. Then add two curved lines to the top for the handle.

4.

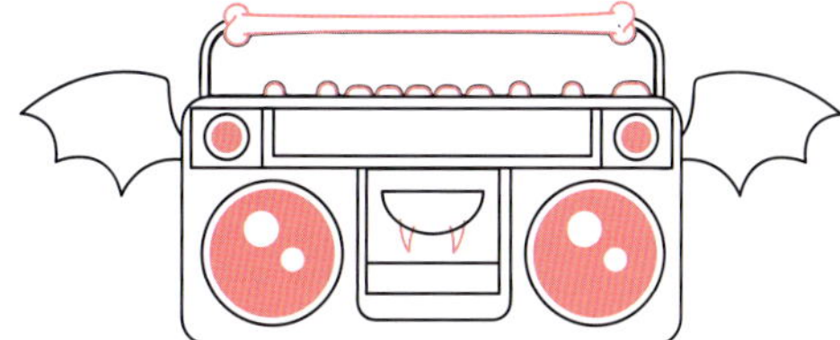

Add a long bone shape to complete the handle. Add buttons to the top of the boom box. Add pointy teeth to the bottom of the half circle, and fill in the speakers, leaving blank spots in larger speakers.

5.

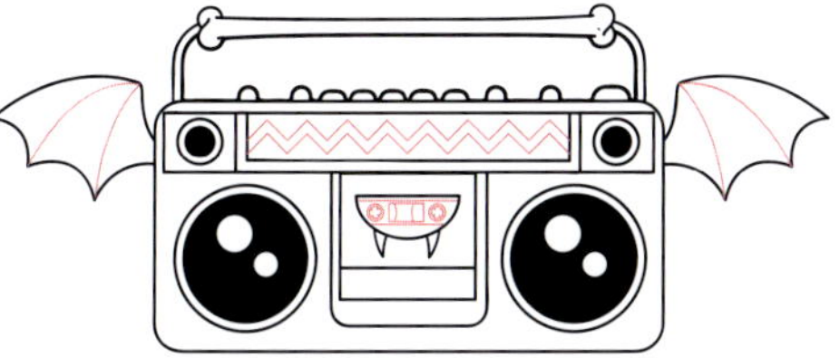

Inside each wing, draw two curved lines joining the top to the bottom points. Then draw two zigzag lines inside the thin rectangle. Inside the half circle, add the details of a cassette tape.

6.

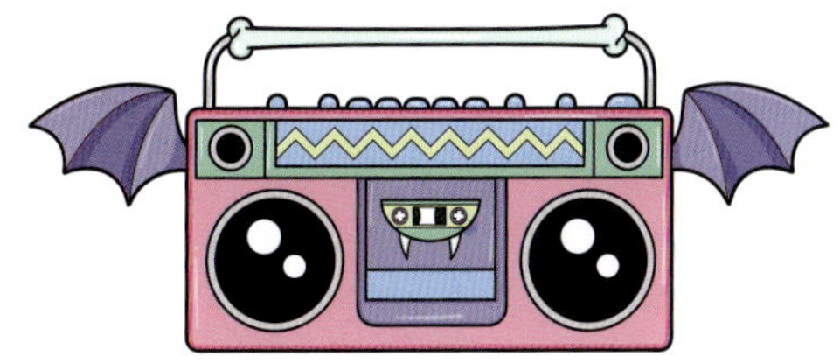

Color in your Batwing Boom Box!

CREEPY MIXTAPE

1. Start by drawing a rectangle with rounded corners.

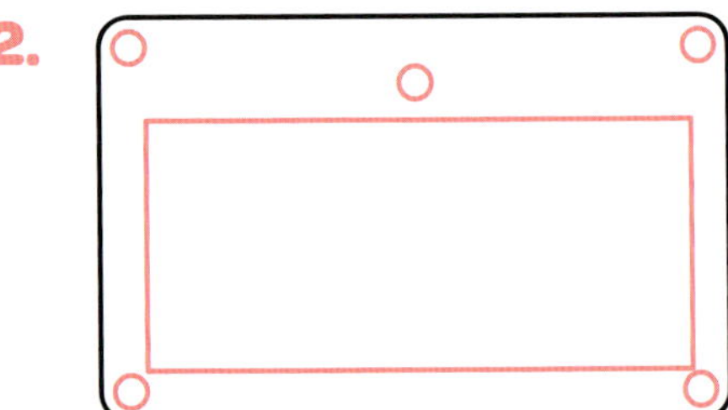

2. Add a smaller rectangle inside, and add small circles to the corners and middle.

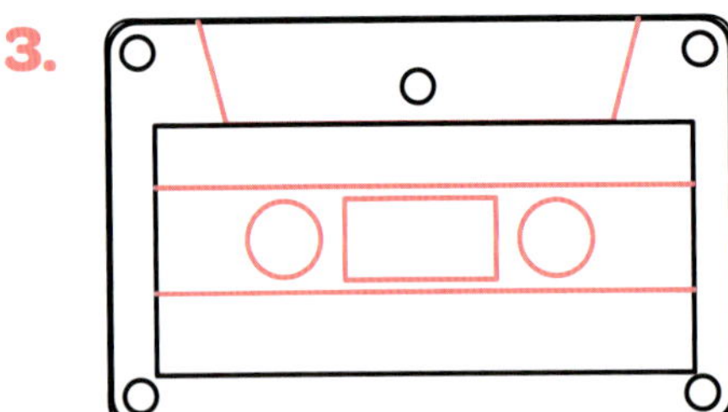

3. Add two slanted lines to the top. Draw two parallel lines inside the smaller rectangle, along with an even smaller rectangle and a circle on either side.

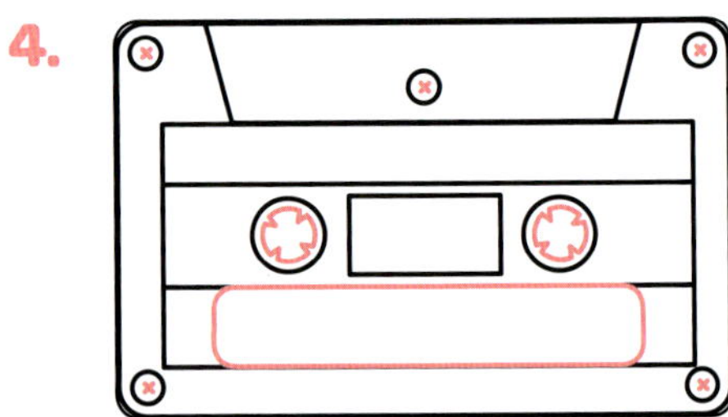

4. Add little X's inside the small circles and larger, rounded crosses inside the larger circles. Then add a rounded rectangle for the mixtape label.

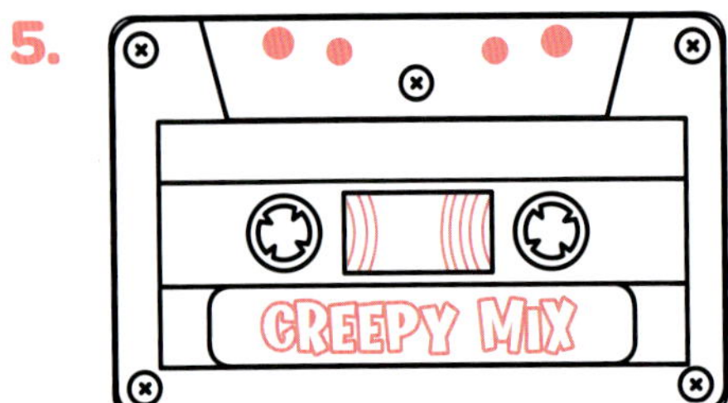

5. Add "CREEPY MIX" in your creepiest handwriting, and draw curved lines inside the middle rectangle. Add four more filled-in circles to the top.

6. Color in your Creepy Mixtape!

HEADPHONE GHOST

1.

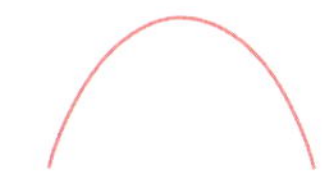

Start by drawing the top of the head: a curved line similar to the top of an egg.

2.

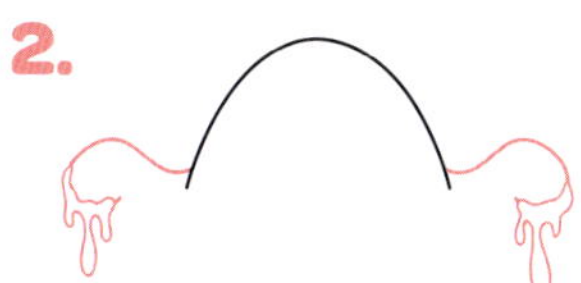

Add the arms with dripping shapes underneath.

3.

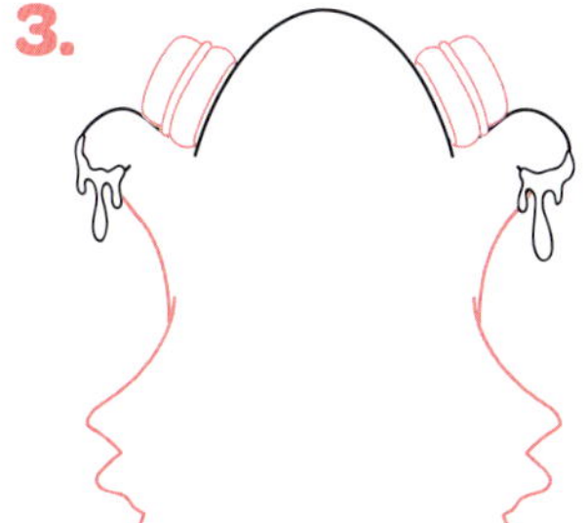

Add the ghost's body shape with a wiggly line at the bottom. Then add headphones to the sides of the head.

4.

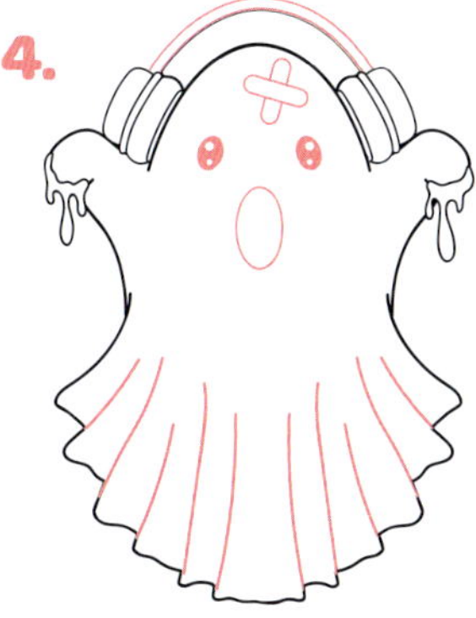

Join the headphones with two curved lines. Draw a large oval for the mouth and two shaded ovals for eyes. Add crossed bandages to the top of the head and lines from the ghost's midsection toward the bottom for creases.

5.

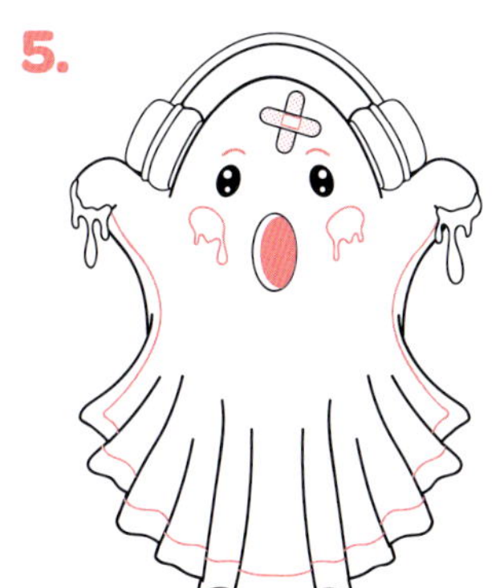

Add detail to the bandages. Then add the eyebrows. Draw dripping ovals for cheeks, and shade in the mouth. Add a second line all along the sides and bottom of the body outline.

6.

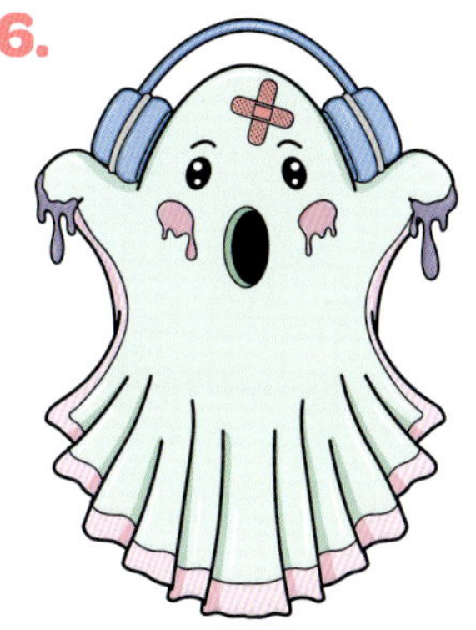

Color in your Headphone Ghost!

WIZARD BOBA

1.

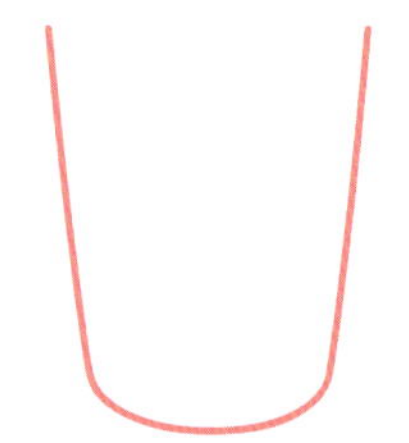

Start by drawing the base of the cup.

2.

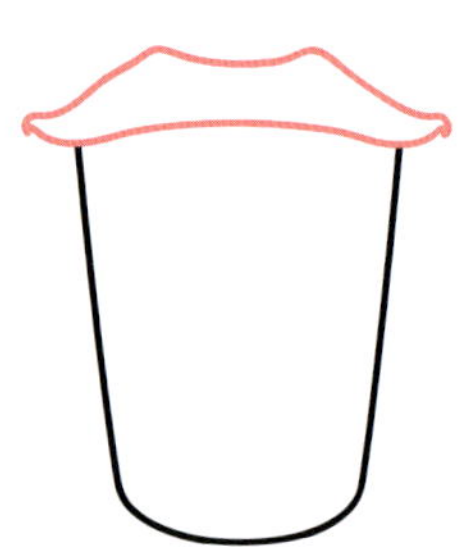

Add the base of the wizard's hat to the top of the cup.

3.

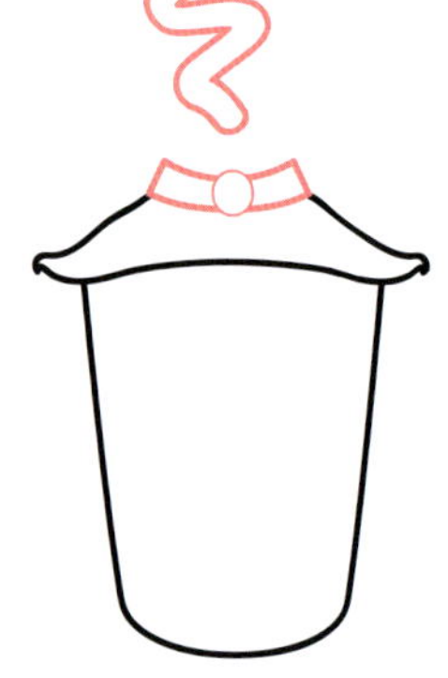

Add a belt shape with an oval buckle in the middle. Then draw a curly shape for the straw.

4.

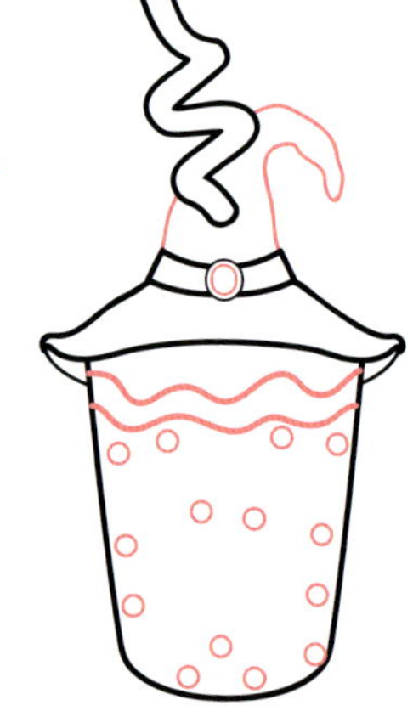

Add the crooked top of the hat. Draw a smaller oval inside the buckle. Then add two wavy lines to the top of the cup. Draw circles for the boba pearls.

5.

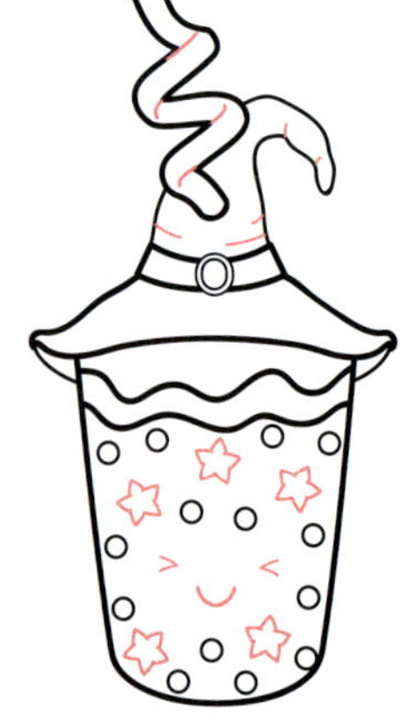

Add a cute face and stars. Draw some detail lines on the hat and straw.

6.

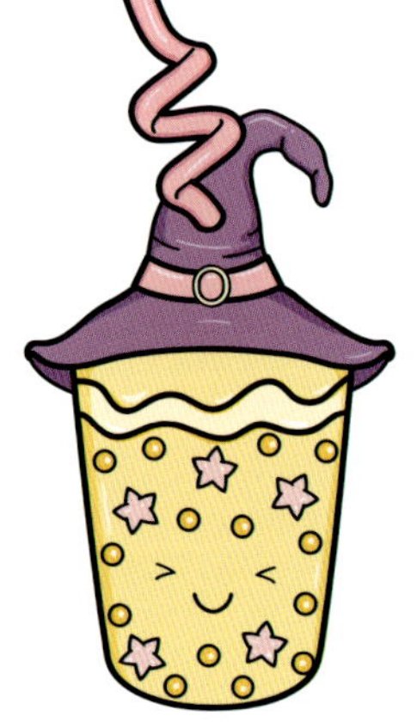

Color in your Wizard Boba!

DEVIL BOBA

1.

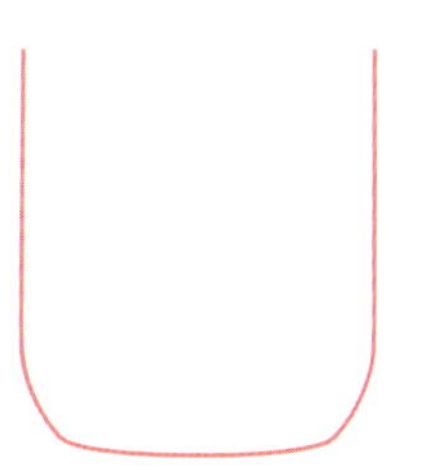

Start by drawing the main shape of the Mason jar, leaving the top open.

2.

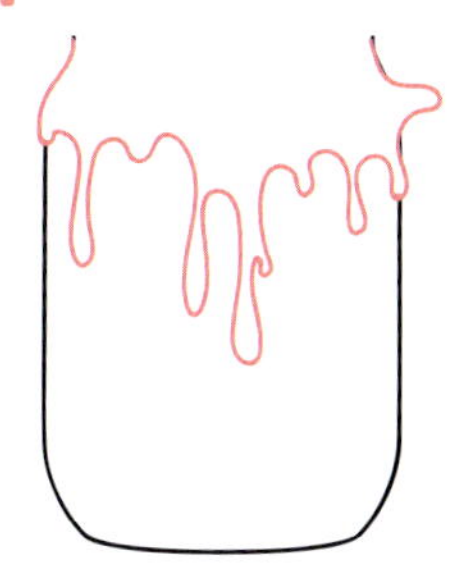

Add a dripping line to the top of the Mason jar.

3.

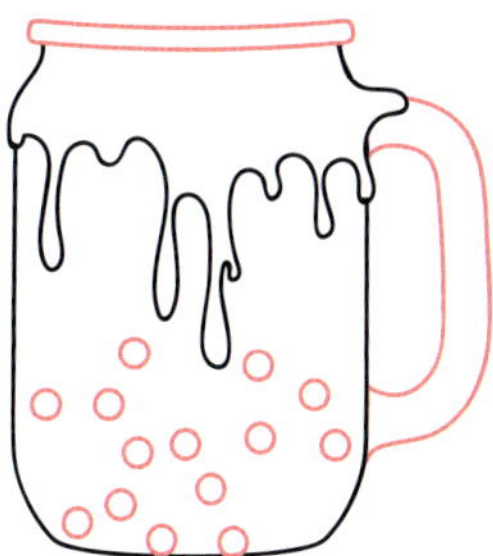

Add the rectangular handle. Then draw a curved rectangle on top for the start of the lid. Draw some circles for boba pearls.

4.

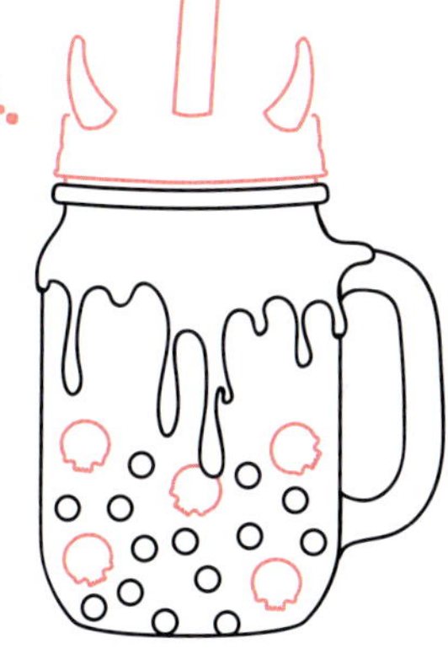

Add the top part of the lid, leaving the top open. Then draw two triangular horn shapes. Draw a cylinder for the straw and some skull shapes inside the jar.

5.

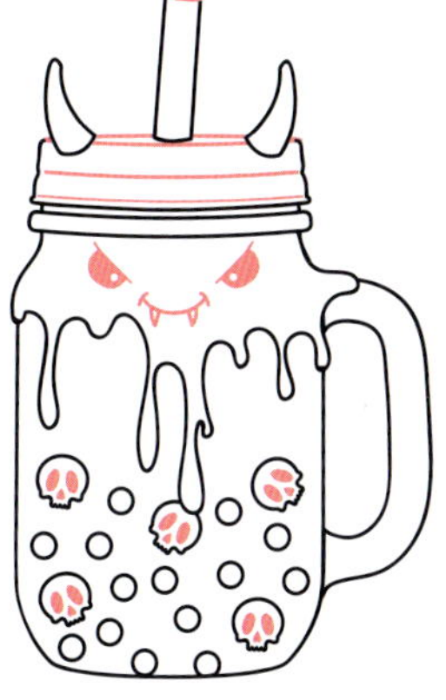

Add a creepy face inside the dripping section. Draw filled-in eye sockets and noses on the skulls. Add the top oval for the lid, two horizontal lines below, and the top oval for the straw.

6.

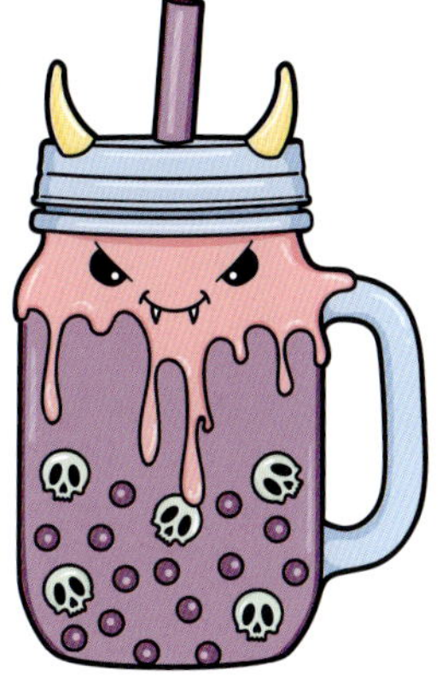

Color in your Devil Boba!

HEDGEHOG PUMPKIN

1.

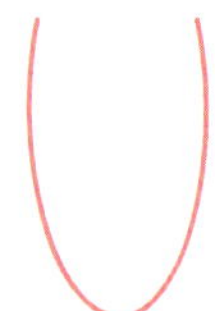

Start by drawing a narrow, upright oval, leaving the top open.

2.

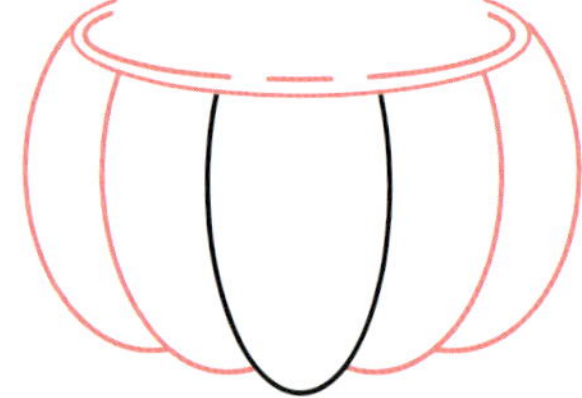

Add two more ovals to each side and a double oval at the top, leaving space for the paws and hedgehog.

3.

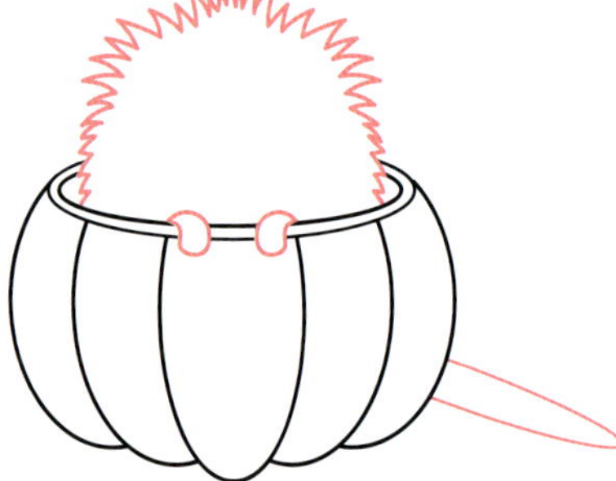

Draw a spiky oval shape in the pumpkin. Then add the paws as two teardrop shapes. Draw a slanted oval beside the pumpkin.

4.

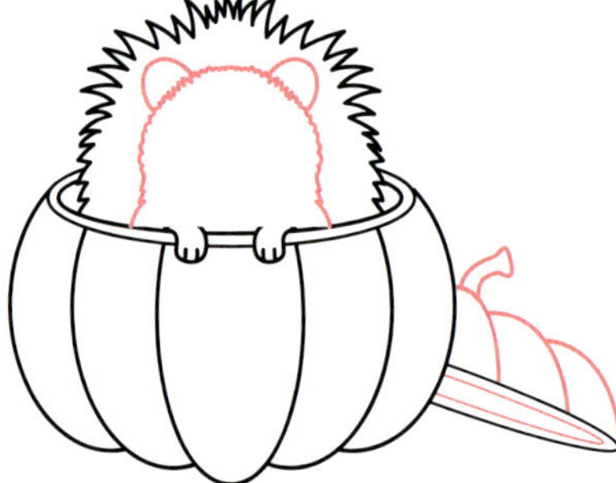

With a furry line, add the body of the hedgehog and two half circles for ears. Then add an inner oval, arch shapes, and a stem to complete the pumpkin top.

5.

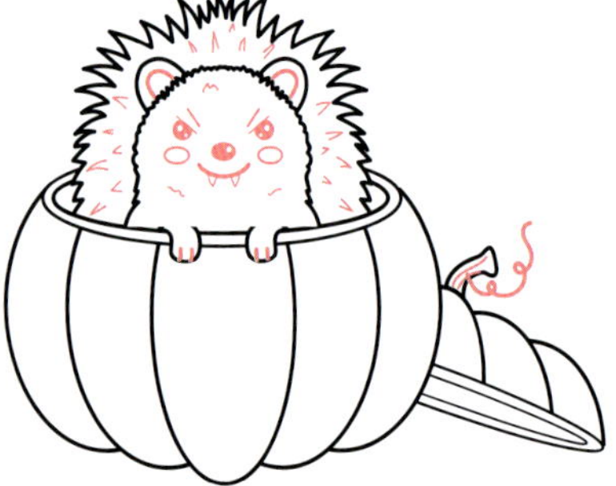

Draw a creepy cute face with pointy teeth. Then add details: half circles inside the ears, wiggly lines for fur, pointy lines for spikes, tiny toes, and a tendril for the pumpkin stem.

6.

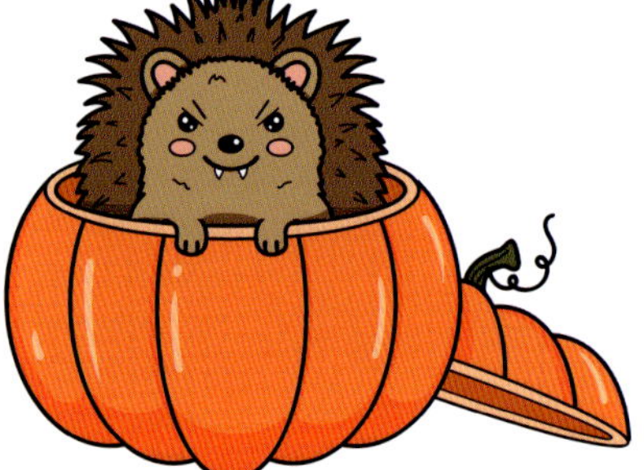

Color in your Hedgehog Pumpkin!

GHOSTLY ACORN

1.

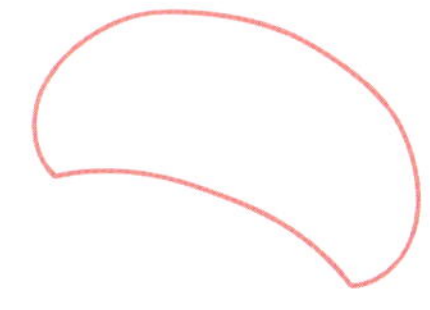

Start by drawing a fat crescent for the cap of the acorn.

2.

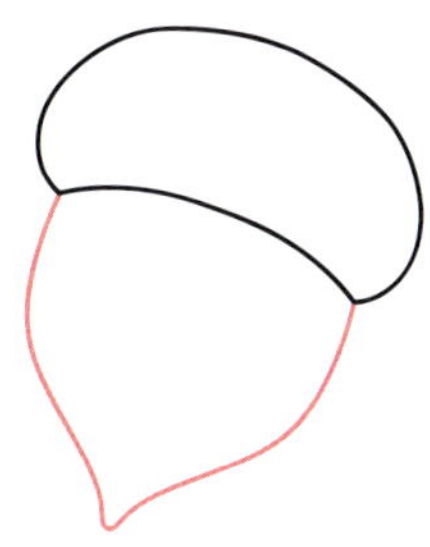

Add a pointed oval for the bottom of the acorn.

3.

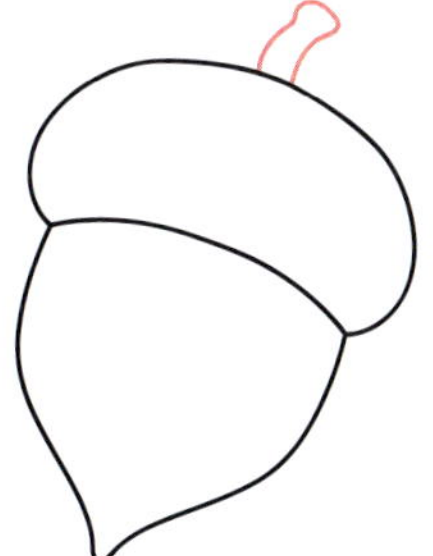

Draw a sturdy stem with a knob on the end.

4.

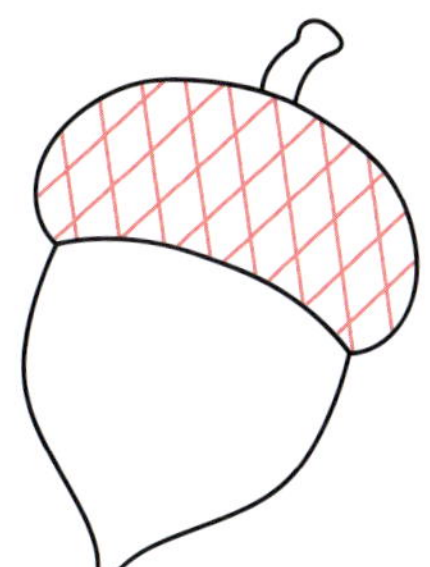

Add cross-hatching to the acorn cap for texture.

5.

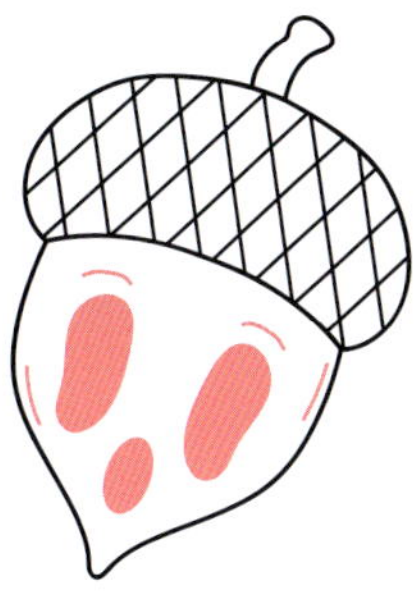

Add two big, filled-in ovals for eyes and a smaller filled-in oval for the mouth. Add some detail lines.

6.

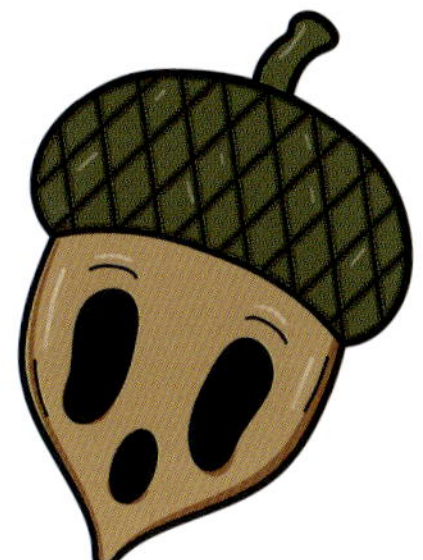

Color in your Ghostly Acorn!

ANGRY MUSHROOM

1.

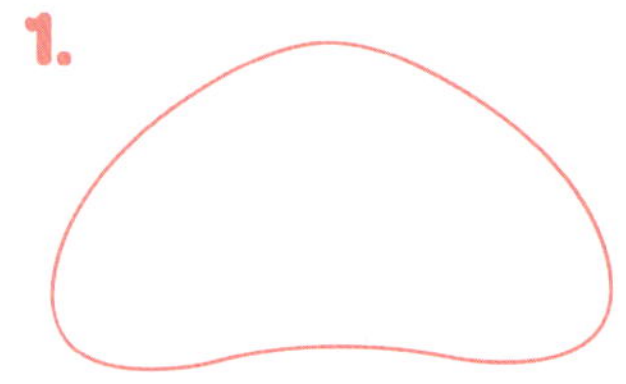

Start by drawing a squished oval for the cap of the mushroom.

2.

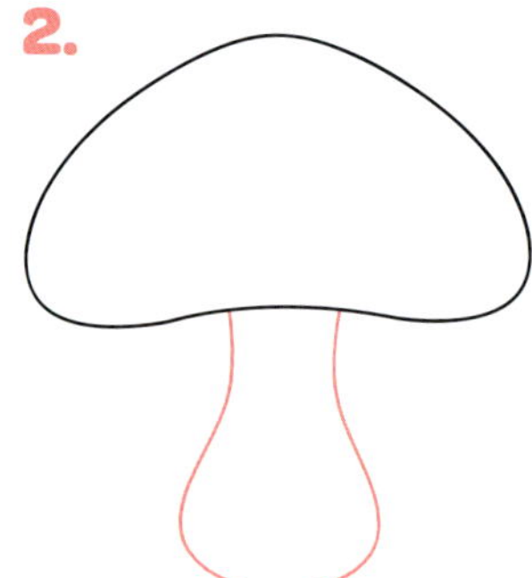

Draw the stalk of the mushroom as a teardrop shape.

3.

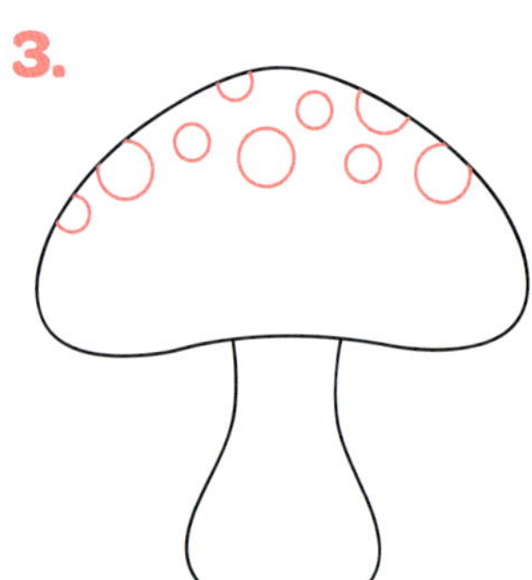

Draw small circles at the top of the mushroom. Leave the bottom half blank.

4.

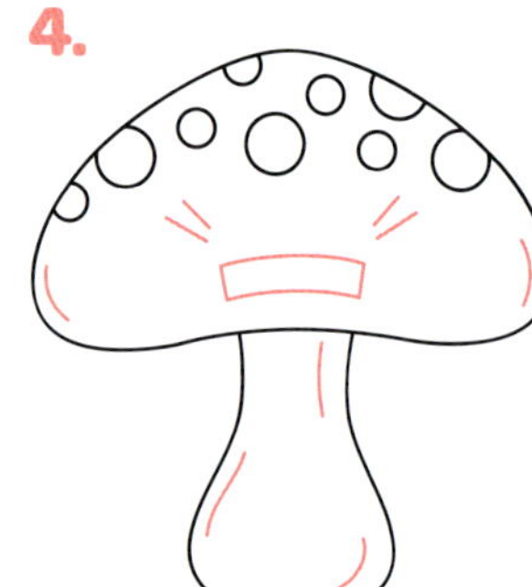

Add two straight lines on either side for the first part of the eyes and a downward-curving rectangle for the mouth. Draw curved lines for wrinkles.

5.

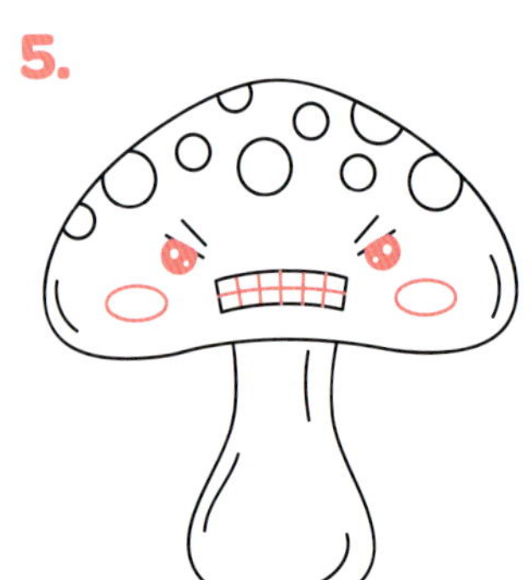

Draw shaded circles for the eyes, and add ovals for cheeks. Add teeth to the mouth.

6.

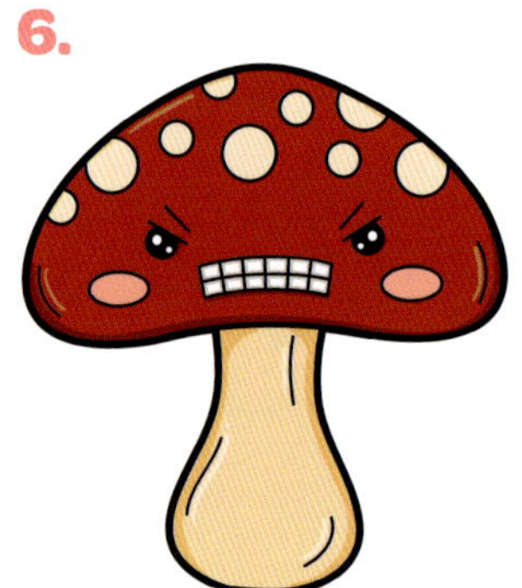

Color in your Angry Mushroom!

HAPPY JACK-O'-LANTERN

1. 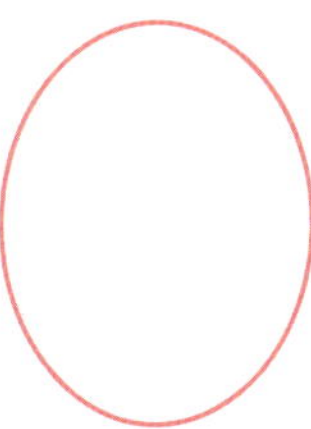

Start by drawing an oval.

2. 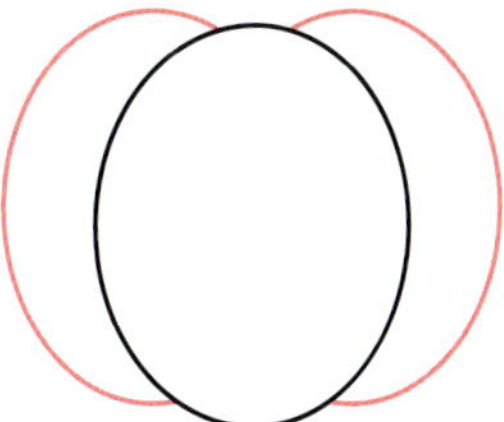

Add another oval on either side, both slightly higher than the first.

3. 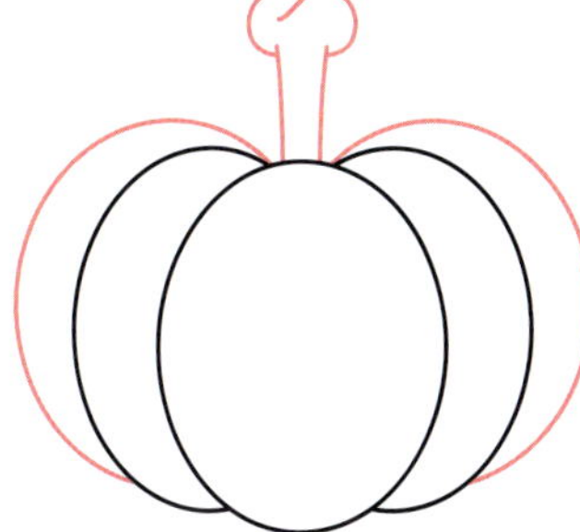

Draw another curved line on each side of the pumpkin. Then add a bone shape for the stem.

4. 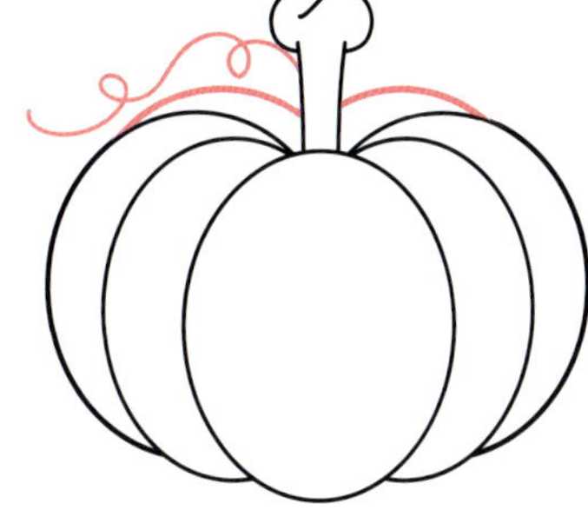

Add a curved line on each side of the stem, and add a curly tendril to the top.

5. 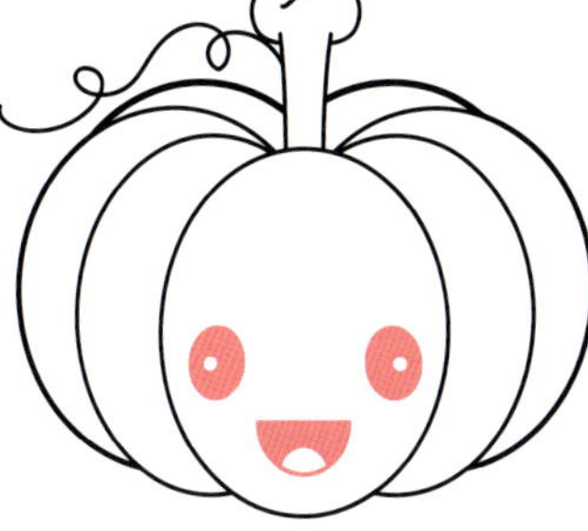

Shade in two oval eyes and a half-circle mouth.

6. 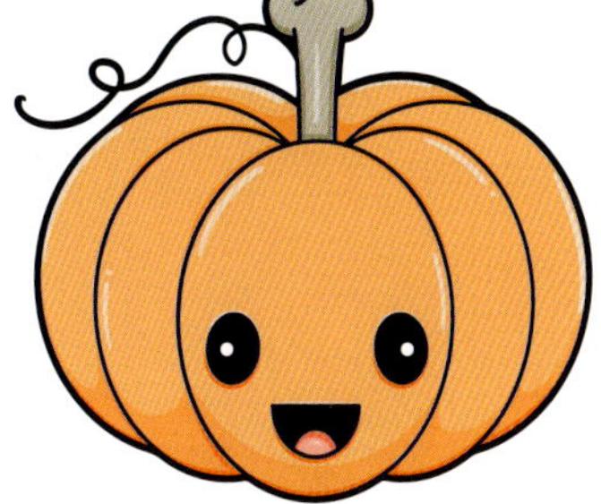

Color in your Happy Jack-O'-Lantern!

GHOSTLY CORNUCOPIA

 **1.**

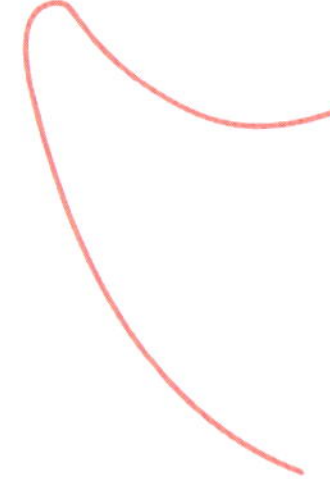

Start by drawing a horn shape, leaving the large end open.

2.

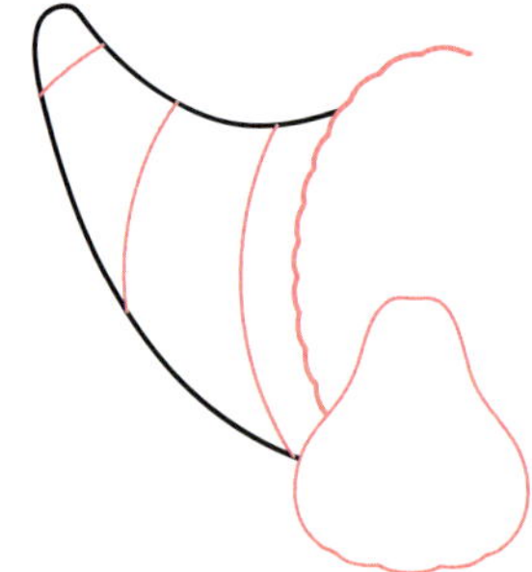

Add a pear shape at the bottom and a round wiggly line for the horn's opening. Add three curved lines to the horn.

3.

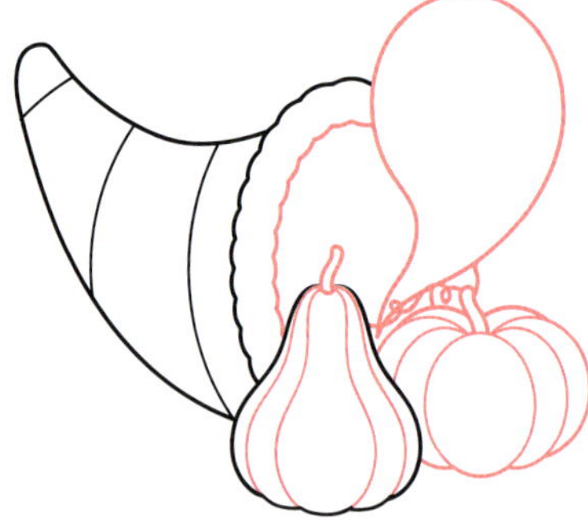

Add an upside-down teardrop shape for the ghost. On the pear, draw curved lines and a stem. Add a little pumpkin.

4.

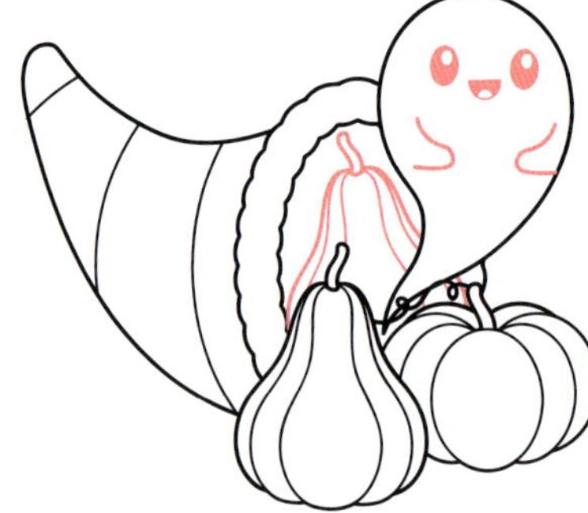

Repeat the pear shape inside the opening of the horn. Draw two little arms and a spooky face on the ghost.

5.

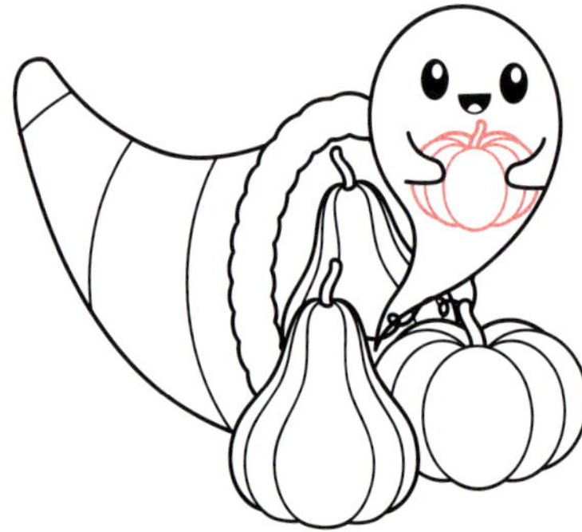

Add another pumpkin in the arms of the ghost.

6.

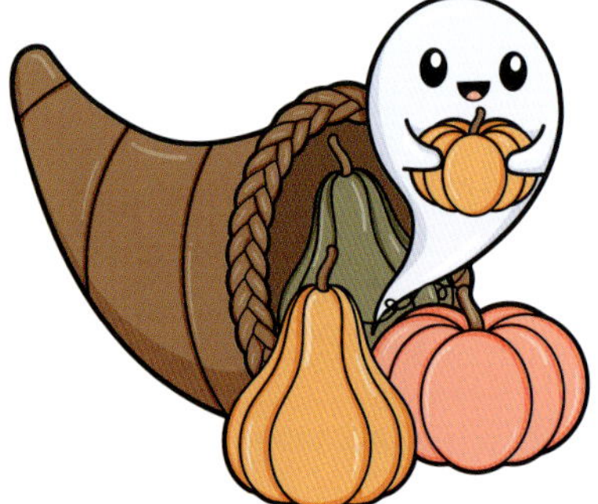

Color in your Ghostly Cornucopia!

GRINNING APPLE

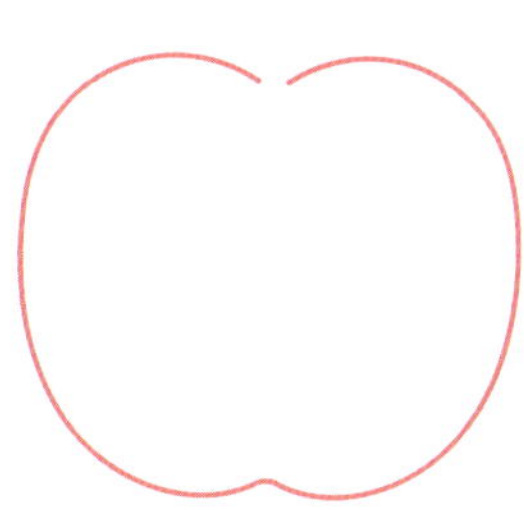

1.

Start by drawing a round apple shape, leaving a small opening for the stem.

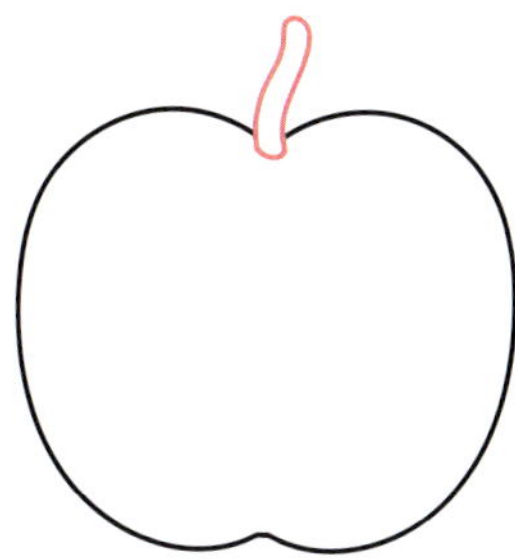

2.

Add a stem to the top of the apple.

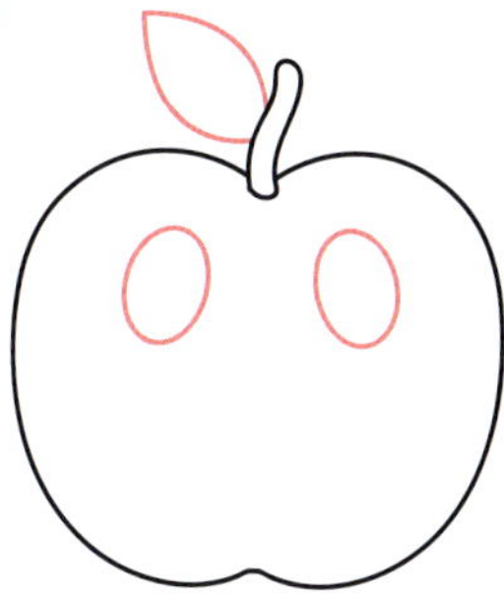

3.

Add a leaf shape to the stem, and draw two big ovals for eyes.

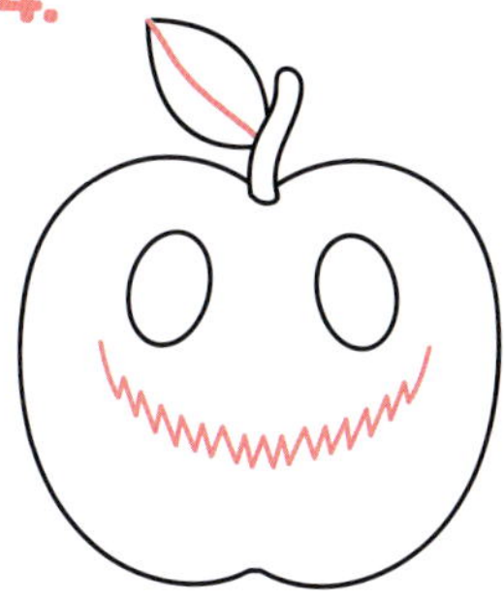

4.

Draw a curved zigzag line for the top of the mouth. Add a line to the middle of the leaf.

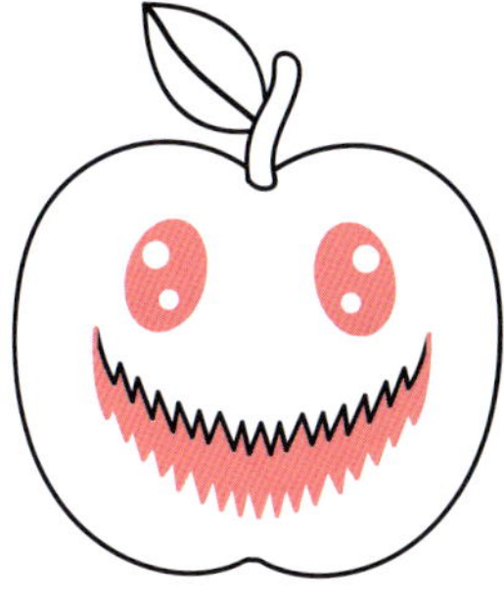

5.

Shade in the eyes, then add another curved zigzag for the bottom of the mouth. Fill in the mouth.

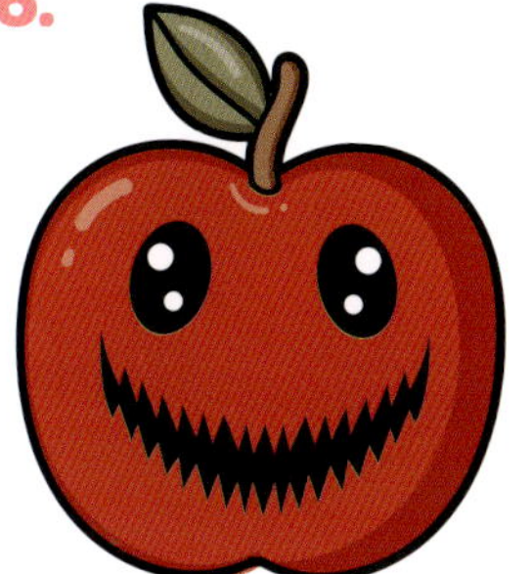

6.

Color in your Grinning Apple!

EYEBALL TEA

1.

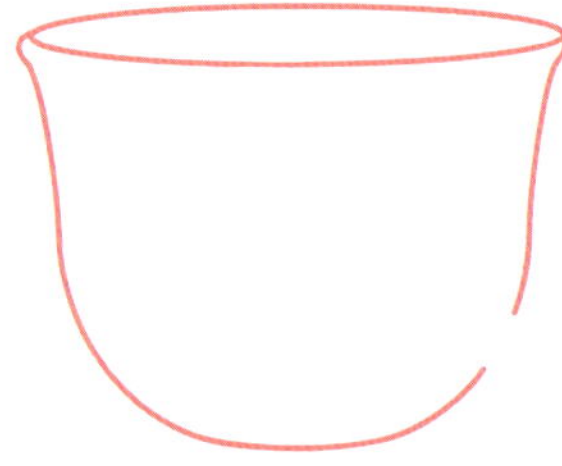

Start by drawing an oval for the top of the teacup. Then add the U shape of the cup, leaving a small opening on the right side.

2.

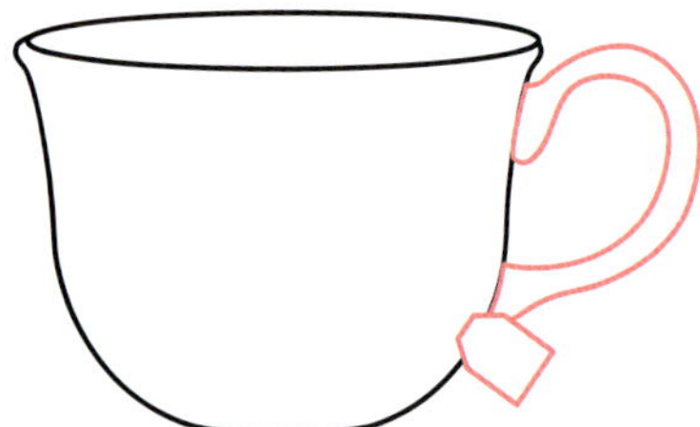

Draw the label of the tea bag as a rectangle with slanted edges. Then add the handle to the side of the cup.

3.

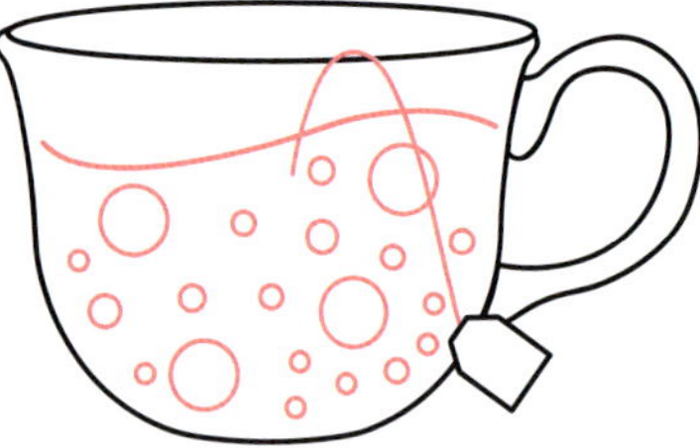

Add a curved line from the tea bag label to the inside of the teacup. Then add circles for eyeballs and smaller circles for bubbles. Add a curved line for the surface of the tea.

4.

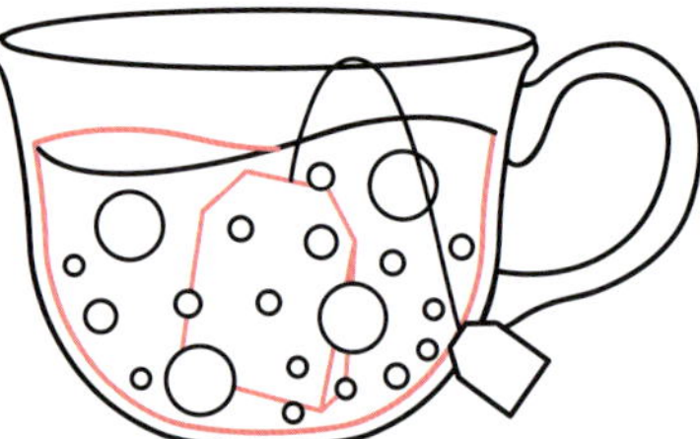

Add a shorter curved line to the top of the tea, then trace along the inside of the cup to show the width of the cup. Draw the tea bag: a rectangle with slanted edges, plus a triangle for the side.

5.

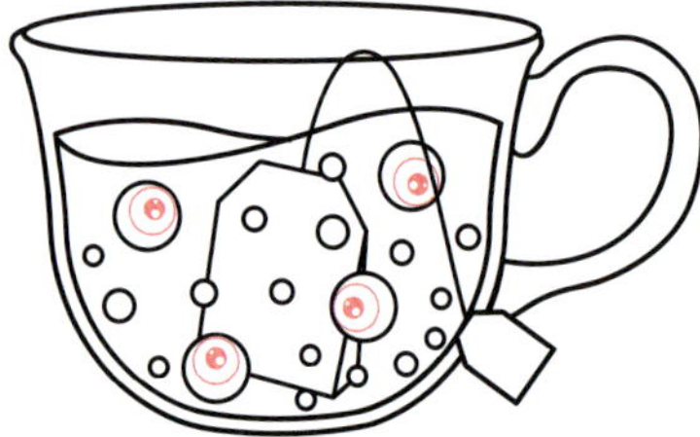

Inside the eyeballs, add irises and shaded pupils.

6.

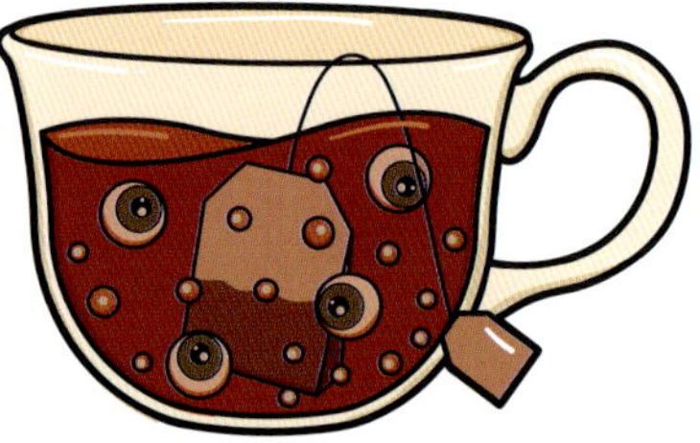

Color in your Eyeball Tea!

SKULL SWEATER

1.

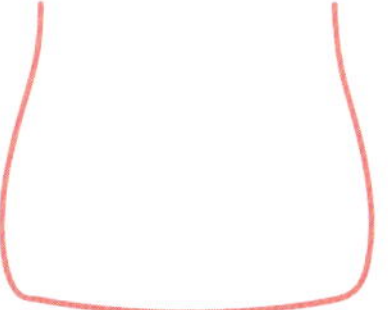

Start by drawing a curvy rectangle for the bottom of the sweater. Leave the top open.

2.

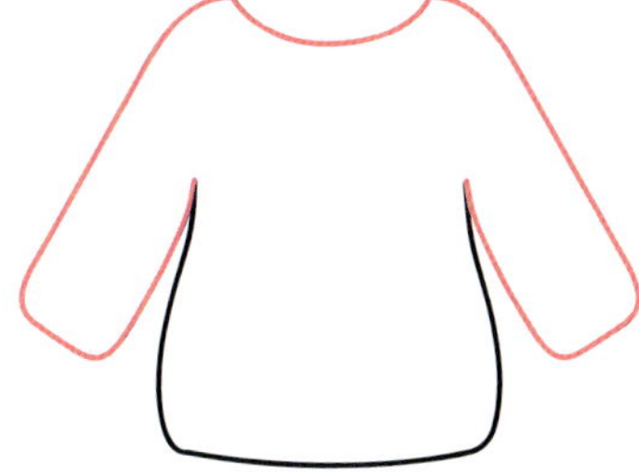

Add a sleeve on each side and a half oval for the neck.

3.

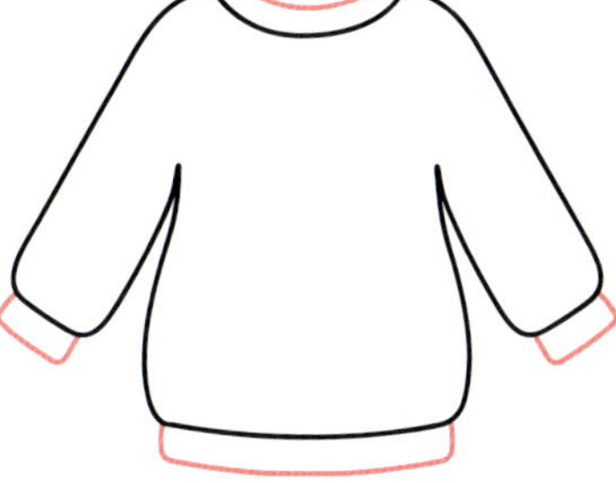

Add the cuffs, hem, and neckline.

4.

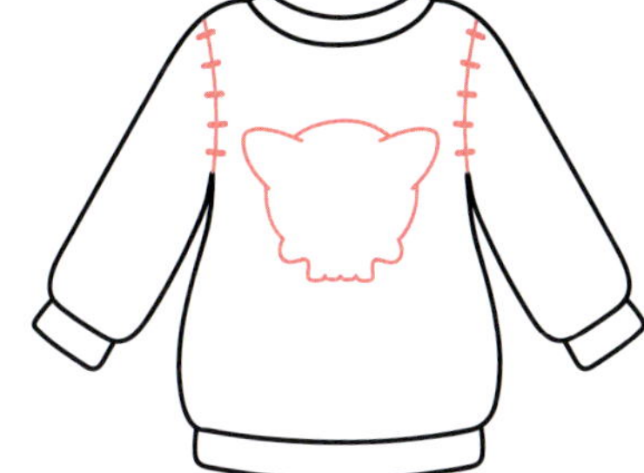

Add a curved line at each shoulder. Draw some smaller lines for stitches. Then outline a skull—a circle with a square jaw and triangles for ears—on the front of the sweater.

5.

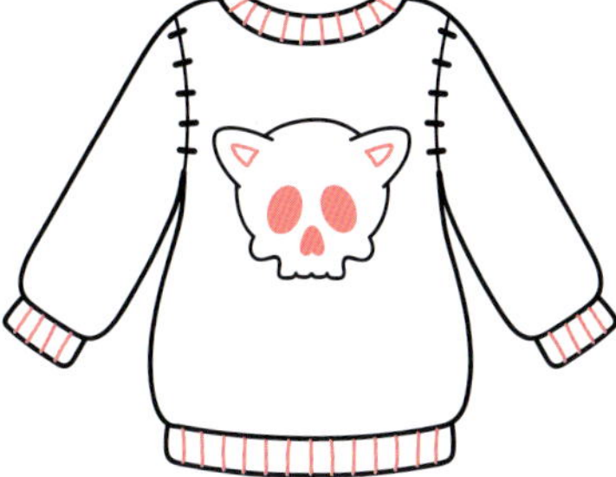

Draw two big, filled-in ovals for eye sockets and a filled-in upside-down heart for the nose. Add a smaller triangle in each ear. Add lines to the cuffs, neckline, and hem.

6.

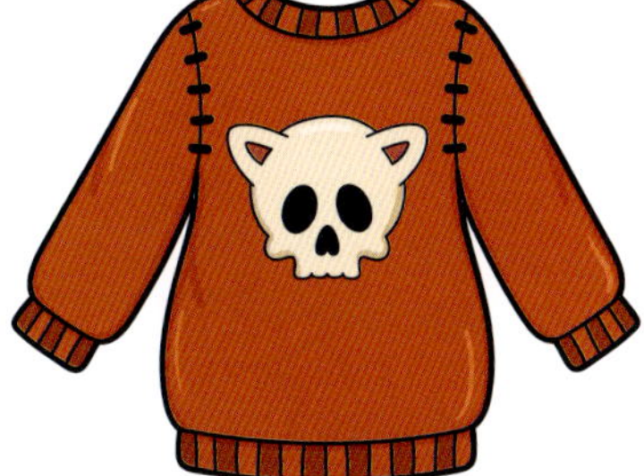

Color in your Skull Sweater!

HAUNTED BOOKS

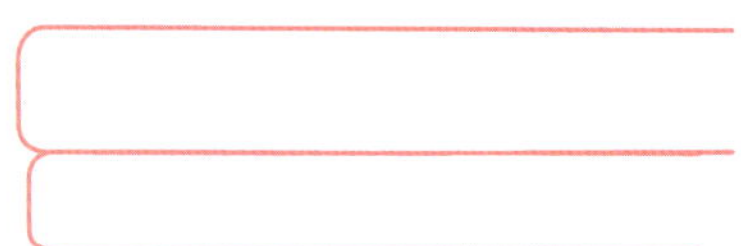

1.

Start by drawing two rectangles with curved edges. Leave the right sides open.

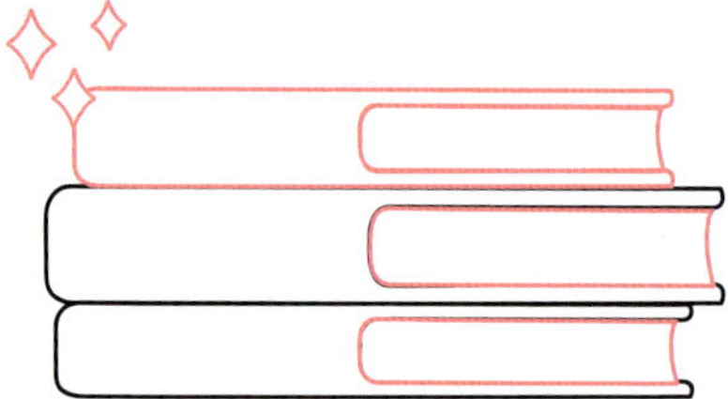

2.

Draw three diamond shapes on the left side, above the books. Add another curved rectangle for the top book. Then add rectangles for the bottoms of the books.

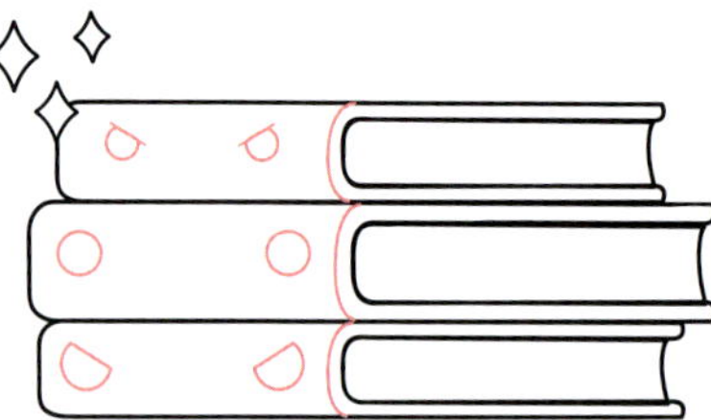

3.

Add a different shape of eye outlines to each book spine, then add a curved line near the bottom of each spine.

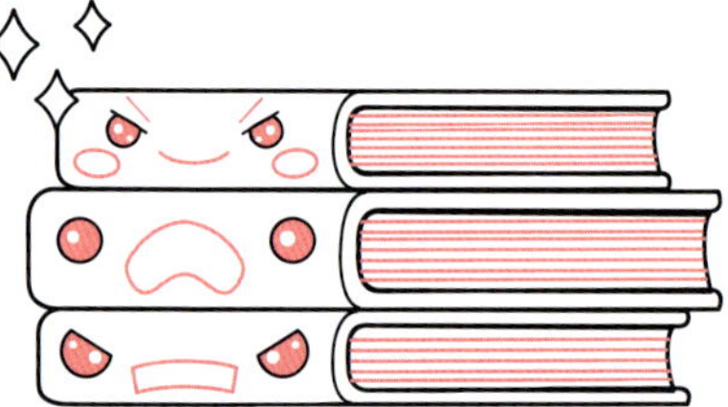

4.

Shade in the eyes, then add mouths, eyebrows and cheeks. Add straight lines for the pages of the books.

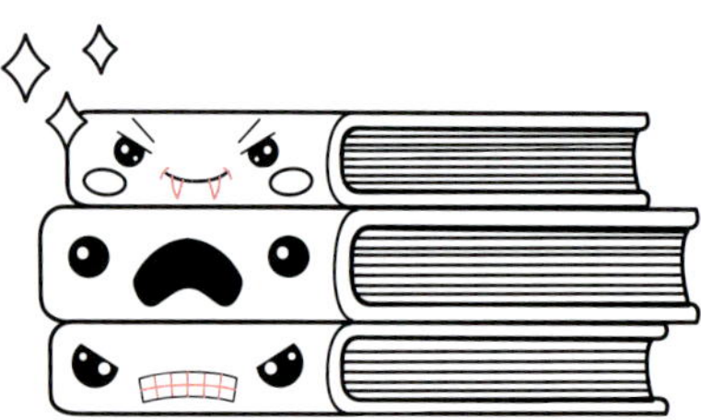

5.

Add some teeth to the spooky faces.

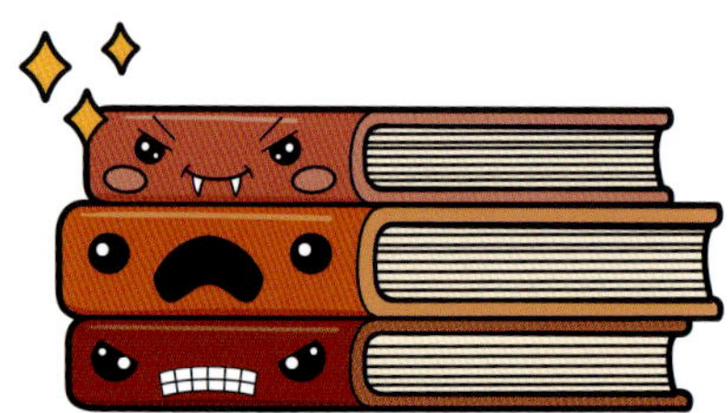

6.

Color in your Haunted Books!

CREEPY CUTE PENCIL

1.

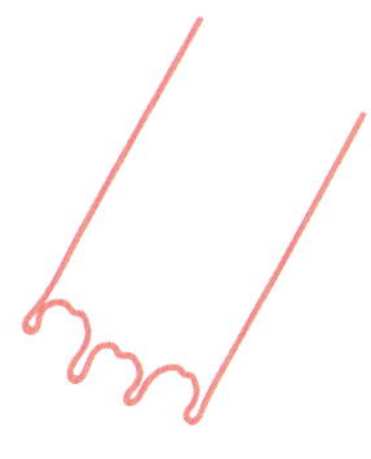

Start by drawing a rectangular shape with a dripping edge. Leave the top open.

2.

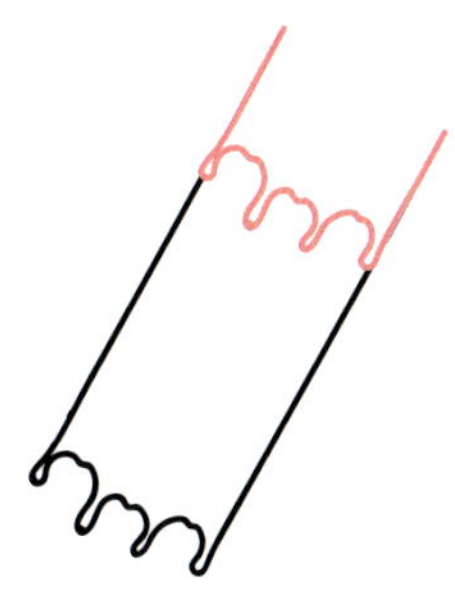

Add another dripping rectangular shape to the top.

3.

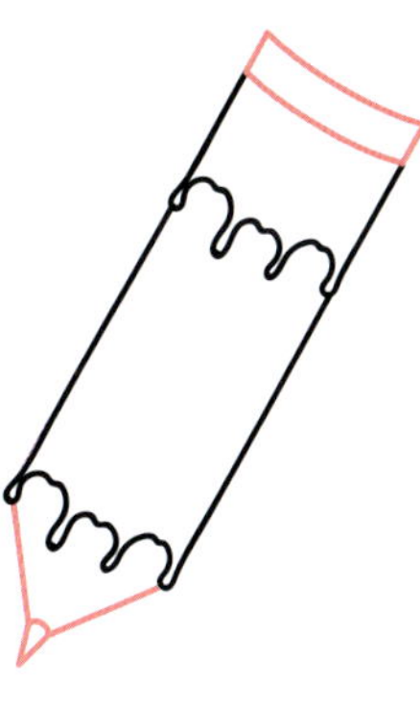

Add a curved rectangle to the top of the pencil. Then, at the bottom, add a triangle with a spike.

4.

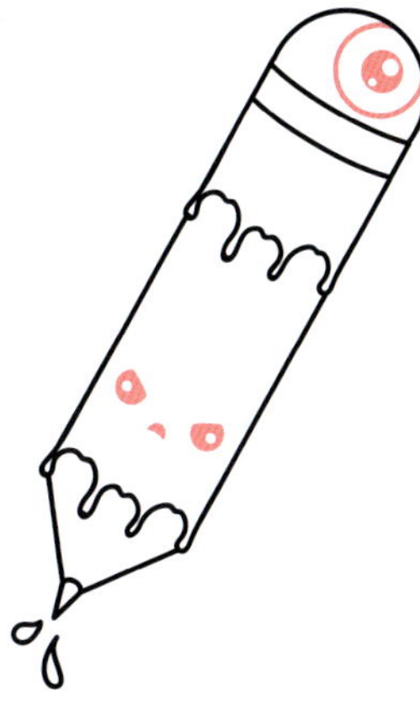

Add a semicircle to the top of the pencil. Then draw some teardrop shapes at the bottom.

5.

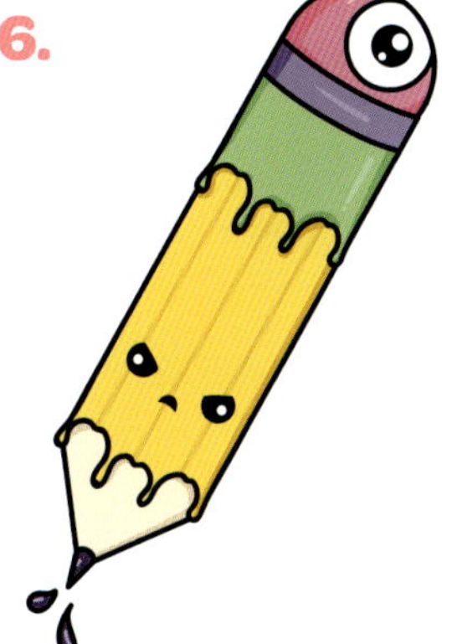

Add a circle for the iris and shade in a pupil. Add a grumpy face.

6.

Color in your Creepy Cute Pencil!

EYEBALL POP

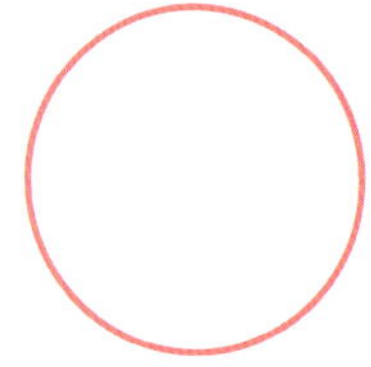

1. Start by drawing a circle for the top.

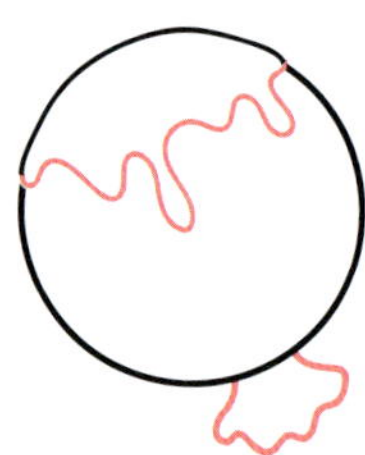

2. Add a dripping topping to the top of the circle and a wavy triangle to the bottom.

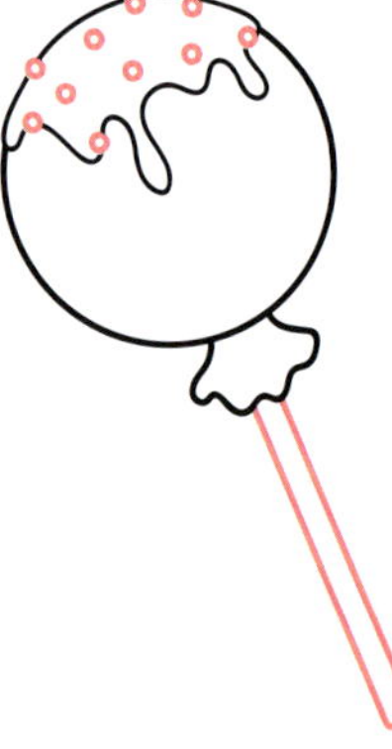

3. Add some round sprinkles. Then draw a stick shape at the bottom.

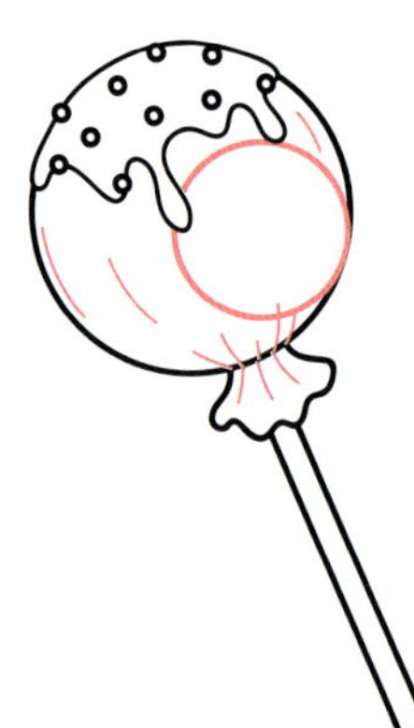

4. Add a circle and some curved detail lines for the creases of the wrapper.

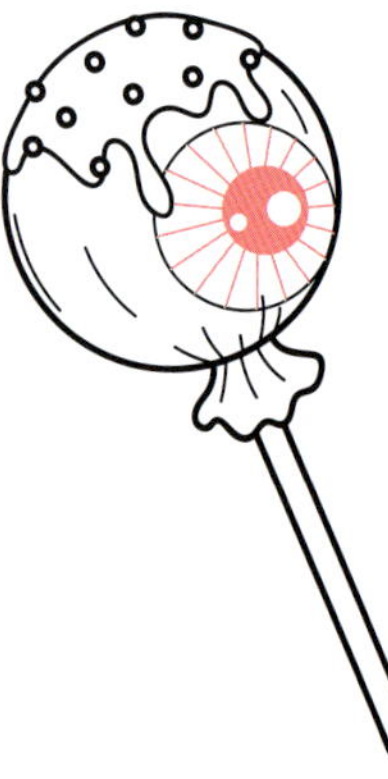

5. Add a shaded circle for the pupil and some straight lines around the iris.

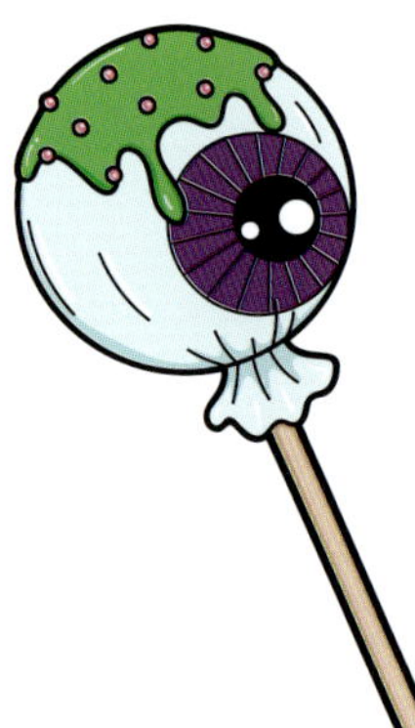

6. Color in your Eyeball Pop!

SPIDER DONUT

1.

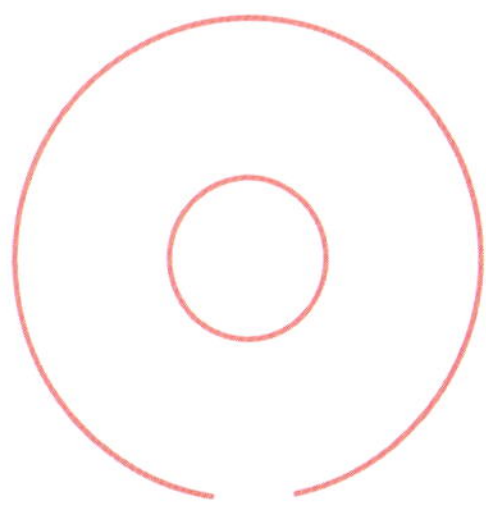

Start by drawing a ring shape, leaving some space at the bottom of the outer circle.

2.

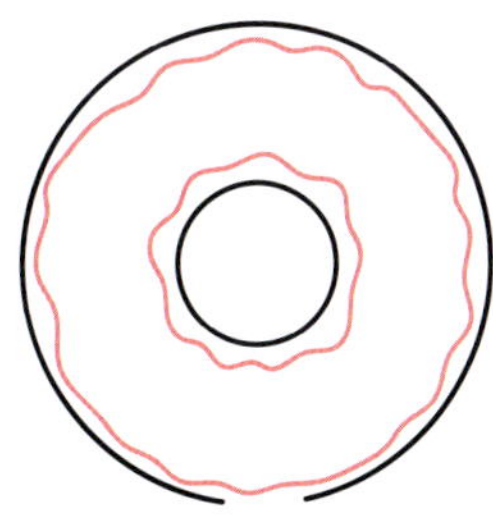

Add two wavy circles inside the donut.

3.

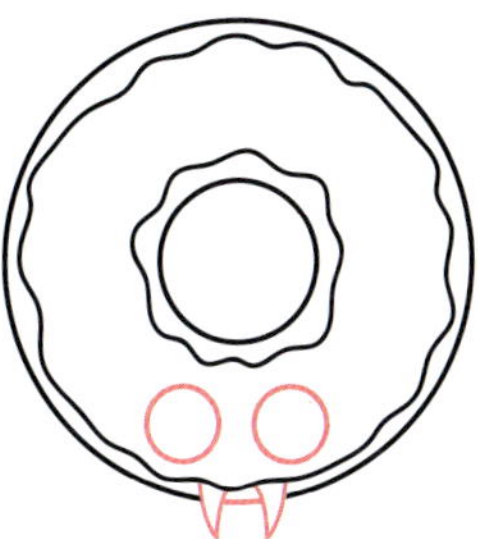

Add two circles for eyes and two pointy triangular teeth. Then complete the circle between the teeth.

4.

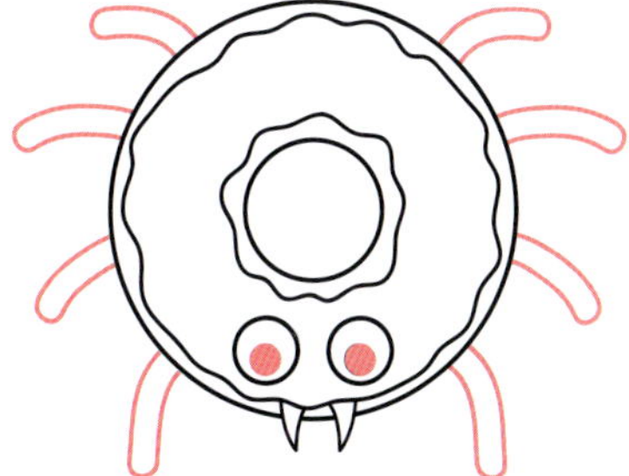

Add four legs to either side and filled-in circles in the eyes for pupils.

5.

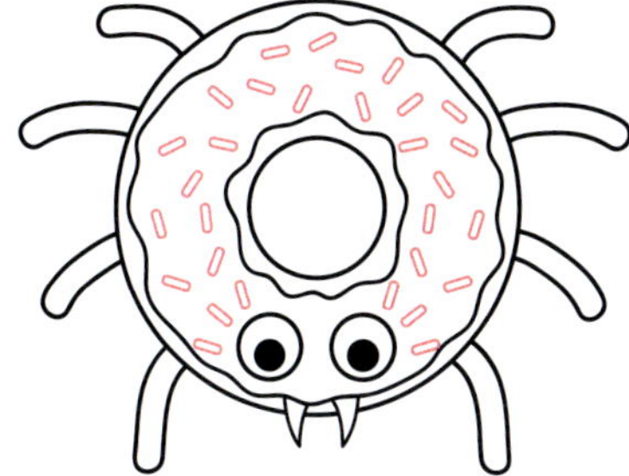

Add some little rectangles for sprinkles.

6.

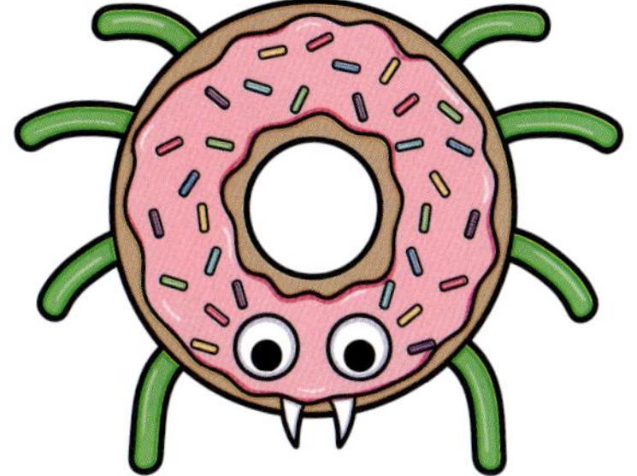

Color in your Spider Donut!

ANGRY CANDY

1.

Start by drawing an oval. Make the line slightly wiggly on the left and right sides.

2.

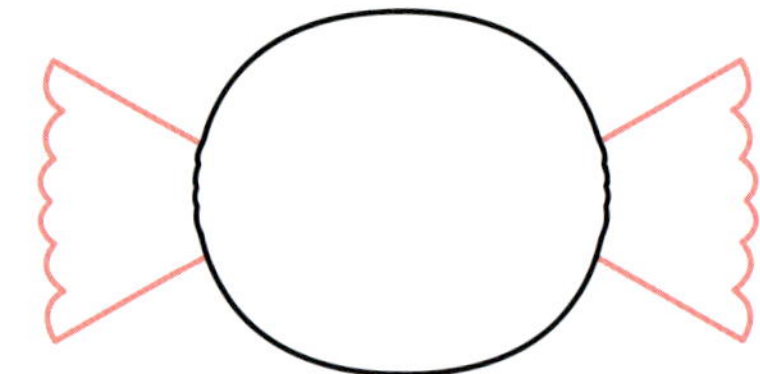

Add a triangle with scalloped edges to each side.

3.

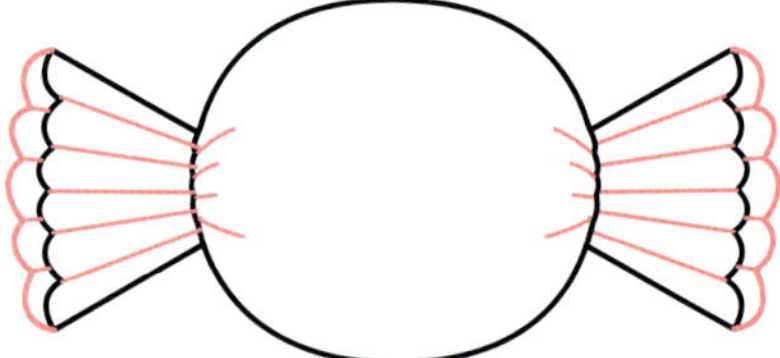

Add another scalloped line outside each triangle, and add detail lines for the creases of the wrapper.

4.

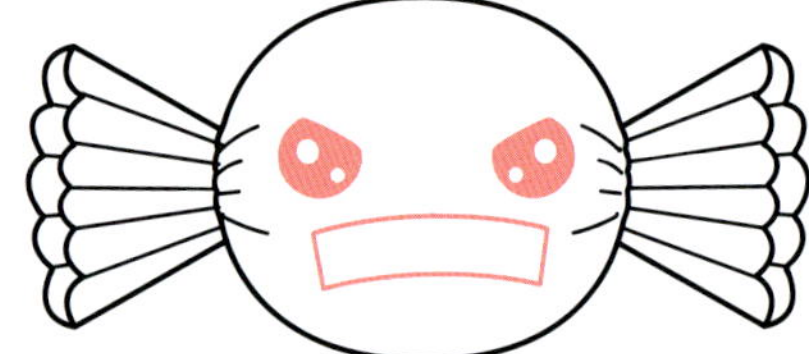

Add a curved rectangle for the mouth and slanted, shaded eyes.

5.

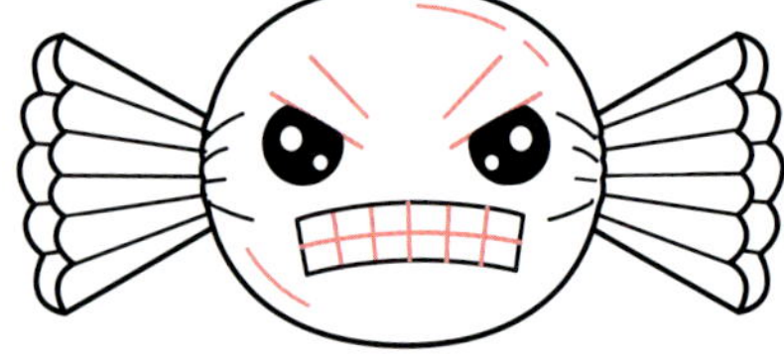

Add lines for the teeth, eyebrows, and wrapper details.

6.

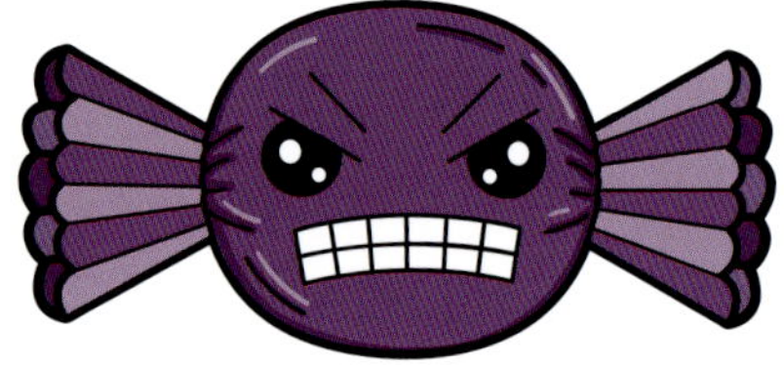

Color in your Angry Candy!

BAT WITH A TICKET

1.

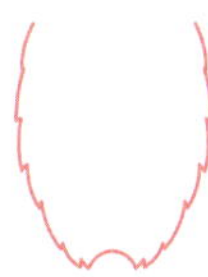

Start by drawing the jagged, oval body shape of the bat.

2.

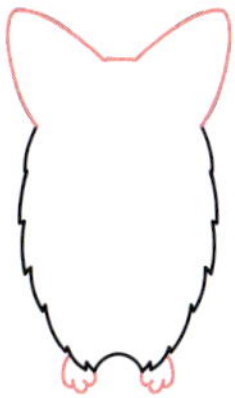

Add two large triangles for ears, and join them in the middle. Then add tiny feet.

3.

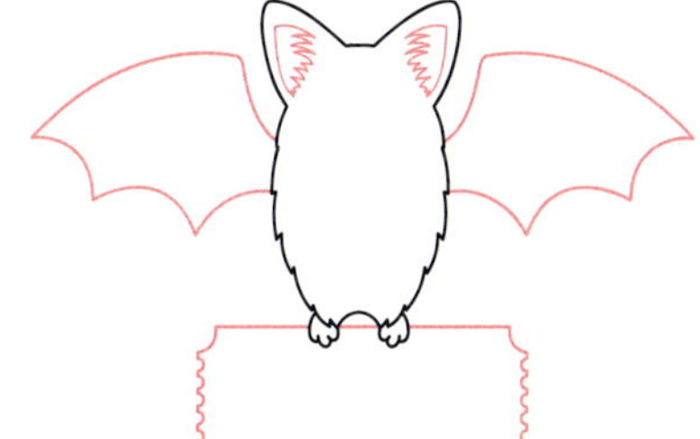

Give the ears furry insides. Draw a wing shape at either side. Then, for the ticket, draw a rectangular shape at the bottom with scalloped edges.

4.

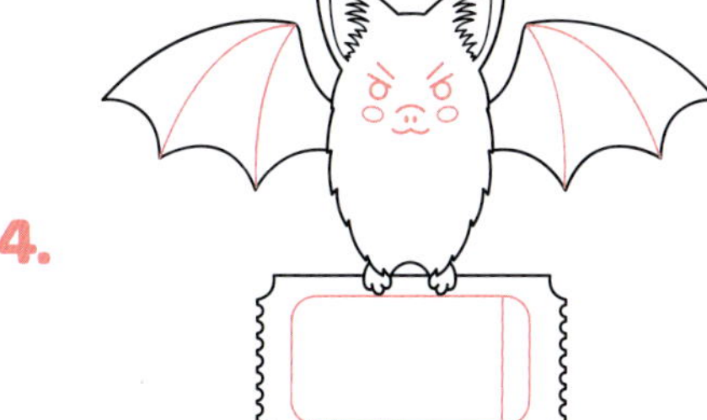

Add two slanted circles for eyes, slanted eyebrows, oval cheeks, and a curved nose. Add two dots for nostrils, and draw a mouth shape. Add curved lines inside wings. Inside the ticket, draw a smaller curved rectangle with a line through one side.

5.

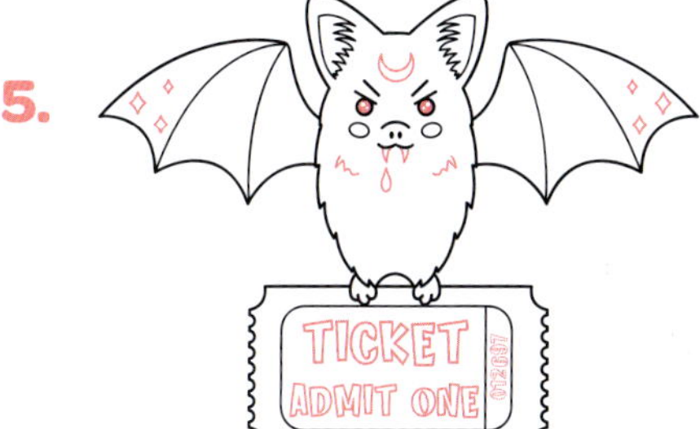

Shade in the eyes and add two pointy teeth with a blood drip. Then add a sideways crescent moon shape to the forehead. Draw some diamonds on the wings, detail lines for fur, and ticket text.

6.

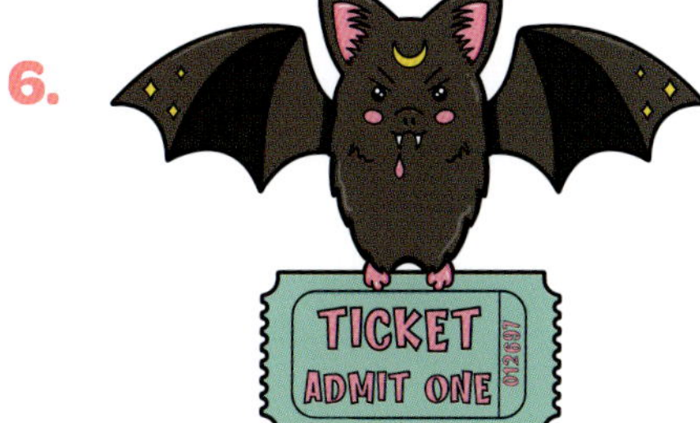

Color in your Bat with a Ticket!

ANGRY CLAPPER

1.

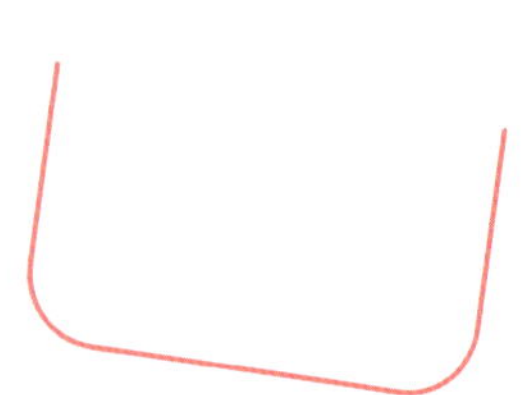

Start by drawing a rectangle with curved bottom edges, leaving the top open.

2.

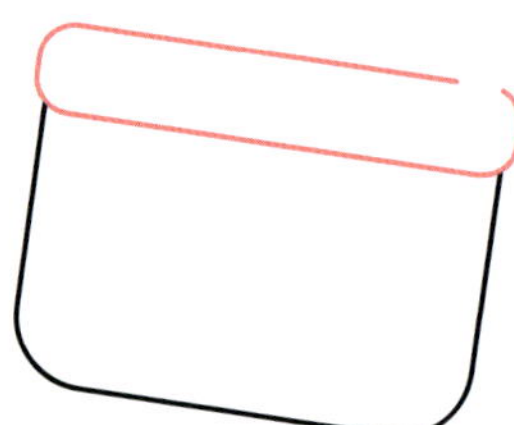

Add another curved rectangle to the top, leaving a little space at the top right corner.

3.

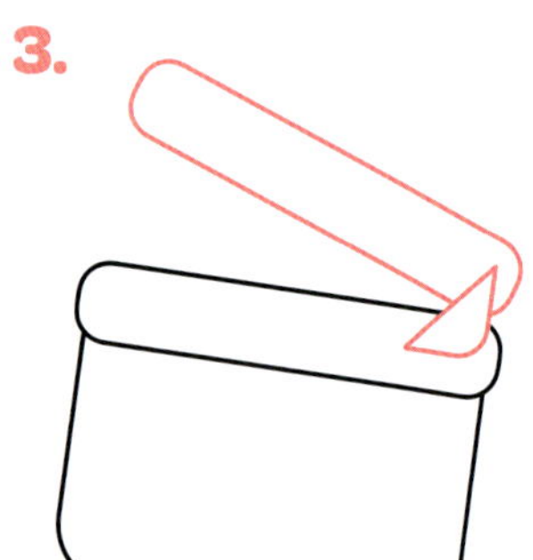

Add a triangle with a curved corner, then draw a slanted rectangle with curved edges at the top.

4.

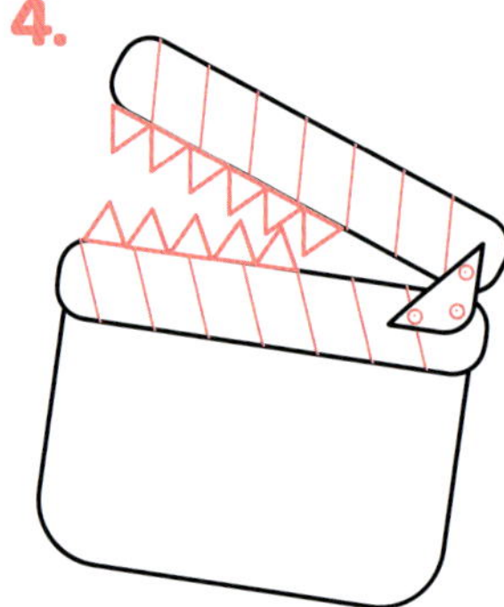

Add slanted stripes to the two top rectangles. Add three small circles with dots in the middle to the triangle, then add some pointy triangular teeth.

5.

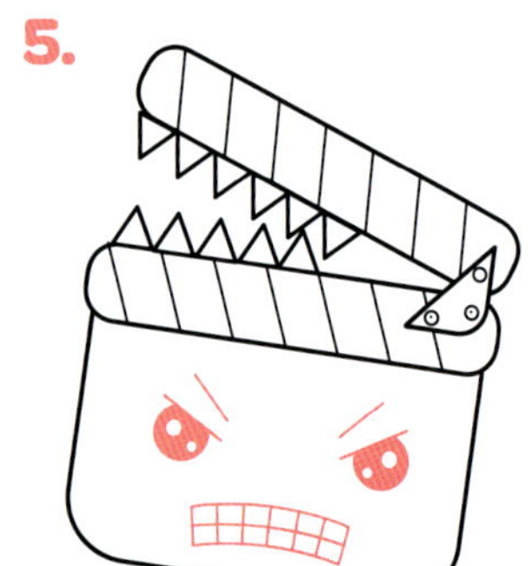

Draw some slanted, shaded eyes, slanted eyebrows, and a curved angry mouth with teeth.

6.

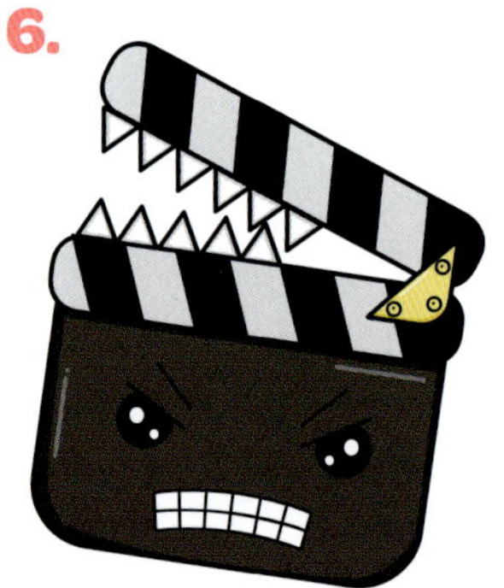

Color in your Angry Clapper!

DEVIOUS FILM ROLL

1.

Start by drawing a ring shape—a circle inside another circle.

2.

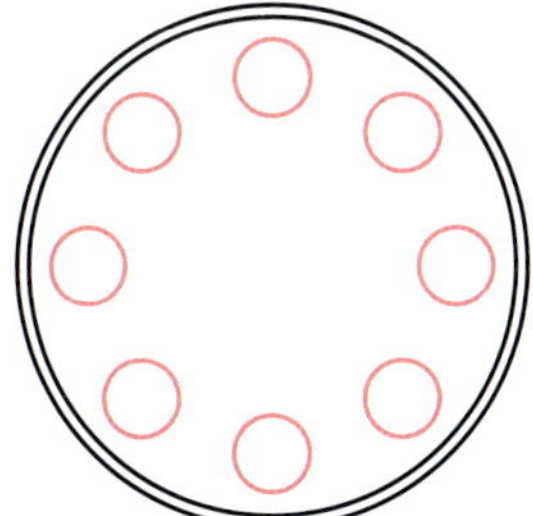

Draw eight circles, spaced evenly inside the edge of the ring.

3.

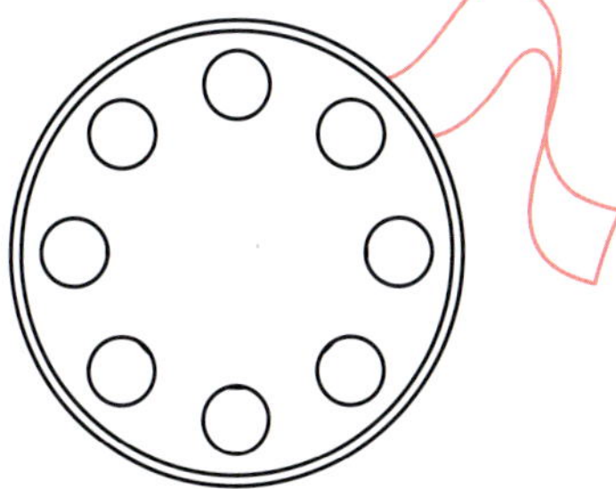

Draw a wavy rectangle for the film.

4.

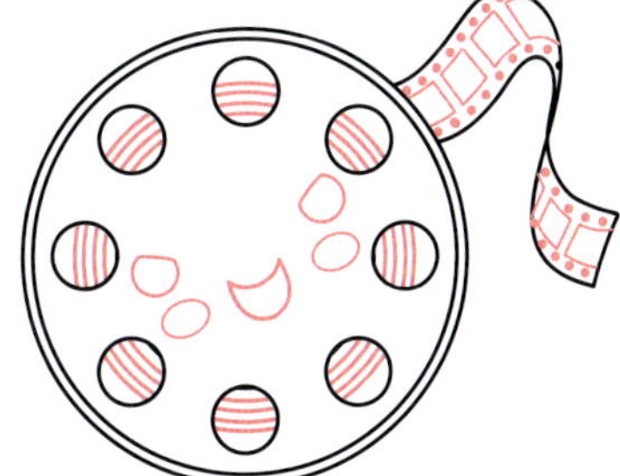

Add four lines inside each of the inner circles. Then draw squares in the film section and dots along the edges of the film. Then add a smile, slanted eyes, and oval cheeks to the middle.

5.

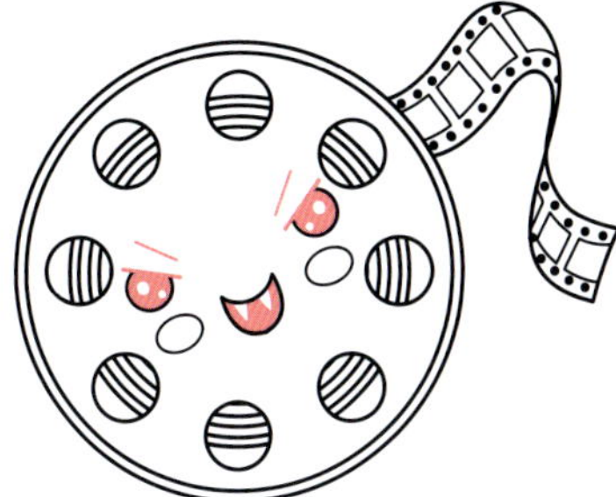

Add sharp teeth, fill in the mouth, shade in the eyes, and add slanted eyebrows.

6.

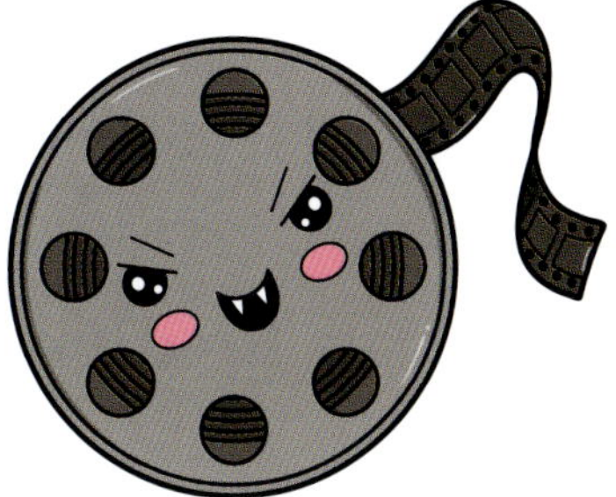

Color in your Devious Film Roll!

BONEY POPCORN

1.

Start by drawing a curved L shape for the side of the box.

2.

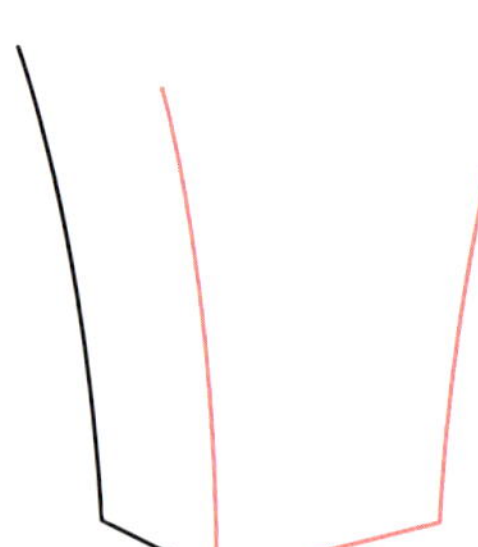

Draw the front of the box, leaving the top open.

3.

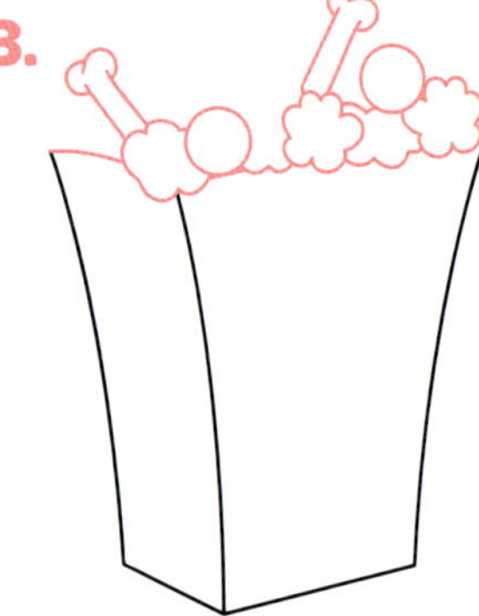

Add some popcorn shapes, circles, and two bone shapes to the top.

4.

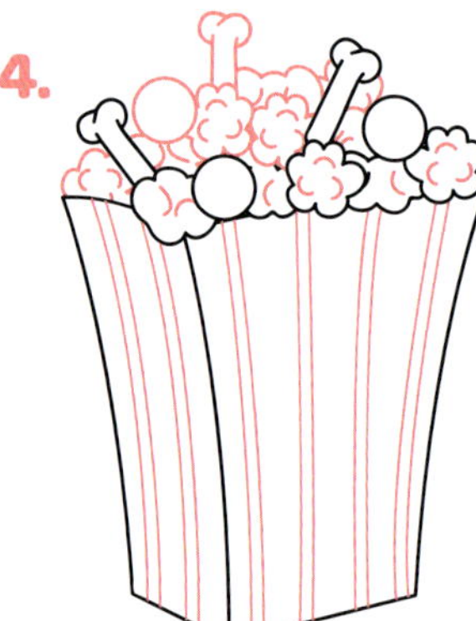

Add more popcorn shapes, circles, and another bone shape to the top. Add curved lines inside the popcorn pieces. Then draw stripes on the popcorn box.

5.

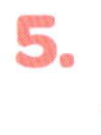
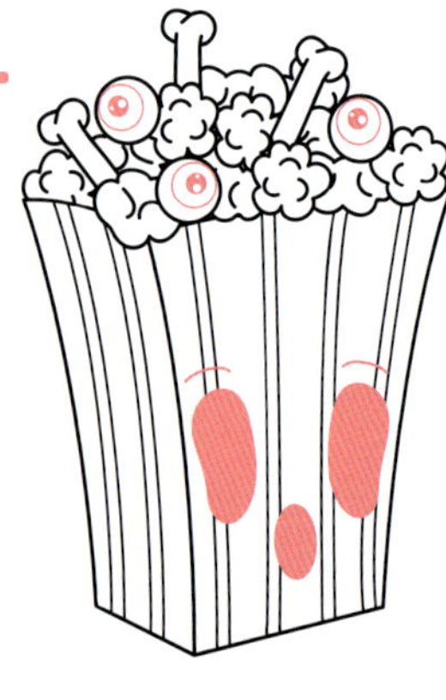

Add circles (irises) and shaded pupils inside the eyeballs. On the front of the box, draw a ghostly face: two big, filled-in ovals for eyes and a smaller, filled-in oval mouth. Add eyebrows.

6.

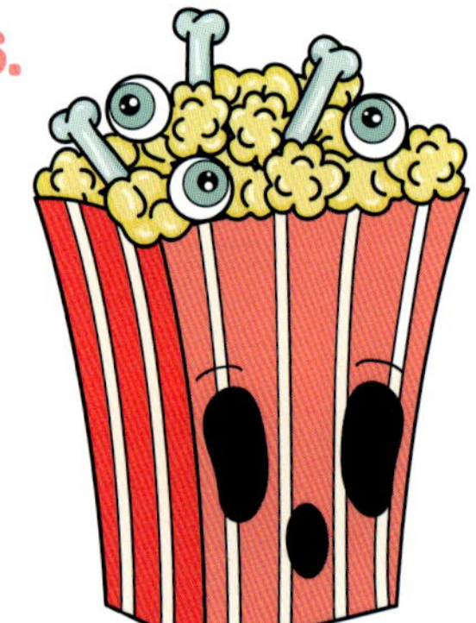

Color in your Boney Popcorn!

UNDEAD CHEERLEADER

1.

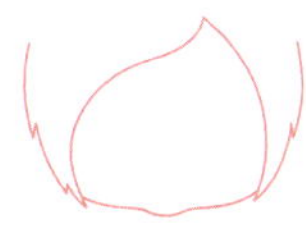

Start by drawing the shape of the chin with jagged hair to the sides.

2.

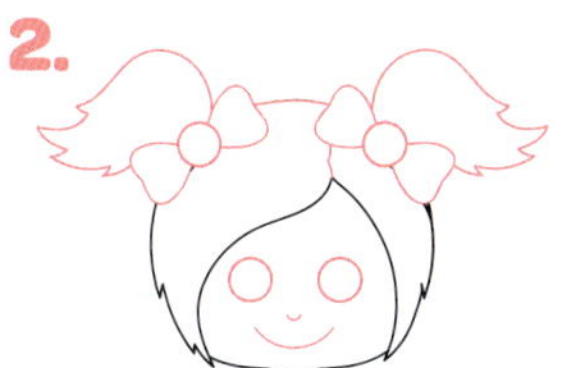

On either side, draw a bow shape and a pigtail. Join them in the middle. Add a hair part, two circles for eyes, and curved lines for the nose and mouth.

3.

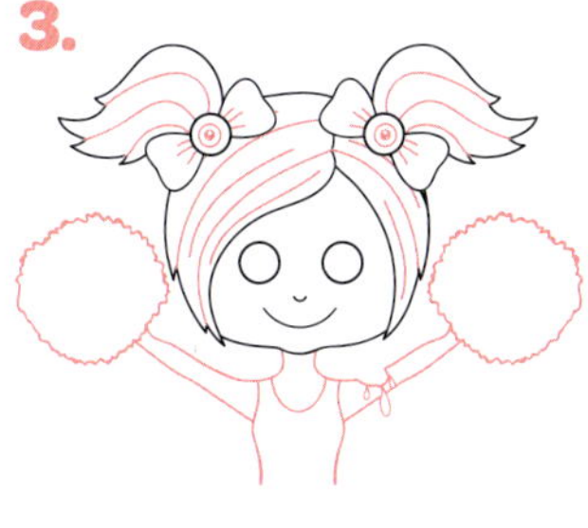

Detail the bows with eyeballs at the centers and fold lines on the sides. Draw lines for hair. Draw the torso and two arms—one of them missing a chunk. Add some teardrop shapes for blood. Draw a wiggly circle at the end of each arm.

4.

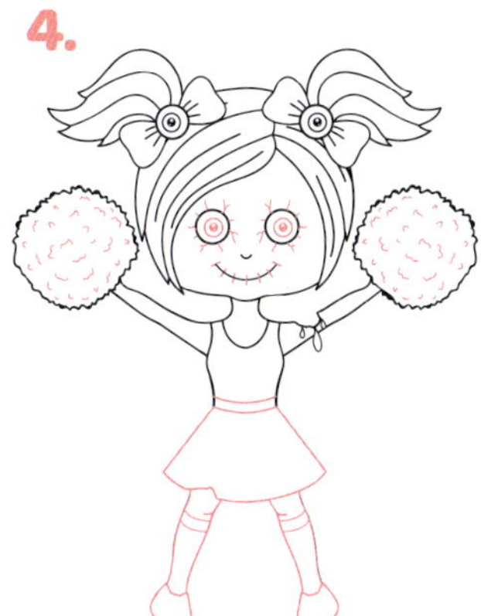

Add two curved lines at the waist and a prism-shaped skirt. Add legs and feet, and draw curved lines for the socks and shoes. Add detail to the pom-poms and eyes and stitches to the mouth.

5.

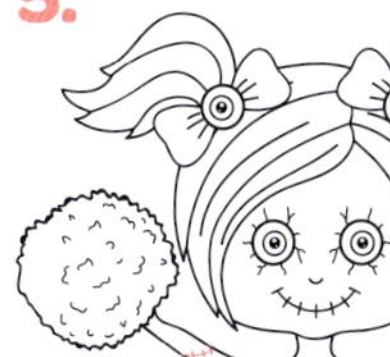

Add a line above the missing chunk in the arm. Draw three triangles on the skirt. Then add details like patches, more stitches, and a cobweb.

6.

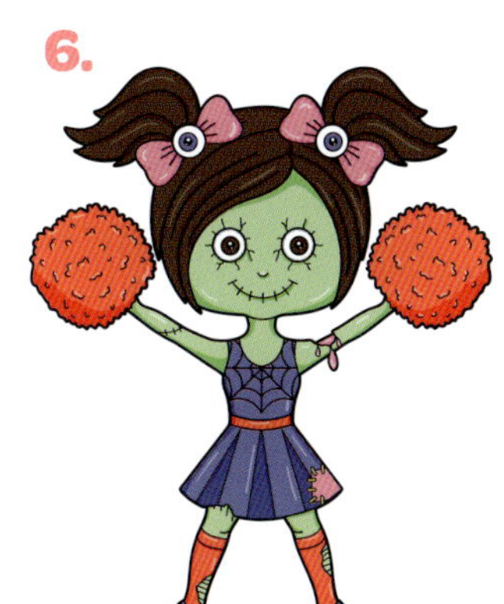

Color in your Undead Cheerleader!

ANGRY FOOTBALL

1.

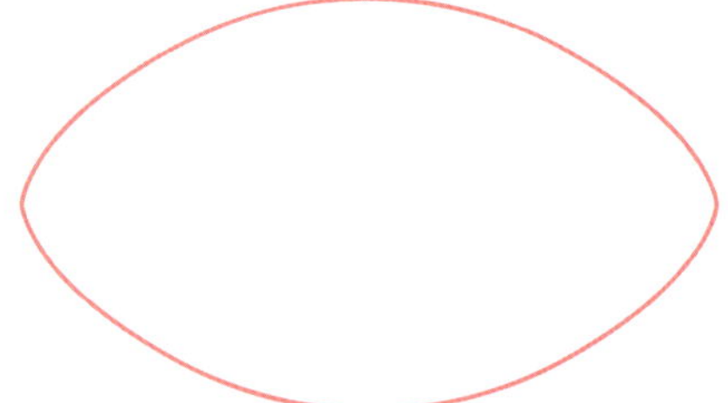

Start by drawing the shape of the football.

2.

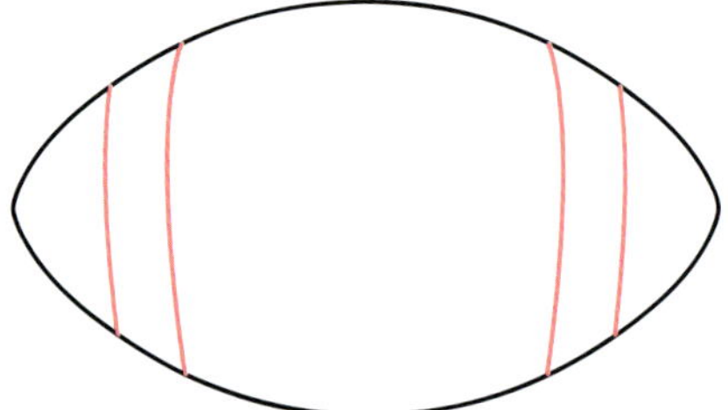

Draw two parallel lines on each side of the football.

3.

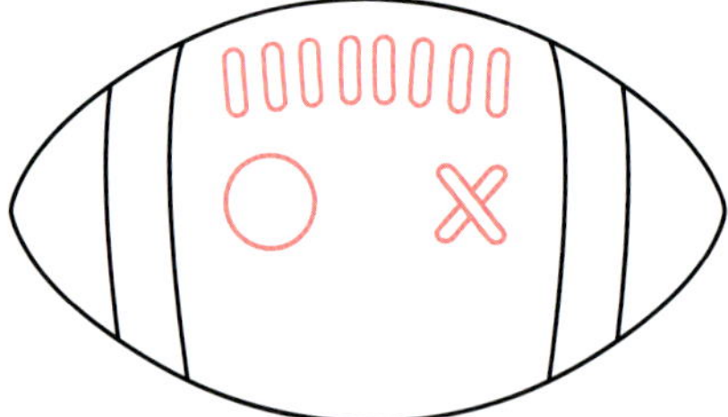

Draw vertical stitches near the top of the football. Then add a circle and an X for eyes.

4.

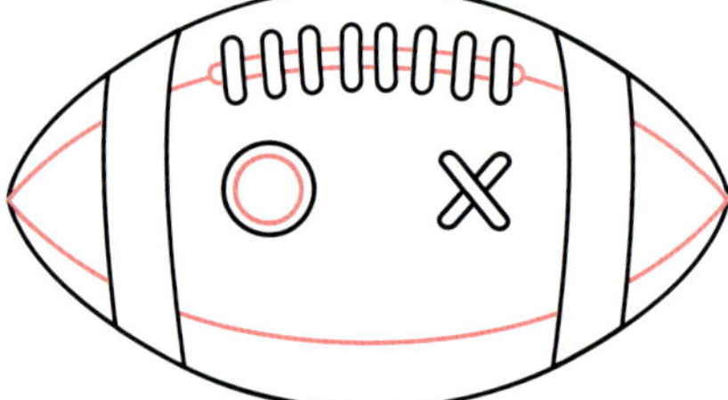

Add a horizonal stitch line to the top of the football. Then add curved horizontal lines to the top and bottom. Add a circle within the circular eye.

5.

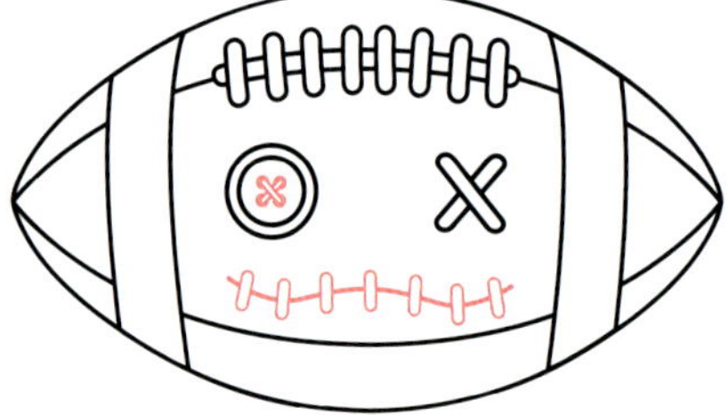

Draw a wavy line with stitches for the mouth. Then add an X to the middle of the circular eye to make it into a button.

6.

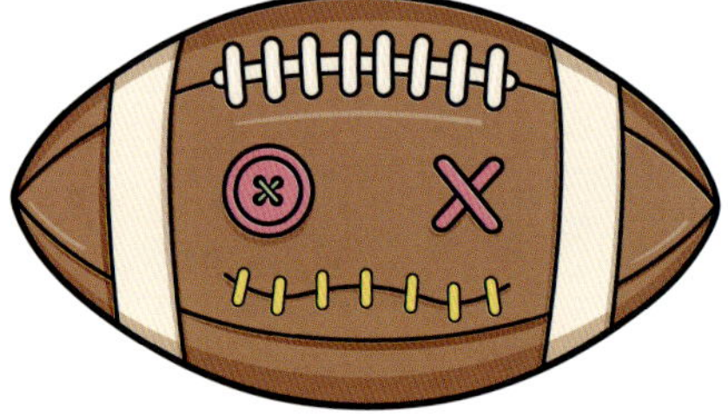

Color in your Angry Football!

HAUNTED GRILL

1.

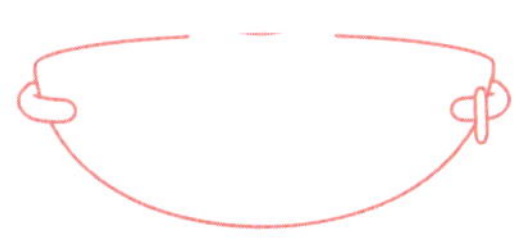

Start by drawing the top of the grill as a half circle with a handle at either side and a smaller oval shape on the right. Leave two open spaces at the top.

2.

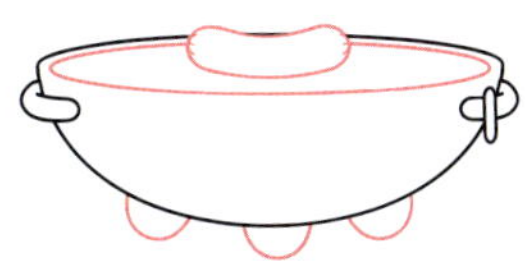

Draw a sausage shape in the middle of the grill. Add an oval inside the top, and add three half circles to the bottom.

3.

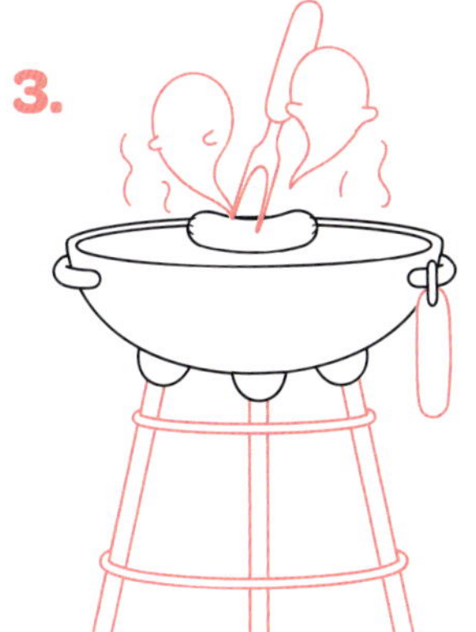

Draw two ghost shapes with arms. Then add the barbecue fork. Add three grill legs and two curved double lines (leg supports). Add an oval to the right side of the grill, and draw heat lines.

4.

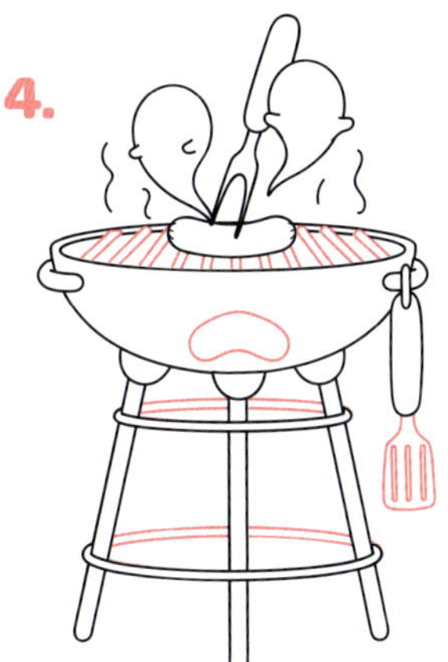

Add double straight lines for the bars of the grill. Add the end of the spatula, and finish the leg supports with double curved lines. Then give the grill a jelly bean–shaped mouth.

5.

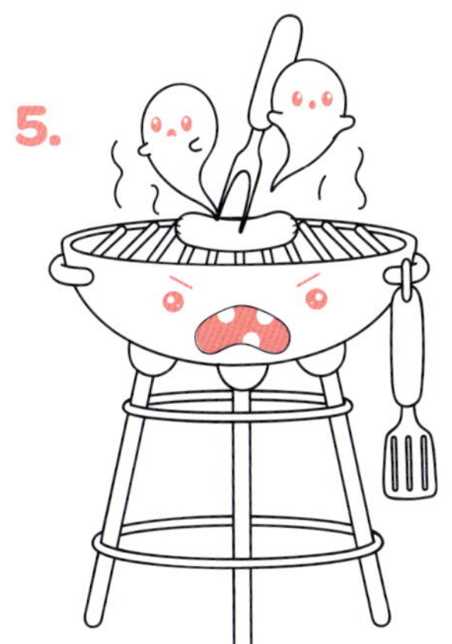

Draw shaded eyes and slanted eyebrows on the grill. Then add teeth and fill in the mouth. Draw spooky little faces on the ghosts.

6.

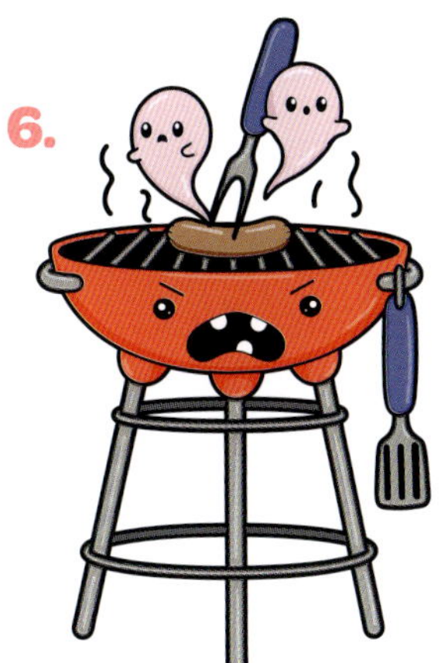

Color in your Haunted Grill!

GHOST IN THE OVEN

1.

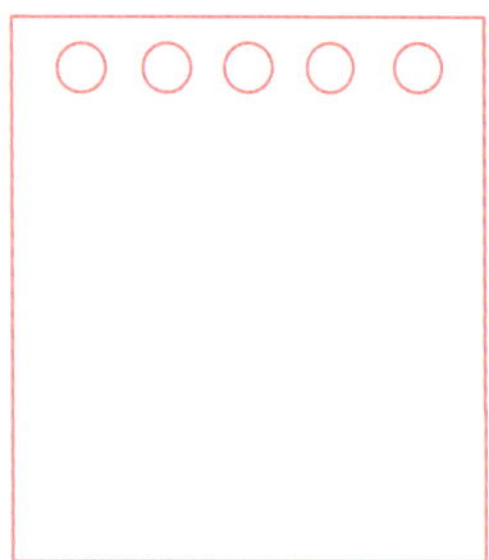

Start by drawing a rectangle with five circles (knobs) along the top.

2.

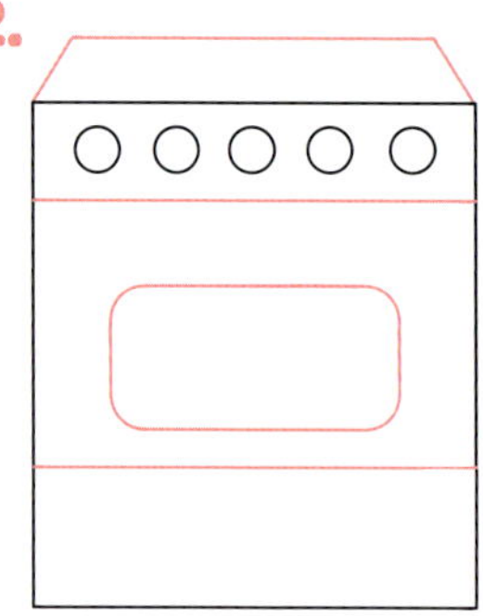

Above that, draw a slanted rectangle. Then add a rectangle with rounded edges (window) in the middle of the oven. Draw a horizontal line below the knobs and another below the window.

3.

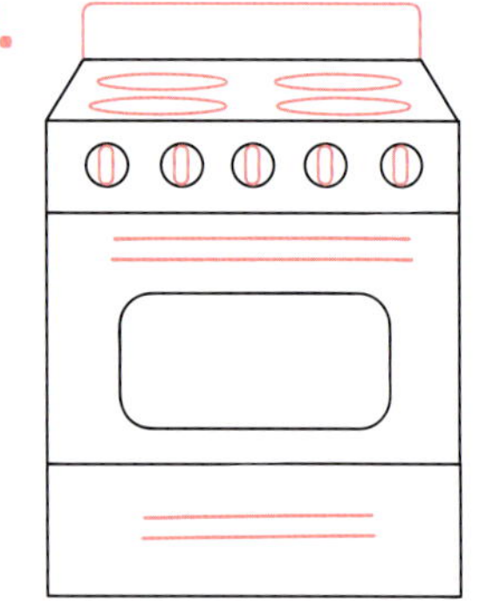

Add a thin rectangle at the top. Then add small rounded rectangles inside the knobs. Add four squished ovals for burners. Draw two horizontal lines above the window for a handle. Draw two horizontal lines within the bottom rectangle for a handle.

4.

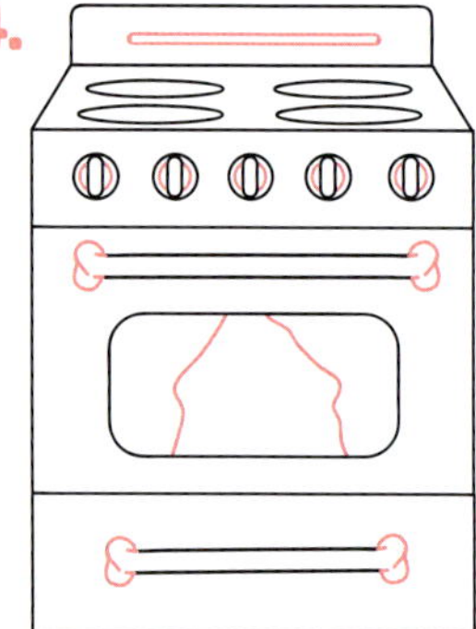

Add another thin rectangle inside the top rectangle. Add circles inside the knobs, and add heart shapes (bone ends) to the ends of the handles. Add two wiggly lines for the ghost.

5.

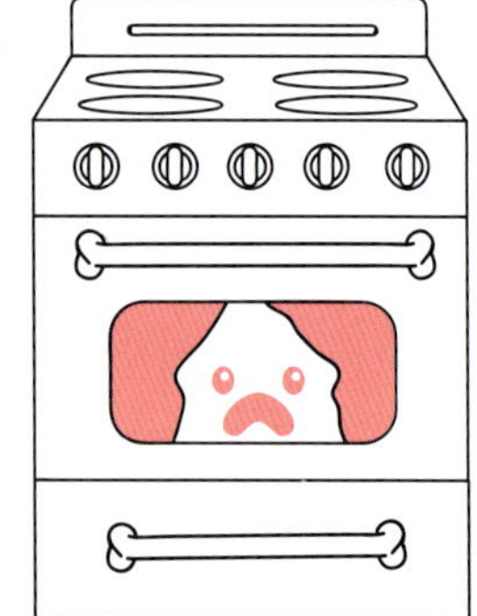

Add a spooky face to the ghost and fill in the space behind it.

6.

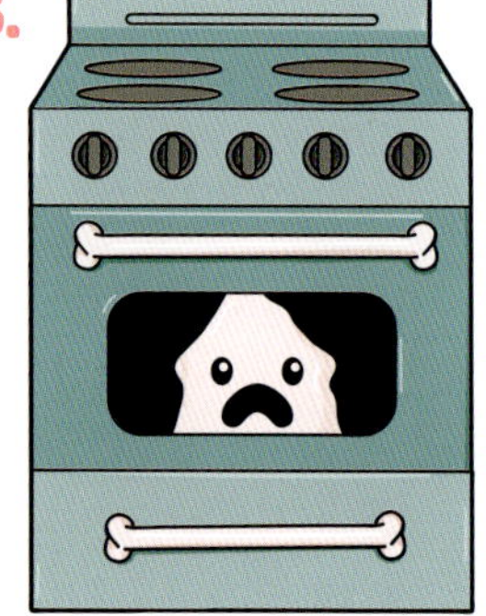

Color in your Ghost in the Oven!

BATTY APRON

1. 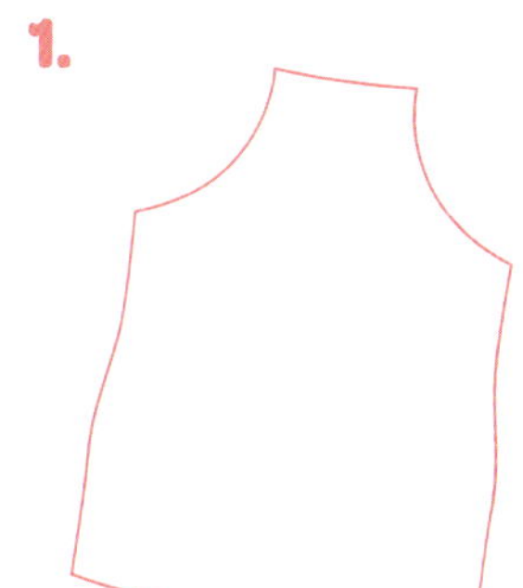

Start by drawing the outline of the apron: a rectangle with curved cutouts at the two top corners.

2. 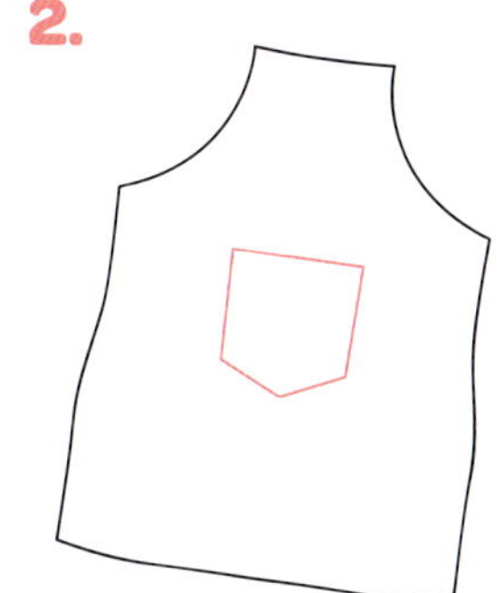

Add a square pocket with a triangular bottom.

3. 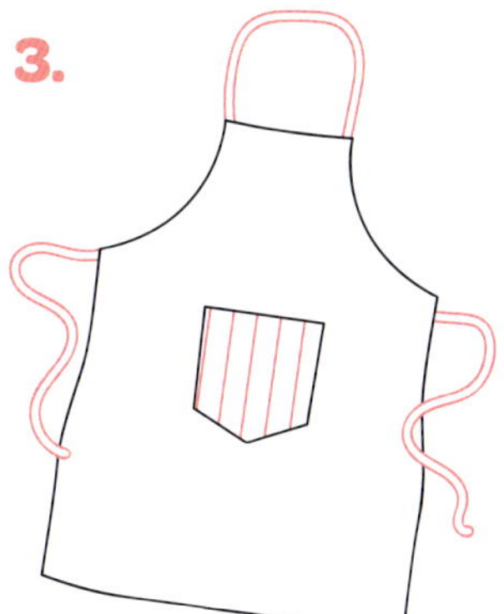

Add stripes to the pocket. Draw squiggly lines for side ties and a neck loop at the top.

4. 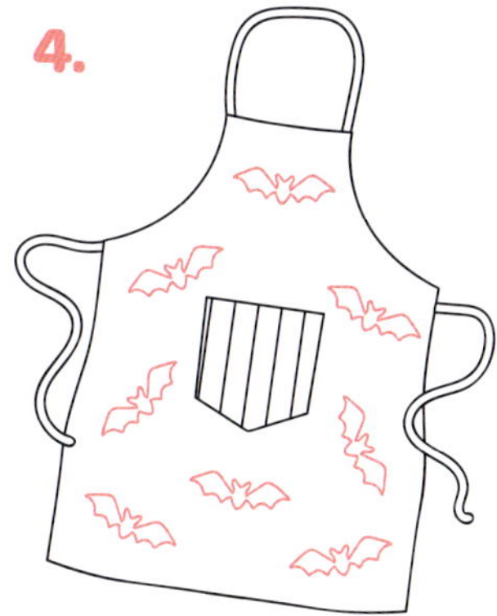

Add bat shapes on apron.

5. 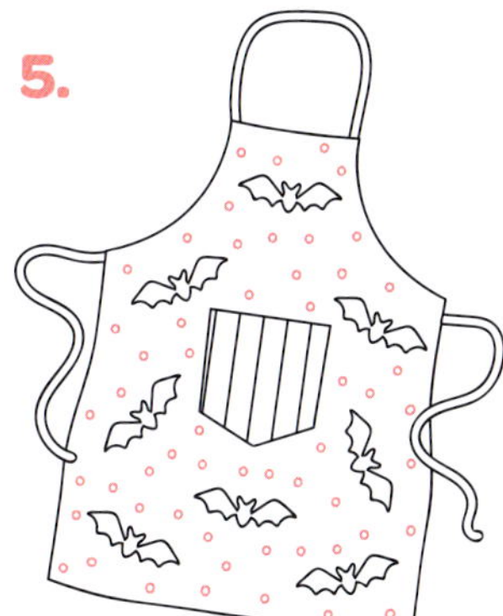

Add little circular dots.

6. 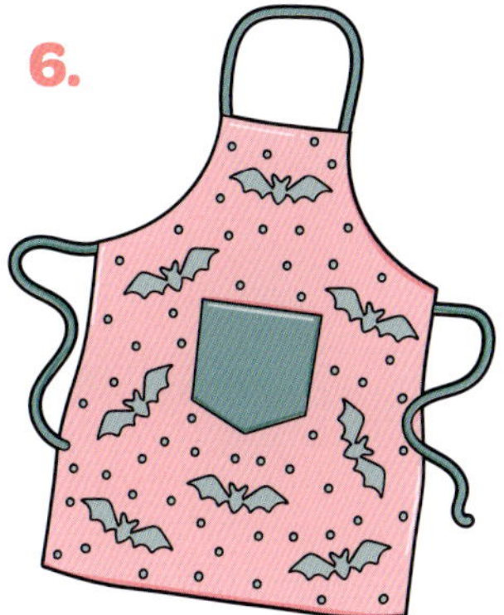

Color in your Batty Apron!

BONEY ROLLING PIN

1.

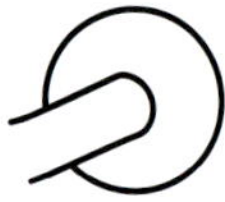

Start by drawing a circle with a slanted cylinder on its side, leaving the left side of the cylinder open.

2.

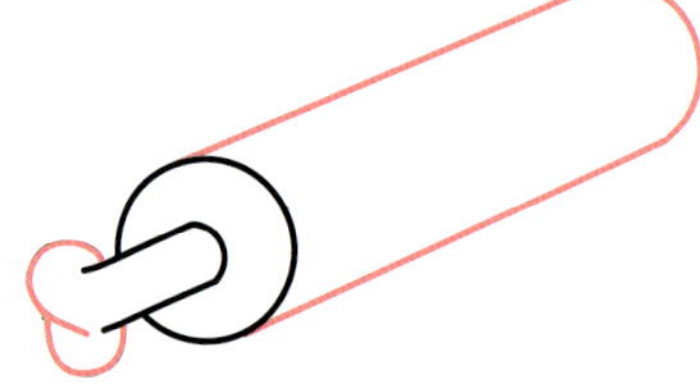

Add a heart-shaped bone end to the cylinder. Then add a long, slanted cylinder to the right side of the circle.

3.

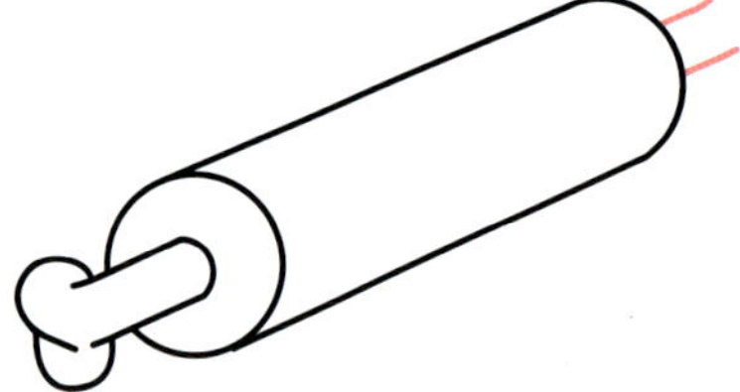

Add two short, slanted lines.

4.

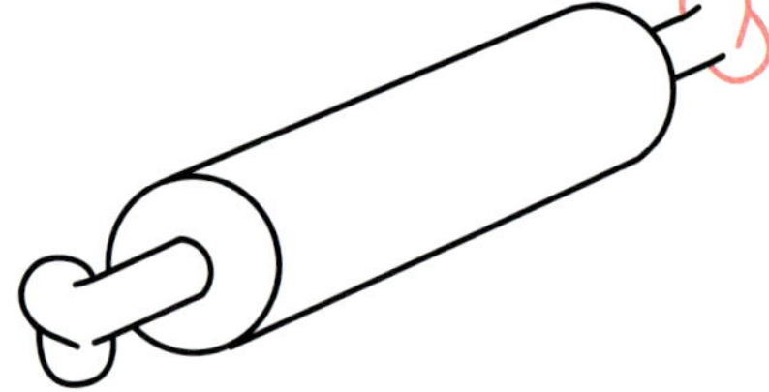

Add a heart-shaped bone end to the right side of the slanted lines.

5.

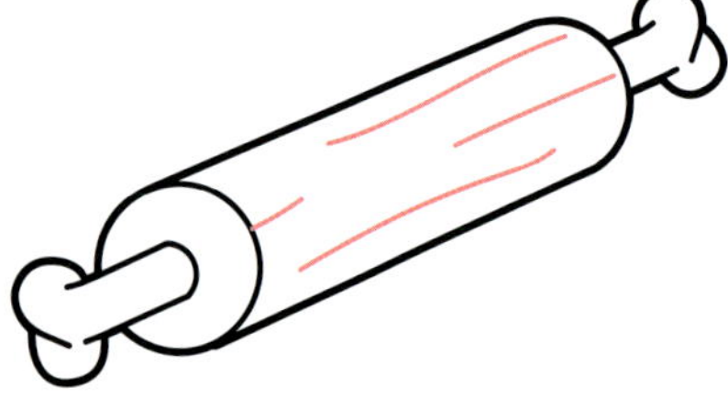

Add lines for texture.

6.

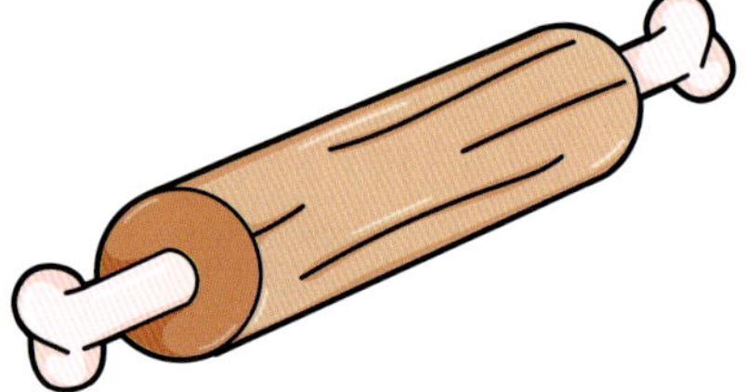

Color in your Boney Rolling Pin!